POLICING

POLICING

Concepts, Strategies, and Current Issues in American Police Forces

Michael J. Palmiotto
Wichita State University

Carolina Academic Press
Durham, North Carolina

Library of Congress Cataloging-in-Publication Data

Palmiotto, Michael.
   Policing : concepts, strategies, and current issues in American
police forces / Michael J. Palmiotto
      p.   cm.
   ISBN 0-89089-867-7
   1. Police—United States. 2. Law enforcement—United States.
I. Title.
HV8138.P35   1997
363.2'0973—dc21   97-13942
                                                    CIP

Carolina Academic Press
700 Kent Street
Durham, North Carolina   27701
Telephone (919) 489-7486
Fax (919) 493-5668
Email www.cap-press.com

Printed in the United States of America

Contents

POLICING

CHAPTER **1**

The Historical Development of Law Enforcement

Major Issues

1. Is an understanding of the historical development of policing important to the modern-day law-enforcement officer?
2. Modern policing replaced an antiquated inefficient and ineffective system.
3. Modern policing reflects the professionalism that is found in such fields as medicine, law, and education.

Introduction

The practice of law enforcement has its origins in primitive societies, and like society, it has evolved. But an evolutionary theory of the police function does not exist. Neither historians nor anthropologists have put much effort into examining the evolution of policing. So, while we know that there are several key issues that have permeated and governed the history of policing—issues like the role of the police in civil disorders, the ambiguity of the police role, the enforcement of unpopular laws, and the personnel problems that face many police departments[1]—the lack of historical information and documentation make it difficult to study the police function.

The historical record of American policing is also sketchy. Throughout America's law enforcement history, police agencies have not maintained accurate historical records of their departments—if they have maintained any historical records at all.

Yet, it is of crucial importance that students of law enforcement living in an age of rapid social, economic, and cultural change develop an understanding of current law enforcement principles—principles that can only be appreciated when contributions from earlier decades are recognized and understood. Ideally, each new generation of law enforcement professionals will make a contribution to the field by adding new concepts and innovative techniques that can be passed on to the next generation. Students of law enforcement need to know that law enforcement has always served a

---

1. Samuel Walker, "The Urban Police in American History: A Review of the Literature," *Journal of Police Science and Administration* 4 (September 3, 1976): 252.

social need and it has always provided a service that other units of the government or the business community have been unwilling or incapable of providing.

An Appreciation of Historical Development

When the law-enforcement professional can appreciate the various phases of the historical development of law enforcement, he or she will be in a better position to implement change. How can law enforcement be improved if the implementer of change does not know how and why policing practices have failed in the past or, for that matter, how and why they have succeeded?

How *did* the police role develop into its present function? For example, do the modern student and the police professional know that the role of women and minorities has changed in policing through the decades? Optimistically, an understanding of the development of law enforcement throughout the ages and in America will allow professionals in the field and those who will have some impact on the law enforcement profession to be creative in improving the field and to avoid the errors of past police agencies and individuals.

The Ancient and Feudal Periods

The history of law enforcement can be traced to ancient times when the family, tribe, or clan assumed the responsibilities of protecting its members. The concept of "kin police" evolved with the idea that an attack against a member of the group was an attack against the entire group. In essence, the people were the enforcers of their own laws. Punishment was retaliatory and often inhumane. Mutilation and branding were used, along with flaying, impaling, stoning, burning, and crucifixion. Contemporary America has a *formal process* of handling the unacceptable behavior of individuals; however, ancient societies had an *informal process* in which individuals handled violations against themselves.

Additionally, the implementation of law precedes the need for its enforcement. As a body of law emerges, the need to enforce those laws evolves concurrently. In other words, before governments establish formal law enforcement agencies they usually have laws in place that need to be enforced. Police agencies are implemented when citizens fail to obey laws voluntarily. Government reacts to the failure of citizens to obey laws by creating an agency that will enforce its laws. Therefore, the formalization of laws can also be traced to ancient times.

History indicates that King Hammurabi of Babylon in the tenth century B.C. codified the laws of Babylon and the means for their enforcement in his kingdom. The *Code of Hammurabi* dealt with commercial and criminal law and established laws for domestic relations, marriage, and divorce. The code had these essential features:

1. It provided for individual responsibility under the law,
2. It guaranteed the sanctity of an oath before God, and
3. It established the necessity of written evidence in all legal matters.

Punishment for crimes was retributive and law enforcement was carried out by *messengers* who were the equivalent of modern day magistrates. The courts were under the control of the priestly class, perhaps because of the oaths required in legal proceedings.

The Code of Hammurabi preceded the *Mosaic Code* which was based on a major moral and religious philosophy of the Middle East. Our modern day classification of *Natural Law* and *Human Law* can be traced to the Mosaic Code. Natural Law reflects God's eternal law and forbids vices and sins. Human Law, instituted by man, is conditional and, therefore, changeable. Also, our society's classification of crime as *mala en se* or *mala prohibita* has its roots in the Mosaic Code. *Mala en se* is an act of evil in itself—like murder, rape, arson, or aggravated assault. *Mala prohibita* refers to acts prohibited by society—acts that are not inherently evil like speeding, failure to pay alimony, and truancy.

Other ancient civilizations contributing to our modern understanding of the legal system include the Assyrian Empire which established a court system to deal with adultery, theft, and murder. Also, the ancient Egyptians, around 1500 B.C., had laws dealing with bribery and corruption and established a judicial system to handle these violations.

Early Greek States

The early Greek states were the first to develop the practice of city policing. Under Pistratus, a ruler of Athens, a guard system was established.

About 620 B.C. Draco was appointed to codify the laws of Athens. Under Draco, the laws were regularized and publicized to make all citizens aware of them. Draco advocated the death penalty for all crimes regardless of their seriousness. Both stealing *and* murder, for example, were capital offenses.

Solon succeeded Draco and established a program of reform. He instituted a court system with juries selected from the citizenry. Athens was ruled democratically with a general assembly of freemen who passed the laws. In addition, the death penalty was rescinded for all crimes except murder and fines were instituted for such crimes as seduction.

Plato, in his treatise, *Laws*, categorized crimes according to the time of day the act was committed—violations committed during hours of darkness, he asserted, were more serious than criminal acts during daylight hours. In addition, he observed that there were various degrees of homicide and he differentiated between voluntary, involuntary, and premeditated homicide—concepts that have been incorporated into our modern criminal laws. Plato also advocated the rehabilitation of offenders and suggested that retribution or retaliation was not necessarily the best punishment.

Romans

The Romans in their conquest of the Mediterranean made significant contributions to the development of law and the enforcement of laws. In the fifth century, B.C., the *Law of the Twelve Tables*—outlining judicial procedures, parental rights, inheritance, ownership, torts, and confession—was developed. The *praetor*, the forerunner of the modern judge, was responsible for administering justice under the Twelve Tables.

Under the influence of the Roman Empire, the sources of law developed and changed. For example, *leges* (legislation) were important enactments made by the emperor or the senate. The *Senatus consulta* were decrees passed by a majority vote of the Senate.

The Emperor Augustus made a number of contributions to law enforcement. He established the *Praetorian Guard* from the military legions to protect the life and property of the emperor. The *urban cohorts*, units of 500–600 men, were created to keep the peace of Rome. The *praefectus urbi*, the perfect of the city, was given the responsibility of maintaining order in the city. The *curatores urbis* came under the direction of the *praefectus urbi* and was responsible for a specific area of the city.

The *vigiles of Rome* were also established by Augustus to assume fire-fighting responsibilities. Rome was plagued with fires and a unit was needed to spot and fight fires. In addition to its fire-fighting duties, the unit was responsible for patrolling the streets.

English Police System

The English police system has its origins in the laws and customs of the Danish and Anglo-Saxon invaders. Originally its citizens were responsible for the peace keeping duties. The establishment of the *mutual pledge* system by Alfred the Great, 870–901, is recognized as initiating the process of modern policing. In structuring the defense of his kingdom, Alfred believed that internal order was important. The mutual pledge system encouraged that social order be maintained through the mutual responsibility of its citizens.

Under the mutual pledge system every man was responsible not only for his own actions but also for those of his neighbors. It was each citizen's duty to raise the "hue and cry" when a crime was committed, to collect his neighbors, and to pursue a criminal who fled from the district. If such a group failed to apprehend a law breaker, all were fined by the crown.[2]

The mutual pledge system enrolled every male over twelve years of age (unless he was excused because of his social position) for maintaining peace and enforcing the principle that all citizens were held accountable for the conduct of their neighbors. At the lowest level of the mutual pledge system was the *tithing*, a group of approximately ten families headed by a *tithingman*. Each member of the tithing was responsible for the other members' behavior. If one member was accused of a crime, the other members had to produce him or they could pay his fine or otherwise make retribution. The next level was called the *hundred* which consisted of a group of ten

---

2. President's Commission on Law Enforcement and Administration of Justice, *Task Force Report: The Police*, (Washington, D.C.: Government Printing Office, 1967), 3.

tithings. Through a *hundred court* judicial authority was exercised. Out of the hundred the role of the *constable* was developed. The constable was responsible for the weapons and the equipment of the hundred. Hundreds were combined to form *shires*, or counties, under the jurisdiction of a shire-reeve or sheriff. The shire-reeve was responsible for maintaining the king's peace in the shire. The shire-reeve had the authority—known as the *posse comitatus*—to call all able-bodied men to pursue a criminal.

Norman Invasion

After the Norman Invasion of England in 1066 the mutual pledge system was modified and came to be known as the *frankpledge*. Typically, a conquered people are placed under strict authoritarian controls, and so the Normans simply centralized their peace-keeping efforts by tightening the mutual-pledge system they found in place at the time of conquest. The Assize of Clarendon in 1166 reflects the mechanism the Normans used to control the Anglo-Saxons. According to the Assize of Clarendon:

> The villagers were required to report to the sheriff's court any suspicions they might harbor about one another, together with any other matter affecting the affairs of the district. These reports, or 'presentments', as they were known, were made by the tithingman (or chief pledge, as he was now sometimes called in his progression to work towards becoming a constable) to a jury of twelve free men of the hundred, who forwarded serious accusations to the sheriff. In this is to be seen the early use of the jury system. Information would be required not only about felons, but also about any suspicious character.[3]

The Constable System: The Thirteenth to the Sixteenth Centuries

By the end of the thirteen century the constable system evolved as the rural form of law enforcement. The constable was elected annually by the parish, a population center of worship, to maintain so-

---

3. T.A. Critchey, *A History of Police in England and Wales 900–1966*, (London: Constable, 1967), 4.

cial order. The constable had the responsibilities of the tithingman, but he was also a royal officer who had the responsibility of keeping the king's peace by the "hue and cry." The principles of the constable system can be summarized as follows:

1. It was a duty of everyone to maintain the King's peace, and it was open to any citizen to arrest an offender,
2. The unpaid, part-time constable had a special duty to do so, and in the towns he was assisted by his subordinate officer, the watchman,
3. If the offender was not caught red-handed, hue and cry was to be raised,
4. Everyone was obligated to keep arms with which to follow the cry when required,
5. The constable had a duty of presenting the offender at the court leet.[4]

The constable system enlisted the entire community and fines were imposed for lack of cooperation and support. In the urban area the *watch and ward* system was implemented and its officers were given the duties of patrolling the streets for fires, guarding the gates of the town between sunset and sunrise, arresting strangers during darkness, and preventing the breaking and entry of the houses and shops.

Both the constable and *watch and ward* systems were defined by the Statute of Winchester of 1285 and the Justice of the Peace Act of 1361. This system marked the transition of the frankpledge, the feudal system of law enforcement, into a rudimentary police system. This policing system remained in effect until the Industrial Revolution.[5]

The Seventeenth to the Eighteenth Centuries

In the late seventeenth century the policing system began to break down in both urban and rural areas. The three main causes for this were

1. The contempt into which the office of constable had fallen,
2. The corruption of many justices of the peace, and

4. Ibid., 7.
5. Ibid., 6–9.

3. The sheer inability of the old police system, in its debilitated and corrupt state, to cope with a social and economic upheaval which in the course of the eighteenth century doubled England's population from 6 to 12 million people, transforming the Metropolis from two overgrown cities into a massive conurbation, and turned vast rural areas into agglomerations of slum, mine, and factory, which lacked the elementary conditions of civilized living.[6]

During this period of time, men paid others to serve as constable, and since many of the men hired to function as constable were incompetent, the office of constable sank to a low when the principle of community service died. It was even possible to pay a fine to a parish fund to avoid serving as a constable.

The magistrate system also contributed to law and order difficulties. The magistrate enacted a fee for every act performed—"The magistrate rewarded in proportion to the number of persons he convicted had little incentive to resist corruption of the times and many submitted to it."[7] Magistrates extorted fees, used blackmail tactics, and traded justice.

In the latter part of the seventeenth century and early eighteenth century, crime began to increase. There were increased numbers of thefts, burglaries, robberies, and swindles and there was also an increase in counterfeiting, gambling, prostitution, and juvenile delinquency. There even existed professional receivers of stolen goods, known as *fences*.

In 1748, Henry Fielding was appointed magistrate of Bow Street. As a police reformer he introduced the concept of crime prevention as a responsibility of the police. He also published the *Covent of Garden Journal* in which he described cases that appeared before him. The Journal was also used to provide descriptions of robberies. Fielding advocated that citizens who were victims of crimes such as robberies and burglaries should report the offense to his office. This initiated the concept of crime victims reporting crimes to the police. Fielding also developed a rapport with pawn brokers, providing descriptions of stolen items, and requesting that they inform him if they became aware of the whereabouts of the contraband. Henry Fielding suggested that policing was a municipal responsibility.

---

6. Ibid., 18–21.
7. Ibid., 19.

In 1750, *thief-takers* were organized to apprehend criminals. The thief-taker received payment on a reward system in which he was paid for apprehending offenders or receiving stolen property.

Fielding also believed that it was important that police should respond to a crime scene quickly to obtain untampered evidence.

John Fielding succeeded his brother Henry as Magistrate of Bow Street. Under John Fielding, a foot patrol and a horse patrol were established. He also described the thief-taker's or Bow Street Runner's role in investigating crime. Another innovation of John Fielding's was that he established Bow Street as a clearing house of crime information. Information sheets describing offenders were distributed and affixed to public places.

Another contributor to the evolution of modern policing was Patrick Colquihoun, a Glasgow merchant. Colquihoun wrote the *Treatise on the Police Metropolis* in which he advocated that policing should be considered a new science with the objectives of preventing and detecting crime. He recommended that offenders be registered and that a trained, well-organized police unit be established for the London area. Colquihoun also created a marine police patrol in 1798.

Between 1780 and 1820, five parliamentary commissions met in London to determine the appropriate action to be taken concerning the public order. It was not until Sir Robert Peel became Home Secretary that a constructive proposal was brought before Parliament and passed.[8] In 1829, Parliament passed "An Act for Improving the Police In and Near the Metropolis"—referred to as the *Metropolitan Police Act*—and on September 29, 1829, the first Metropolitan Police marched out of Scotland Yard to begin duty. Two commissioners of police were given the authority to mold the "*new*" police: Colonel Charles Rowan, an ex-soldier, to enforce discipline, and Richard Mayane, an attorney. By May 1830, the Metropolitan Police had a force of approximately 3,000 officers. This was a period of high turnover mainly because dismissals for drunkenness were high. Many of the Peelian Reform principles are applicable for our contemporary police agencies:

1. The police must be stable, efficient, and organized along military lines;

---

8. Samuel G. Chapman and T. Eric St. Johnson, *The Policing University Heritage in England and America*, (East Lansing, MI: Michigan State University), 13.

2. The police must be under government control;
3. The absence of crime will best prove the efficiency of police;
4. The distribution of crime news is essential;
5. The deployment of police strength by both time and area is essential;
6. No quality is more indispensable to policemen than a perfect command of temper: a quiet, determined manner has more effect than violent action;
7. Good appearance commands respect;
8. The securing and training of proper persons is at the root of efficiency;
9. Public security demands that every police officer be given a number;
10. Police headquarters should be centrally located and easily accessible to the people;
11. Policemen should be hired on a probationary basis; and
12. Police records are necessary for the correct distribution of police strength.[9]

Development In America

The first colonies with their small population and primitive living conditions were not concerned with law enforcement. The established church of the early colonists functioned as the agent of social control. The religious influence on the initial settlers created a social bond.

When the first settlers felt the need to establish control, they implemented the law enforcement institutions they were familiar with—the sheriff, the constable, and the watch. In the Northern colonies the settlers formed towns and implemented the system of having a constable overseeing a watch, while in the South the settlers formed agricultural communities with the county as the seat of local influence. The office of sheriff seemed to be the most acceptable method for the rural community to enforce its laws.

9. A.C. Germann, Frank D. Day, and Robert R.J. Gallati, *Introduction to Law Enforcement and Criminal Justice*, (Springfield, IL: Charles C. Thomas, 1973), 60–61.

The first night watch was instituted by the town of Boston in February of 1636 to be staffed by citizens appointed by the town government. New York, under Dutch influence, established a citizen's Rattle Watch in 1652 in which citizens used rattlers to announce their presence and to communicate with each other. A few years later in 1658, a paid watch of eight watchmen replaced citizen volunteers. New Haven, Connecticut, appointed two constables in 1673 while Philadelphia established a night watch in 1700.

The quality of this early police system—sheriff, constable, and watch—was ineffective and inefficient. Some watchmen slept on duty while some citizens paid substitutes to serve for them. At times, service as a watchman was a sentence of punishment. Fees were paid to constables and sheriffs for testifying in court, serving papers, and other tasks. As in England, unscrupulous officials became entrepreneurs.

Law Enforcement is Forced to Change

However, law enforcement was forced to change in England and America because of the pressures of social, economic, and cultural trends. As towns increased in population and became cities, the old police system of constable and watch was unable to maintain order. With the advent of industrialization in the early nineteenth century and with cities attracting people with diverse socio-economic and ethical problems, social unrest and crime was bound to increase. To use a modern term, a crime wave was occurring. According to one author,

> New York City was alleged to be the most crime-ridden city in the world, with Philadelphia, Baltimore, and Cincinnati not far behind... Gangs of youthful rowdies in the larger cities... threatened to destroy the American reputation for respect for the law....Before their boisterous demonstrations the crude police forces of the day were often helpless.[10]

Both England and America had a law enforcement system that was unable to cope with the social unrest and the crime. As we know, England attacked this problem with the creation of the Met-

---

10. *Task Force Report: The Police*, 5.

ropolitan Police in 1829. Concurrently within the same time frame as England's adoption of the "*New Police*," officials of American cities were examining models of maintaining order. In 1833, Philadelphia became the first city to face this problem. Stephen Girald, a wealthy Philadelphian, left in his will a provision for the establishment of a competent police agency. A day watch was established with twenty-three men and a night watch of 120 men. Boston, in 1838, created a day watch of six men. However the day and night watches were, in both cities, distinctly separate entities.

The Development of Municipal Policing

New York City initiated the modern municipal policing concept in America. In 1844, the New York State legislature provided funds for a day and night watch. A year later New York City consolidated its forces. Under this concept, policing in New York was centralized and services were provided around the clock. New Orleans and Cincinnati followed New York in 1852, Philadelphia and Boston in 1854, Chicago in 1855, and Baltimore in 1857. By the 1860s the New York Model had been accepted by many cities though with some modifications. While the basic principles of the New York model were largely acceptable, the new police system confronted three issues:

1. A controversy over the adoption of uniforms,
2. A concern about arming the police, and
3. The issue of appropriate force in making arrests.[11]

The purpose of the uniform was to make the police readily visible to victims, to deter potential offenders, and to compel officers to perform their duty and avoid hiding. In 1853, New York City became the first city to require officers to wear uniforms. The Commissioner refused to hire any officers who refused to wear the uniform. There were many arguments, however, against wearing uniforms. Some felt that the uniform would simply make officers more visible to thieves, that it was un-American, or that it undermined officers' masculinity.

---

11. David R. Johnson, *American Law Enforcement: A History*, (St. Louis: Forum Press, 1981), 28.

Firearms

In the 1840s, there was a sharp increase in the use of firearms in individual disputes. In the late 1840s and 1850s, officers were occasionally shot in the line of duty. During the 1850s, it was a matter of personal choice for an officer to carry firearms for protection. Eventually, carrying firearms became an acceptable practice for police officers. Generally, many Americans felt that law enforcement was for the other fellow and not for them, and so, during periods of social turmoil when violence was acceptable behavior for specific segments of society, the establishment found the "use of force" an acceptable form of police behavior.[12]

Police Administrative Boards

Many city governments in the middle of the nineteenth century created police administrative boards as a means of eliminating improper political influence and corruption from municipal policing. These boards had the authority to appoint the top management of the police department. However, the administrative boards were unsuccessful at freeing municipal policing from unscrupulous political meddling in law enforcement.

Another attempt to eliminate the political influence of state control was made by state legislatures. For example, the New York legislature created a metropolitan commission in 1857 to curtail corruption and inappropriate political meddling in the New York City Police Department.

The basic rationale for state control was

> That the police were engaged primarily in executing the laws of the state; in the performance of this function, they were serving as agents of the state; the interest of the state in the efficient administration of the police was vital and permanent; and state control was less subject to improper local influence.[13]

Many states followed New York's example, and police operations had some form of state control in America's largest cities, and yet,

---

12. Ibid., 28–31.

13. George D. Eastman, *Municipal Police Administration*, 7th ed., (Washington, D.C.: International City Managers Association, 1971), 2a/3.

state control was as ineffective as administrative boards. This system merely substituted state politics for local politics. In the twentieth century most cities regained control of their police departments.

A tragedy in 1881 played a role in curtailing political interference in governmental operations when President James Garfield was assassinated by a deranged office seeker. The result of this abomination was the creation of the Federal Civil Service system with the passage of the *Pendelton Act* in 1883. State and local governments followed the example of the federal government in establishing civil service commissions.

Another breakthrough in the latter part of the nineteenth century was the organization of the National Chiefs of Police Union in 1871. One resolution adopted by the members indicated that one purpose for the organization's existence was "to assist each other on all occasions, by arresting and detaining any criminal who may be called for, or any person to have committed a crime in any other city or state."[14] Other areas of mutual interest to the organization's members were uniform standards of civil-service rules for police-officer selection, a uniform system of identification, the need for a central bureau of information, classification of police officers, and uniform arrest practices for felony arrests committed in other states. In 1902 the organization adopted its current name, The International Association of Chiefs of Police.[15]

Police Professionalism

An early president of the International Association of Chiefs of Police, Chief Richard Sylvester, was Superintendent of the District of Columbia Police from 1898 to 1915 and head of the police association from 1901 to 1915. As president of the International Association of Chiefs of Police he encouraged the idea of professionalism and made the chiefs' association a major advocate for the police.[16]

---

14. Donald C. Dilworth, *The Blue and the Brass: American Policing 1890–1910*, (Gaithersburg, MD: International Association of Chiefs of Police, 1976), 5.

15. Ibid., 5–6.

16. Geoffrey P. Albert and Roger G. Dunham, *Policing Urban America*, (Prospect Heights, IL: Waveland Press, 1988), 28.

One acceptable approach to policing during the first two decades of the twentieth century was the social-work approach in which the police played a part in reforming or assisting law violators. One police historian believes that the social work approach to police work could still be viable. He writes that "this aspect of police history has been lost from view. Police professionals eventually came to be defined almost exclusively in terms of administrative efficiency. By the 1930s under the influence of August Vollmer, O.W. Wilson and J. Edgar Hoover, the crime fighter became the ideal police type."[17]

A Decade of Surveys

The concept that police officers should function as social workers and not merely make arrests was the belief of many police administrators before the 1930s. They advocated that the police had a role in preventing crime by working to save the criminal offender. In order to gauge the effectiveness of the law enforcement community and its methods, the 1920s became a decade of surveys. Cleveland, Ohio, initiated the first crime survey. The Missouri Crime Survey of 1925 examined the state processes of law enforcement, judicial procedures, and correctional practices. In 1926, the Illinois Crime Survey investigated the criminal justice process and organized crime in Cook County, Chicago. The crime problem of the 1920s led President Herbert Hoover to create an investigative commission known as the *National Commission on Law Observance and Enforcement*, with former U.S. Attorney General George W. Wickersham as its chairman.[18] The *Wickersham Commission* examined various aspects of the criminal justice process. The Commission found that there was a need for honest, efficient, and effective patrol officers. The commission recommended that officers should receive training and discipline while incompetent police officers should be fired. The commission's study also discovered a lack of adequate communication systems and equipment necessary to effectively enforce the law. Another finding that may still be appropriate today is that too many duties were given to the patrol force.[19]

---

17. Samuel Walker, *A Critical History of Police Reform*, (Lexington, MA: Lexington, 1977), 79–80.

18. James A. Inciardi, *Criminal Justice*, 2d ed., (Orlando: Harcourt Brace Jovanovich, 1987), 23.

19. National Commission on Law Observance and Enforcement, *Report on*

The Decades of the 1930s and 1940s

Although law enforcement has had its problems with inappropriate political influence, inefficiency, and corruption, there has also been progress. The radio, the patrol car, and the telephone were major contributions that have significantly influenced police work. The use of automobiles as a method of patrol increased during the 1920s. Radios were first used in police cars in 1929. The advent of the radio in patrol cars, claimed some police administrators, gave police officers a great advantage in deterring crime and apprehending offenders. They also gave the police more mobility and quicker response time in emergency situations. In 1930 there were only one thousand radio- equipped patrol cars in service; by 1949 there were five thousand.[20]

The decades of the 1930s and 1940s were both decades of crisis for Americans. During The Great Depression of the 1930s and World War II during the 1940s when America had its energies focused on priorities higher than law enforcement, we could not have expected major reforms. However, the effects of education and training began to be recognized. Some departments established crime laboratories while others improved their organizational structure, implemented better recruitment procedures, or improved police benefits. But because soldiers were needed for World War II, many police officers were drafted, and many police departments had to be manned by police reserves.

State and Federal Law Enforcement

Although law enforcement in America has traditionally been a local responsibility and function, there does exist a role and need for state and federal law enforcement agencies. Only two states, Texas and Massachusetts, had state police agencies prior to the twentieth century.

The first form of state police were the Texas Rangers, formed in 1835. The Rangers dealt primarily with outlaws and cattle rustlers. Then Massachusetts, in 1865, created a state police agency that had the authority to handle general crime problems, but their primary

the Police, (Washington, D.C.: Government Printing Office, 1931), 5–7.

20. Jonathan Rubenstein, *City Police*, (New York: Farrar, Straus, and Giroux, 1973), 23.

mission was to enforce vice laws. But because of the unpopularity
of the agency, they were abolished in 1875.

The first state in the twentieth century to create a state police
was Pennsylvania. In 1905, Governor Pennypacker, in response to
labor violence, created the Pennsylvania State Police and the era of
modern state law enforcement began. Between 1908 and 1923,
fourteen additional states established police agencies similar to Pennsylvania's. The primary reasons for establishing state police agencies
were

1. To coordinate state and local enforcement agencies,
2. To ensure the uniformity of law enforcement practices,
3. To compensate for the lack of police protection and services in
   rural areas,
4. To counteract the hesitancy of local law enforcement to enforce laws that are unpopular,
5. To compensate for the inability of local law enforcement
   agencies to cope with crime problems,
6. To establish a coordinated system to control crimes of mobility,
7. To counteract the effects of political influence on local law enforcement,
8. To counteract the mismanagement, corruption and inefficiency
   that characterized many local police departments, and
9. To assist with the increase in the volume of automobile and
   traffic accidents.[21]

Federal law enforcement activities were slow in developing primarily because state and local authorities had to contend with
many of these responsibilities. But the U.S. Constitution provides
the federal government with authority over counterfeiting, inter
state commerce, and postal services, and gradually, agencies were
established to bring these responsibilities under federal control. For
example, in 1789, the Revenue Cutter Service was inaugurated to
prevent smuggling; the Post Office in 1829 initiated the investigation of mail fraud; the U.S. Attorney General began to investigate
crime against the federal government in 1865; and the Secret Ser-

21. George T. Felkenes, *The Criminal Justice System: Its Functions and Personnel*, (Englewood Cliffs, N.J.: Prentice-Hall, 1973), 41.

vice in 1865 was given the responsibility of investigating counter-feiting.[22]

As the preceding indicates, the federal government's role in law enforcement in the nineteenth century was limited, it concentrated on the mail, counterfeiting, and smuggling, but the early twentieth century saw two issues—narcotics and national security—become major concerns.

In 1914, the Harrison Act was passed which regulated the importing, manufacturing, and distribution of narcotics. The Treasury Department through its Internal Revenue section had the responsibility of enforcing the law. The Attorney General of the United States established the Bureau of Investigation in 1908 to investigate business crime and corruption. With the passage of the White Slave Act (The Mann Act) in 1910, the Bureau was given the responsibility of enforcing this law. During World War I the Espionage Act of 1917 and the Sedition Act of 1918 increased federal law enforcement powers. With the success of the Russian Revolution in 1917, a "Red Scare" developed in America. J. Edgar Hoover was placed in charge of the Intelligence Division of the Justice Department by Attorney General A. Mitchell Palmer. The Intelligence Division under Hoover "had prepared dossiers on 450,000 people, 60,000 of whom he designated as important radicals."[23] Acting on the information contained in these dossiers, federal officials made mass arrests of citizens who were suspected of being communists. Eventually, the "Red Scare" subsided in 1920.

In 1924, J. Edgar Hoover assumed the Directorship of the Bureau of Investigation. The name was to be changed to the Federal Bureau of Investigation in 1934. Under Hoover's tutelage the Bureau improved its image. Once a corrupt political organization, it became an efficient and professional law enforcement agency. Hoover hired college graduates, created a crime laboratory, and established the *National Police Academy*. He also obtained Congressional approval for agents to carry weapons and expanded their power to investigate interstate crime. Ultimately, it was Hoover who is responsible for creating the image of the *"crime fighter."* Criminal investigative authority and intelligence investigative powers for national security purposes both grew under Hoover's Direc-

---

22. German et. al., 68–69.
23. Johnson, 172.

tor.hip. The war of the 1940s and the "Red Scare" of the 1950s both helped Hoover's influence grow in collecting intelligence information for national security.

Modern Law Enforcement

Following World War II, the concept of professionalism and police efficiency had come to be associated with California. William H. Parker, appointed Police Chief of the City of Los Angeles after a corruption scandal in 1950, is credited with being a police administrator who incorporated many operational innovations into the Los Angeles Police Department. Although the California Professionalism was to be attacked in the 1960s, because it led to an insensitivity to minorities, some of Parker's operational innovations are still appropriate for today's law enforcement agencies. These include:

1. The formation of an internal affairs division to investigate citizen complaints of police misconduct,
2. The Co-authorship of a city Board of Rights procedure guaranteeing the separation of police discipline from politics,
3. The creation of a bureau of administration, which included two new components: the intelligence and the planning and research divisions,
4. The establishment of an intensive community relations program,
5. The deployment of a fleet of patrol helicopters, and
6. The enactment of a strict firearms use policy that included an internal department review of all weapons discharged.[24]

The 1960s was a decade of turmoil marked by assassinations, civil rights demonstrations, riots in our streets, and demonstrations against the Vietnam War. The drug culture also gained impetus during this decade. During the '60's the U.S. Supreme Court, through its numerous court decisions, curtailed law enforcement procedures relating to such areas as search and seizure, interrogations, the questioning of suspects, and the right of defendants to an attorney. In the 1964 Johnson-Goldwater Presidential campaign, crime became an issue. Barry

---

24. Donald O. Schultz and Eric Beckman, *Principles of American Enforcement and Criminal Justice*, 2d ed. (Sacramento, CA: Custom, 1987), 129.

Goldwater, the Republican Presidential candidate, evoked the *"law and order"* slogan to emphasize the seriousness of violence in American society. The 1960s was also a decade when law enforcement agencies were closely scrutinized and criticized. In response, prominent groups such as the International Association of Chiefs of Police and the International Association of Police Professors (now the Academy of Criminal Justice Sciences) began to issue public statements in support of higher education for law enforcement personnel.[25]

Further impetus was provided by the President's Commission on Law Enforcement and Administration of Justice in their report, *The Challenge of Crime in a Free Society*. The Commission, although it was created in 1965 by President Johnson, issued its report in 1967. The President's Commission had the following to say about the quality of police personnel:

> The Commission believes that substantially raising the quality of police personnel would inject into police work knowledge, expertise, initiative, and integrity that would contribute importantly to improved crime control.[26]

The 1960s was a decade of social disruption and violence. It was common in that era for police to be involved in confrontations with university students and with anti-Vietnam-War protesters. The police were charged not only with being ineffective in controlling disorders, but also with aggravating and precipitating violence through harassment of minority ghetto dwellers, student dissidents, and other citizens. The National Advisory Commission on Civil Disorders discovered that, in the cities, aggressive police patrolling and harassment resulted from society's fear of crime. But this practice only created hostility and conflict between police and minorities. According to the Commission's report

> In Newark, in Detroit, in Watts, in Harlem—in practically every city that has experienced racial disruption since the summer of 1964—abrasive relationships between police and ne-

---

25. Richard W. Kobetz, "Law Enforcement and Criminal Justice Education Directory, 1975–76," *The Police Chief* 43 (1977), 7.

26. The President's Commission on Law Enforcement and Administration of Justice, *The Challenge of Crime in a Free Society*, (Washington, D.C.: Government Printing Office, 1967), 107.

groes and other minority groups have been a major source of grievance, tension, and ultimate disorder.[27]

Historically, the federal government has refrained from interfering in local law enforcement activities. Yet, the influence of federal activities in the mid-1960s had a profound effect on the actions and emphasis of local agencies in the development of their programs and priorities. The establishment of a President's Commission on Law Enforcement and the Administration of Justice, by President Johnson in 1965, and the Law Enforcement Assistance Act were the first steps in providing federal grants-in-aid programs designed for the purpose of assisting state and local crime reduction capabilities.[27] President Johnson, in a message to Congress, explained his *"war on crime"* as follows:

> This message recognizes that crime is a national problem. That recognition does not carry with it any threat to the basic prerogatives of state and local governments. It means, rather, that the Federal Government will hence forth take a more meaningful role in meeting the whole spectrum of problems posed by crime. It means that the federal government will make a national effort to resolve the problem of law enforcement and the administration of justice—and to direct the attention of the nation to the problems of crime and the steps that must be taken to meet them.[28]

Congress, six months later, enacted the Law Enforcement Assistance Act of 1965 (LEAA). The Attorney General administered the program through the Justice Department's Office of Law Enforcement (OLEA). Over the next three years, OLEA awarded nearly $19 million for over 300 separate projects. Also, because of OLEA's special project program, twenty-seven states established new criminal justice planning committees or broadened the activities of exist-

27. *Report to the National Advisory Commission on Civil Disorders*, (Washington, D.C.: Government Printing Office, 1970), 8.

27. Advisory Commission of Intergovernmental Relations, *Making the Safe Streets Act Work: An Intergovernmental Challenge*, (Washington, D.C.: Government Printing Office, 1970) p. 8.

28. President's Message to the Congress, "Crime, Its Prevalence and Measures of Prevention," *1965 Congressional Quarterly Almanac* (March 8, 1965), 1396–1397.

ing committees, seventeen states began police science courses and college degree programs, twenty states initiated or expanded police standards and training systems, twenty states started planning for statewide integrated in-service correctional training systems, and thirty-three large cities developed police and community relations programs.[29] The Safe Streets and Crime Control Act was developed by the Johnson Administration in 1967 to implement many of the recommendations proposed by the President's Commission on Law Enforcement and the Administration of Justice.[30]

Another change that began to occur in 1968 was that females began performing similar functions in policing as men.

In the 1970s police agencies began to be examined with much more vigor than in prior decades. Organizations such as the Police Foundation and the Police Executive Research Forum have contributed to the research revolution that is currently occurring. Issues studied have included police response time, preventive patrol, management of investigations, and team policing—to name only a few areas. In addition, new concepts such as crime analysis, profiling of criminals, and community oriented policing have been accepted by many agencies. The use of computers has increased, and along with automation, the location of fingerprints on file is becoming a reality. Additionally, most states now require basic recruit training. We can also observe an increase in the number of minorities and females as police chiefs.

Modern law enforcement is not what it was twenty years ago, For that matter, even the last ten years have seen significant changes.

Summary

Law enforcement has its origins in primitive society. Law enforcement can be traced to ancient times when the family, tribe, or clan assumed the responsibility of protecting its members. The concept of "kin police" evolved with the idea that an attack against a member of the group was considered an attack against the entire group.

---

29. *Making the Safe Streets Act Work*, 7.
30. Ibid., 10.

History indicates that King Hammurabi of Babylon in the eighteenth century, B.C., codified the laws of Babylon and their enforcement in his kingdom. The Code of Hammurabi preceded the Mosaic Code which is based on major moral and religious philosophy that originated in the Middle East. Other ancient civilizations contributed to our modern understanding of the legal system such as the Greek states which began to develop city policing. The Romans made significant contributions to the development of law and the enforcement of laws. For example, the Romans established the position of praetor, the forerunner of the modern judge.

The English, under Alfred the Great, established the mutual pledge system which encouraged that social order be maintained through the mutual responsibility of its citizens. Under the English, the offices of constable and sheriff were also developed. In the mid 1700s the position of thief-taker, which evolved into the modern detective, was established for the apprehension of criminals. During this period, foot patrols and horse patrols were also established. The founding of the first modern policing organization is credited to Sir Robert Peel who in 1829 founded the Metropolitan London Police Department. Many of the concepts pioneered by Sir Robert Peel are still in effect today. These include probationary periods, wearing uniforms, and the use of some form of identification such as a badge number.

Early police systems in America—the sheriff, constable, and watch—were ineffective and inefficient. Some watchmen slept on duty and fees were paid to constables and sheriffs for testifying in court. In 1844, New York City initiated the modern municipal police concept in America. A day and night watch were combined under the authority of one department head. During the Nineteenth and early twentieth centuries, administrative boards and state control of municipal police agencies were common. Administrative boards were created to eliminate improper political influence and corruption from municipal policing.

During the 1930s the concept of police professionalism became defined almost exclusively in terms of administrative efficiency. Also, during this decade, the notion was born that the crime fighter was the ideal police type. During the war years of the '40's policing was given a low priority. Because of municipal police agencies' inability to curtail crime, state police agencies were created to assist them. Also, the role of federal law enforcement agencies in solving federal crimes that did not fall under the jurisdiction of state or municipal police agencies grew in importance over the years.

Following World War II, the concept of professionalism and police efficiency had become associated with California. This philosophy of policing was challenged during the 1960s, a decade of social turmoil. Most importantly, it was felt that the police were insensitive to minorities. Because of the violence in American society, President Johnson created the President's Commission on Law Enforcement and Administration of Justice. This Commission recommended that the quality of police personnel be improved and that police officers receive mandatory basic training. They also recommended that police officers be college graduates.

Historically, the federal government has refrained from interfering in local law enforcement activities. Yet, the influence of federal activities in the mid 1960s had a profound effect on the actions and emphasis of local agencies in the development of their programs and priorities. For example, President Johnson initiated a "war on crime" and he enacted the Law Enforcement Assistance Act which awarded millions to police agencies for special projects. The Safe Streets and Crime Control Act was passed with the purpose of implementing many of the recommendations proposed by the President's Commission on Law Enforcement and the Administration of Justice.

The 1970's observed the requirement of mandatory training for all police recruits. Research on policing increased substantially and included such areas as preventive patrol, management of investigation, and team policing. This push to improve policing has not abated. New concepts and strategies are constantly being developed and implemented.

Key Terms

Assize of Clarendon	Mosaic Code
constable	natural law
Covent of Garden Journal	New Police
crime fighters	OLEA
curatores urbis	Pendelton Act
Draco	Plato
Espionage Act	praetorian guard

frankpledge	President's Crime Commission
hue and cry	rattle watch
human law	Sir Robert Peel
hundreds	Sedition Act
Justice of the Peace Act	shire-reeve
kin police	Statute of Winchester
King Hammurabi	tithings
LEAA	Twelve Tables
leges	vigiles of Rome
mala en se	White Slave Act (Mann Act)
mala en prohibita	Wickersham Commission

Review Questions

1. Why is the development of law enforcement considered an evolutionary process?
2. What characterized the policing of ancient times?
3. What is the difference between the formal and informal processes of handling unacceptable behavior?
4. What role did the Greeks and Romans play in the evolution of policing?
5. Explain the evolution of the English police system.
6. What contribution did Sir Robert Peel make to modern policing?
7. Explain the development of policing in America.
8. Explain the federal government's role in policing during the 1960s.

References

Advisory Commission on Intergovernmental Relations. *Making the Safe Streets Act Work: An Intergovernmental Challenge.* Washington: Government Printing Office.

Albert, Geoffrey P. and Roger G. Dunham. *Policing Urban America.* Prospects Heights, IL: Waveland Press, 1988.

Chapman, Samuel G. and T. Eric St. Johnson. *The Policing University Heritage in England and America.* East Lansing, MI: Michigan State University.

Critchey, T.A. *A History of Police in England and Wales: 900–1966*. London: Constable Co., 1967.

Dilworth, Donald C. *The Blue and the Brass: American Policing 1890–1910*. Gaithersburg, MD: International Association of Chiefs of Police, 1978.

Eastman, George D. *Municipal Police Administration*. 7th ed. Washington: International City Managers Association, 1971.

Felkenes, George T. *The Criminal Justice System: Its Functions and Personnel*. Englewood Cliffs, NJ: Prentice-Hall, 1973.

Germane, A.C., Frank D. Day, and Robert R. J. Gallati. *Introduction to Law Enforcement and Criminal Justice*. Springfield, IL: Charles C. Thomas, 1973.

Inciardi, James A. *Criminal Justice*. 2d ed. Orlando, FL: Harcourt Brace Jovanovich, 1987.

Johnson, David R. *American Law Enforcement: A History*. St. Louis: Forum Press, 1981.

Kobetz, Richard W. "Law Enforcement and Criminal Justice Educational Directory, 1975–76, *The Police Chief* 43 (1977).

National Commission on Law Observance and Enforcement. *Report on the Police*. Washington: Government Printing Office, 1931.

President's Commission on Law Enforcement and Administration of Justice. *Task Force Report: The Police*. Washington: Government Printing Office, 1987.

President's Message to the Congress. "Crime, Its Prevalence and Measures of Prevention," *1965 Congressional Quarterly Almanac* (March 8, 1965).

Report to the National Advisory Commission on Civil Disorders. Washington: Government Printing Office, 1970.

Rubenstein, Jonathan. *City Police*. New York: Farrar, Strauss and Giroux, 1973.

Schultz, Donald O. and Eric Brockman. *Principles of American Law Enforcement and Criminal Justice*. 2d ed. Sacramento, CA: Custom, 1987.

Walker, Samuel. "The Urban Police in American History: A Review of the Literature." *Journal of Police Science and Administration* 49, No. 3 (1976).

CHAPTER 2

The Functions and Levels of American Policing

Major Issues

1. Is the decentralization of American law enforcement a good concept?
2. Is the police mission outdated?
3. Do the news and entertainment media focus too much on law enforcement activities in big cities?
4. Should there be major differences between the three levels of law enforcement: federal, state, and local?

Introduction

The structure of American law enforcement has its historical roots in Anglo-Saxon England. When the British colonists settled on the eastern shores of what is currently the United States they brought the English system of justice with them. This included the legal and order-maintenance mechanisms employed in England.

The English law enforcement structure located order maintenance at the local level giving the responsibility to counties, cities, and villages. England did not establish a centralized policing system under the control of the central government, but instead, it established a decentralized system under the control of local government—the county, the city, the town, or the village.

Historically, America has had a decentralized policing system. Since colonial days America has placed primary emphasis on enforcing law and maintaining the peace on local levels of government. This philosophy of policing still holds true in contemporary America.

The practice of policing in America has evolved dramatically since the Colonial Period and its rate of change does not appear to be slowing down. The evolution of policing has been a gradual process, however, and at times, it has stabilized for decades.

The structure of law enforcement can be divided into three categories: federal, state, and local. The United States Constitution allows the federal government to pass laws to protect the central government and to establish law enforcement agencies to enforce federal laws. The Tenth Amendment of the Constitution reserves for the states, or for the people, those powers not provided to the federal government. State governments do not have the right to pass laws that violate the state constitution. Local police are divided into cities, towns, and villages dependent upon state laws, or county police departments and/or the sheriff's department.

Local Police Departments

Before discussing local police departments it may be best to explain the meaning of the concept of local government. Local government includes any level of government that clearly cannot be identified as either federal or state. A *local law enforcement officer* can be defined as "an employee of a local government agency who is an officer sworn to carry out law enforcement duties."[1] Examples of local law enforcement officers include *sheriffs*, *deputy sheriffs*, *chiefs of police*, sworn police officers, and special police officers that include state college and university police. A local police officer should not be confused with either a *federal law enforcement officer* or a *state law enforcement officer*. These officers are employees of either the federal government or state government. Although there are local police agencies that employ part-time police officers for their departments, the majority of local police departments are manned by permanent, full-time police officers. The communities that employ part-time officers are usually found in rural communities with small populations.

In the 1990s there are an estimated 12,000 local police departments in the United States. Municipal police departments account for ninety-nine percent of the total number of local police departments while county police account for less than one percent. The vast majority of police departments are small. Approximately fifty percent of police agencies employ ten or fewer police officers. Ninety-one percent of local police departments employ fifty or fewer officers, and ninety percent of the police departments serve a population of less than 25,000. Three out of four police departments in the nation serve a population of less than 10,000. This can be contrasted with less than two percent of local police departments serving a population of 100,000 or more and less than one percent of local police departments serving a population of 250,000. Cities

---

1. *Dictionary of Criminal Justice Data Terminology*, 2d ed., (Washington, DC: U.S. Department of Justice, Bureau of Justice Statistics, 1981), 127.

Table 1
Local Police Departments by Number of Sworn Officers, 1990

Number of Sworn Personnel	Departments Number	Percent
1,000 or more	38	.3%
500–999	34	.3%
250–499	81	.7%
100–249	356	2.9%
50–99	575	4.7%
25–49	1,495	12.2%
10–24	3,279	26.7%
5–9	2,910	23.7%
2-4	2,561	20.8%
1	959	7.8%
Total	12,288	100%

Note: Table includes both full-time and part-time employees. Detail may not add to total because of rounding.

Source: Brian A. Reaves, *A LEMAS Report,* "State and Local Police Departments, 1990," (Washington, DC: U.S. Department of Justice).

with a population of one million average about 5,000 police officers while communities with a population of less than 2,500 average three police officers. Although small communities comprise the majority of police agencies in America the vast majority of police officers are employed in communities with a population of 100,000 or more.[2] The responsibility for policing lies primarily with local government with most of police agencies being operated by small police agencies controlling crime in small populated communities.

The Mission of Policing

The primary reason for establishing police forces in America in the 1830s and afterward was to maintain order in American cities. The period between the 1830s and 1870s was a period of disorder. Conflict occurred between ethnic groups and racial conflict was prevalent. The economic situation of the country also generated vi-

---

2. Brian A. Reaves, *A LEMAS Report*, "State and Local Police Departments, 1990," (Washington, DC: U.S. Department of Justice, Office of Justice Programs, Bureau of Statistics), 1–3.

olence and bankrupted investors. Banks that failed were ransacked and workers decimated the property of their employers. Also, questions of public morality were settled by mob violence.[3]

American political leaders in the nineteenth century did not support the creation of a formal police force. Questions remained about the police mission, function, and structure. Another important factor was that the existence of a permanent police force was unprecedented. Since the establishment of police departments as a component of our city governments over 100 years ago, political arguments have often revolved around whether or not to add more officers to the city's police department to curtail crime.

Today, municipal police departments are accepted as an important element of city government.

The primary purpose for establishing a police department has always been to maintain social order. This was true in the 1830s and it holds true for the year 2000. The police mission can be defined as the "maintenance of social order within carefully prescribed ethical and constitutional restrictions."[4] The police mission suggests that law enforcement officers have the following responsibilities:

1. *Prevention of Criminality*. This activity views the police role in constructive terms and involves taking the police into sectors of the community where criminal tendencies are bred and individuals motivated to indulge in antisocial behavior, and it includes seeking to reduce the causes of crime,

2. *Repression of Crime*. This activity stresses adequate patrol plus a continuous effort toward eliminating or reducing hazards as the principal means of reducing the opportunities for criminal actions,

3. *Apprehension of Offenders*. This activity views quick apprehension as the means of discouraging the would-be offender. The certainty of arrest and prosecution has a deterrent quality which is intended to make crime seem less worthwhile. Additionally, apprehension enables society to punish offenders, lessens the prospect of repetition by causing suspects to be incarcerated, and provides an opportunity for the rehabilitation of those convicted,

---

3. Samuel Walker, *A Critical History of Police Reform,* (Lexington, MA: Lexington Books, 1977), 4.

4. George D. Eastman, Ed., *Municipal Police Administration,* (Washington, D.C.: International City Management Association, 1972), 3.

4. *Recovery of Property*. This activity seeks to reduce the monetary cost of crime, as well as to restrain those who, though not active criminals, might benefit from the gains of crime,

5. *Regulation of Noncriminal Conduct*. This aspect of the police mission involves sundry activities that are only incidentally concerned with criminal behavior, such as the enforcement of traffic and sanitary code provisions. The main purpose is regulation, and apprehension and punishment of offenders as a means of securing compliance. Other methods used to obtain compliance are education (e.g. observance of laws) and the use of warnings, either oral or written, to inform citizens of the violations without taking punitive actions,

6. *Performance of Miscellaneous Services*. This involves many service activities peripheral to basic police duties and includes, for example, the operation of detention facilities, search and rescue operations, licensing, supervising elections, staffing courts with administrative and security personnel, and even such completely extraneous things as chauffeuring officials.[5]

The Functions of Policing

According to the American Bar Association's report, *The Urban Police Function*, "The police in this country have suffered from the fact that their role has been misunderstood, the fact that demands upon them have been so unrealistic, and the fact that the public has been so ambivalent about the function of police"[6]—a comment that is as valid today, as we approach the twenty-first century, as when it was made in 1973. The functions of policing are complicated. The range of police functions remain broad and intertwined as to make separation of these functions impossible. The police functions are not only entangled in the functions of the other criminal justice components like courts and corrections but also with diverse governmental and social service agencies.

The police are assigned a wide variety of functions usually without any degree of governmental planning. The priorities or objectives of the police functions are not specified. The police operate in a rather broad mission with broad functions responding, often, to

5. Ibid, 3–4.

6. American Bar Association, *The Urban Police Function*, (New York: American Bar Association, 1973), 1.

the influence of local, state, and federal governments. Factors that influence the police function include "broad legislative mandates to the police; the authority of the police to use force lawfully; the investigative ability of the police; the twenty-four-hour availability of the police; and community pressure on the police."[7] American police are assigned a variety of miscellaneous functions to which no other government agencies are normally assigned. For example, police are asked to report burnt-out street lights that they observe or to report pot holes that they discover while on patrol.

But what do the police actually do? Are they primarily *crime fighters* as has been suggested by police reformers since the 1930s? A movement, once known as *Professional Policing*, emphasized, that the police should be concerned with serious crimes and not with social services, disorderliness, or economic crimes. In *Professional Policing* the *image of the police* was more important than the officer's rapport with the community. A close relationship with the community, it was thought, could create an image of improbity which is to be avoided at all costs. The police were placed in patrol cars and were to have limited contact with the people they served. With police cars, radios, and telephones the police were to be responsive to citizens' *complaints*. The police were to respond to citizen complaints *rapidly*, handle the *situation*, and get back in *service* to handle more citizen complaints.

Studies of police activities show that most police tasks revolve around non-criminal activity. Approximately eighty to ninety percent of police functions involve handling family disturbances, dealing with traffic accidents, finding missing persons, directing traffic, and dealing with a myriad of hazards and dangers. Since the advent of telephones and radios in patrol cars in the 1930s the police have provided a *reactionary* approach to policing. Police officers respond to *calls for service* or to *incidents*. For example, a citizen telephones the police to report an automobile accident or disturbance and the police dispatcher assigns a patrol unit to handle the *call*.

With the arrival of the *911* service in the 1970s, *response time* became extremely important. The universal police 911 number made it easy for a citizen to call the police—which in turn made it possible for the police to service a citizen with a complaint.

---

7. *The Urban Police Function*, (New York: American Bar Association, 1973), 47.

The *proactive* approach to policing is the opposite of the reactive approach to policing. In the reactive approach, police respond to a service call. In the proactive approach the police initiate the action as they do when they make a drug buy or establish a sting operation. Although the reactive function of policing will not disappear, the proactive role of the police has become increasingly common in the 1990s.

One misconception about the police is that they are concerned with all types of crime. The police are concerned, primarily with *predatory crime* like murder, rape, burglary, and theft. Generally, the police have no authority when it comes to economic crimes, civil rights violations, or labor law violations. Herman Goldstein, in discussing police functions, writes:

> To analyze the *totality* of police functioning and the police *as an institution*, it is essential to break through the confining criminal justice framework, for it is now clear that it is not sufficiently comprehensive to encompass all that goes on in the daily operations of a police agency. The bulk of police business, measured in terms of contact with citizens, takes place *before*, invoking the criminal justice system (for example, checking suspicious circumstances, stopping and questioning people, maintaining surveillance), makes use of system for *purposes other than prosecutions* (to provide safekeeping or to investigate), or occurs in its entirety *outside* the system (resolving conflict, handling crowds, protecting demonstrators).[8]

Police work deals with *specific situations*. These situations involve behavior prohibited by either state or local law. When a law has been violated the police have the option of arresting and prosecuting or informally handling specific incidents.[9] "The total police function includes the objectives of the police and the methods they employ."[10] The American Bar Association delineates the objectives and priorities for police service as being:

---

8. Herman Goldstein, *Policing A Free Society*, (Cambridge, MA: Ballinger, 1977), 32–33.

9. Ibid., 34.

10. Ibid., 35.

1. To identify criminal offenders and criminal activity and, where appropriate, to apprehend offenders and participate in subsequent court proceedings;
2. To reduce the opportunities for the commission of some crimes through preventive patrol and other measures;
3. To aid individuals who are in danger of physical harm;
4. To protect constitutional guarantees;
5. To facilitate the movement of people and vehicles;
6. To assist those who cannot care for themselves;
7. To resolve conflict;
8. To identify problems that are potentially serious law enforcement or governmental problems;
9. To create and maintain a feeling of security in the community;
10. To promote and preserve civil order; and
11. To provide other services on an emergency basis.[11]

When citizens call the police, they want action and they want it immediately. Citizens consider their problems important and they want the police to handle these *situations* right away. Occasionally an officer on a murder call may encounter a citizen who feels that his own complaint about a noise problem is more important. The key to good police-citizen relations depends upon effective police intervention in handling situations that citizens find disturbing. Usually, a citizen assumes that the police officer has the authority to handle—in a timely and efficient manner—a situation that agitates them. In order to intervene effectively a police officer can take various actions depending on the circumstances. These actions include:

- Conducting an investigation,
- Stopping and questioning,
- Conducting a frisk,
- Taking a person into custody for further investigation,
- Taking a person into protective custody (a person attempting suicide, for example),
- Issuing an order to desist (as from loud noises or fighting),
- Issuing an order to leave (to a disorderly customer, for instance),
- Issuing an order to separate (as in domestic quarrels),

---

11. *The Urban Police Function,* (New York: American Bar Association, 1973), 53.

- Issuing an order to move on (to a street-corner gathering or streetwalking prostitutes, for example),
- Issuing an order to freeze a situation pending further investigation (as, for using force or threatening to use force.[12]

A Big-City Focus

Policing in America has a big-city focus—a focus underscored by the attention of the entertainment industry and news media. Since network television stations and big-city newspapers emphasize big-city news over small-town news, the city becomes the center of attention. For example, the three major networks, ABC, NBC, and CBS, are located in New York City. With the networks located in a big city with more sensational crime and a police agency of approximately 30,000 people, it should be expected that big-city crime will be emphasized over suburban and rural crime.

New York City has more violent crime than the suburban areas that surround it. The City's police department has had more scandals and more crises than the surrounding suburban area. Of course, the crises and scandals of the small police agencies don't get the press of the big-city news media.

The entertainment media makes movies and television shows that are generally located in the big cities. The action-packed police dramas are usually located in Chicago, Los Angeles, New York City, Miami, San Francisco, and Las Vegas and involve a serial murder or at least a homicide. How many police movies and television shows are located in rural and suburban communities and involve a simple case of mailbox vandalism?

In the late 1980s the *Bureau of Justice Statistics* published a report on municipal police departments in cities with a population of 250,000 or more. These big city departments employed 120,000 full-time sworn police officers having 2.3 officers per 1,000 residents. Approximately twenty percent of the big city departments had fixed-winged aircraft and about fifty percent of these agencies had a helicopter. These big city departments made extensive use of computers and maintained computer files on criminal histories, calls for service, and arrests. All the big city departments had special operating units such as crime prevention, child abuse units, or drug

---

12. Herman Goldstein, *Policing a Free Society*, (Cambridge, MA: Ballinger, 1977), 38.

education. It was reported that the majority of big city police officers were white males but that fourteen percent were black, eight percent Hispanic, and nine percent were women.[13]

In the late 1980s the Police Foundation and the six largest police departments agreed to work together to share knowledge that could improve the effectiveness of their police departments. These cities—New York, Los Angeles, Chicago, Houston, Philadelphia, and Detroit—known as "The Big Six" each had a population of over one million. The six cities had 7.5 percent of the country's population, 12.8 percent of the nation's sworn police officers, eleven percent of our country's property crimes, and twenty-four percent of the nation's violent crimes.[14] There are striking differences between the Big Six departments due to a variety of factors such as demographic characteristics, per-capita income, and the ethnic composition of the cities. An examination of the Big Six leaves many unanswered questions. For instance,

- Why are almost twenty-seven percent of the employees of the Los Angeles Police Department civilians, while in Philadelphia less than 11 percent of police personnel are civilian?
- Why are almost thirty-nine percent of Chicago's city employees working for the police department, while police employees comprise only nine percent of New York City's employees?
- Similarly what accounts for the fact that Los Angeles has only 2.0 sworn officers per square mile, while Detroit, Philadelphia, and Chicago have more than twice that ratio?
- Why are blacks in certain departments (e.g., Detroit and Los Angeles) more proportionately represented than in others?
- Similarly, why does Detroit have a notably higher percentage of female officers than any of the other Big Six Departments?
- Why does the New York City department have almost sixty-seven percent of its sworn personnel assigned to patrol, whereas Los Angeles has less than half of its officers in patrol units?

13. *Bureau of Justice Statistics: Special Report*, "Police Departments in Large Cities, 1987," (Washington, DC: U.S. Department of Justice, Office of Programs, 1987), 1.

14. Police Foundation, *The Big Six,* (Washington, DC: Police Foundation, 1991), 3.

- Why are almost eighty-seven percent of Chicago's sworn personnel in the rank of patrol officer, compared to only sixty-seven percent in Los Angeles?
- What are the reasons for, and the consequences of, the enormous differences among the Big Six, in terms of the number of available patrol units per capita—ranging from less than four per 100,000 in Los Angeles during the night shift to almost twenty-five per 100,000 all day in Philadelphia?
- Why do citizens of Philadelphia make almost twice as many calls for police service as those in any of the other Big Six cities?
- Why does the Chicago department dispatch a police unit to over 65 percent of the calls for service they receive while Los Angeles sends units to less than thirty percent?
- What factors account for the fact that Philadelphia and Houston record significantly fewer violent crimes per capita than any of the other Big Six?
- Why does the Philadelphia department make almost sixty-one percent of violent crime arrests for every 100 recorded violent crimes whereas in Chicago the ratio is less than nine per 100?[15]

Rural Police

Rural law enforcement agencies are small and many of them are unable to provide around-the-clock, seven-days-a-week service. Many of these agencies turn over their police services to the state police or they simply provide a limited, on-call service, responding only when they receive a complaint. Small police agencies often lack the sophisticated equipment or police personnel to perform complex investigations.

Generally, the rural police agency looks to the state police or the state investigative agency for assistance. For instance, small agencies often do not have the personnel necessary to investigate homicides. Because of the lack of advanced equipment and trained personnel, the federal government in governmental studies has recommended the consolidation of small police agencies. One advantage of the small police agencies, though, is that they *do* know the citizens in their community. They can often settle complaints in an informal manner rather than through the complex and more costly criminal justice process.

---

15. Ibid., 17–19.

In a fifty-two-county study of rural police in Illinois, it was found that rural police generally perform the following functions: patrol, community service, the maintenance of order, and administrative work. The residents of the communities and the police found that police activities were appropriate and that no one activity superseded all others.

The rural police have wide-ranging responsibilities. The Illinois study found that rural police officers spend sixty percent of their time on patrol and on law enforcement duties, but they are also asked to perform many disparate tasks. For example, since rural communities do not have specialized social service agencies the rural police are normally the only agency called when social services are required.[16]

County Police

Several counties in the United States have established County Police Departments to police unincorporated areas of the state. County Police are given law enforcement duties when the Sheriff's Department has limited jurisdiction. Several of the better known county police agencies in the country are the Baltimore County Police Department, the Nassau County Police Department, and the Suffern County Police Department—all counties with urban populations of sufficient size and with resources adequate enough to provide full law enforcement services. County police departments can be a combined county-city department or be a county department that provides services to unincorporated areas of the county. County police departments can also provide support to incorporated communities that have their own police departments. There are fifteen potential service areas in which county departments can assist local departments:

Patrol	On-Line Information
Central Dispatch	Training
Emergency telephone	Legal Advisor
Detective Services	Budget
Scientific Evidence Gathering	Purchasing

---

16. Branden Maguire, William Faulkner, Richard Mathers, et al., "Rural Police Job Function," *Police Studies* 14, No. 4, 180–187.

Criminal Histories   Marine Patrol
Complaint Records   Air Patrol [17]

The Nassau County Police Department, located on Long Island New York, serves a population of over 1.2 million people for a 287 square mile area. The department has almost 4,000 members, approximately 2,800 sworn personnel, and 1,119 civilian employees. The Nassau County Police Department functions as a big city police department except that it has county-wide police jurisdiction. But like other large departments, it has a Commissioner of Police, a Chief of Operations, a Chief of Detectives, a Chief of Patrol and a Chief of Support.

The County Sheriff

The office of Sheriff has its roots in Anglo-Saxon England from approximately 700 to 800 A.D. Initially known as a *shire-reeve*—since he was responsible for maintaining the peace in the shire (forerunner to the county)—the sheriff was appointed by a nobleman to maintain order. After the Norman Conquest, the sheriff was appointed by the king and given greater responsibilities such as collecting taxes and serving as chief law-enforcement officer.

The office of Sheriff was brought to America by the early colonists. "The most important aspect of the Sheriff's office in the early decades of colonization was that which made the Sheriff responsible for the preservation of the peace and...empowered [him] to make arrests, raise the *posse comitatus* to pursue felons and runaway slaves and commit malefactors to prison."[18]

The county sheriff is unique in policing since the sheriff is elected by the people of the county usually for a term of four years. In many instances the Sheriff has prior law-enforcement experience as either a state patrol officer or a city police officer. The Sheriff's duties can vary from county to county and from state to state; however, these responsibilities often include being a tax collector, a coroner, an assessor, and/or overseeing the maintenance of county

17. S. Anthony McCann, *County-Wide Law Enforcement: A Report on a Survey of Central Police Services in 97 Counties*, (New York: National Association of Counties Research Foundation, 1975), 5.

18. I. Gladwin, *The Sheriff: The Man and His Office*, (London: Victor Gollanez, 1974), 384.

highways. Normally, the Sheriff's office has charge of a detention facility. Most of the prisoners there await trial, but at times, prisoners serve their sentences in the county jail rather than in the state prison. The Sheriff's Department usually has the task of executing criminal warrants and serving civil papers. Another function of the Sheriff's Department includes the security of the county courthouse. Many Sheriff's Departments function like a municipal police agency, performing routine police tasks and doing criminal investigations. Sheriff's deputies perform routine police work in unincorporated areas where city police do not have jurisdiction.

Generally, the state constitution provides that the Sheriff is the chief law enforcement officer of a county. The services rendered by the Sheriff's office vary from county to county and often from state to state. In some cases a Sheriff can have, practically, no responsibilities at all or he can provide a full range of law enforcement services. The variety of functions provided by the sheriff can be summed up as follows:

- To provide traditional police service to the unincorporated areas of the county. This may include road patrol, marine patrol, search and rescue, air patrol, detective services, radio dispatch, juvenile services, scientific investigation, crime lab, police records, training, traffic enforcement, crime prevention, and narcotic enforcement,
- To maintain the county jail and its prisoners, including the jail, farms and work release programs,
- To execute both criminal and civil processes, including the service of warrants and various writs of attachment and execution,
- To serve the county by carrying out its orders and serving as court bailiff,
- To be present at the meeting of the county board of supervisors for the purpose of maintaining order, and serving notices and subpoenas,
- To investigate public offenses, and
- To serve as tax collector for the county.[19]

The full-service sheriff's office provides patrol, courts, and correctional services. As a model of the full-service sheriff's office, the Los

---

19. Lee P. Brown, "The Role of the Sheriff" in Alvin W. Cohn's *The Future of Policing*, (Beverly Hills: Sage, 1978), 232–233.

Table 2
Sheriffs' Departments by Number of Sworn Personnel, 1990

Number of Sworn Personnel	Departments	
	Number	Percent
1,000 or more	12	.4%
500–999	21	.7%
250–499	64	2.1%
100–249	191	6.2%
50–99	295	9.5%
25–49	522	16.9%
10–24	953	30.8%
5–9	684	22.1%
2–4	335	10.8%
1	17	.5%
Total	3,093	100%

Note: Table includes both full-time and part-time employees Detail may not add to total because of rounding.

Source: Brian A. Reaves, *A LEMAS Report,* "State and Local Police Departments, 1990," (Washington, DC: U.S. Department of Justice).

Angeles Sheriff's Office is the largest Sheriff's office in the United States. The Los Angeles Sheriff's office provides policing services for the unincorporated areas of Los Angeles County and contract police services for incorporated cities within the county. The Sheriff's Department has a police academy, crime laboratory, investigation unit, air patrol, marine patrol, and communication systems to assist in the performance of its police services. The Los Angeles Sheriff's Department also operates the largest jail in the country.

There are approximately 3,100 Sheriff's Departments at the local level and about 1,500 special police operating at the local level. Ninety-eight percent of the Sheriffs' departments perform court related work, ninety-seven percent function as law enforcement officers, and eighty-seven percent are involved in jail-related activities. Generally, Sheriffs' Departments are small with approximately one-third employing fewer than ten officers, and two-thirds of them employing fewer than twenty-five sworn officers. Approximately one-half of the Sheriffs' departments serve counties with a population of less than 25,000. Sheriffs' departments that serve counties with a population over 250,000 employ about one-half of all deputy sheriffs. Those Sheriffs' departments that serve counties with populations of one million or more employ over a one-fifth of the sheriffs' deputies.[20] Although two-thirds of the departments employ fewer than twenty-five deputies, the department serving most of the counties with a population over 250,000 employs the vast majority of deputies.

Miscellaneous Agencies

Special Police

Special police have jurisdiction limited to the enforcement of liquor laws or wildlife conservation, parks, transit systems, college and university campuses, school systems, and airports.[21]

The Constable

The constable has its roots in Anglo-Saxon England but in modern day America it is almost non-existent. Many states and counties in the United States do not use the services of the constable, but Pennsylvania is one state in which the *Office of Constable* is alive and well. The constable obtains office by election and has the primary duty of serving papers for a District Magistrate, a low-level judicial office. The constable receives a monetary fee for each paper he serves.

The Coroner

The office of the coroner can also trace it roots to Anglo-Saxon England where its mission was to safeguard the monetary interests of the king. The coroner had the charge of handling contraband and the relinquished property of felons, murders, and suicides. With the colonization of America the early colonists brought the office of coroner to colonial America.

The duties of the coroner now require that he or she investigate the death of citizens whenever there appears to be an indication of foul play. Usually, state laws do not require that coroners be medical doctors. Often, morticians seeks these positions since they have ex-

---

20. Brian A. Reaves, *A LEMAS Report* "Sheriffs' Departments 1990," (Washington, DC: U.S. Department of Justice, Office of Justice Programs, Bureau of Justice Statistics), 1.

21. Ibid., 2.

perience working with dead bodies. Depending upon state law, the coroner may be either an elected official or an appointed official of a county. Typically, before a dead body can be removed from a crime scene, the police or medical emergency team must obtain the permission of the coroner—whose job it is to determine whether or not foul play occurred. If it seems that a crime might have taken place, then an *inquest* is conducted by the coroner. Generally, a police investigator provides information about the case, including interviews with witnesses who often do not attend the inquest.

The Medical Examiner

The medical examiner—who is a medical doctor—replaces the coroner. In 1939, Maryland was the first state in the country to establish a state-wide medical examiner. Since then a number of other states have passed medical examiner laws. The medical examiner reviews "any death occurring as a result of an accident, homicide, suicide, or natural means wherein there is absence of an attending physician....In addition, any death of a suspicious nature shall become a medical examiner's case."[22] The Kansas Medical Act states that the medical examiner shall conduct an investigation in the case of human deaths in the following causes:

a. Violent deaths, whether apparently homicidal, suicidal or accidental, including but not limited to death due to thermal, chemical, or radiation injury and deaths due to chemical abortion, whether apparently self-induced or not;

b. Deaths not caused by readily recognizable disease, disability or infirmity;

c. Deaths under suspicious or unusual circumstances;

d. Deaths within 24 hours after admission to a hospital or institution;

e. Death of inmates of prisons;

f. Death of inmates of institutions maintained in whole or in part at the expense of the State or county, where the inmates were not hospitalized therein for organic disease;

g. Death from causes which might constitute a threat to public health;

---

22. Irvin M. Sopher and William C. Masemore, "The Police Officer and the Medical Examiner System," *Police* 16, No. 3, (1971), 23.

h. Deaths related to disease resulting from employment or to accident while employed; and

i. Sudden or unexpected deaths of infants and children under 3 years of age and fetal deaths occurring without medical attendance.[23]

State Law Enforcement

During the nineteenth century only two states, Massachusetts and Texas, established police agencies. Other states generally delegated policing to local government. Prior to Texas' independence, an unofficial militia, known as the Rangers protected settlers from raids. By 1936, when Texas became independent, the Rangers became an appendage of the government and their duties took on the characteristics of more general police work. In 1865, Massachusetts created a state force to handle liquor enforcement; however, the force was disbanded in 1875.[24] Now all states, except Hawaii, have some form of state police agency.

Ultimately, the violence between labor and management in the first decade of the twentieth century led to the formation of the first modern state police agency. Because of labor disputes between workers and the coal and iron companies and the violence occurring as a result of labor disputes, the Governor of Pennsylvania, Samuel Pennypacker, saw the need for creating a state police agency to maintain order within the state. Because he felt that the Coal and Iron police could not be impartial when dealing with Coal and Iron workers, Governor Pennypacker believed an impartial state unit should be established to oversee any disagreements between labor and industry. Consequently, the Pennsylvania State Police were created in 1905 with a compliment of 228 men modeled after the Royal Irish Constabulary.[25]

---

23. Kansas "State Medical Examination Act 52:17B-78." Effective Jan. 1, 1968.

24. David R. Johnson, *American Law Enforcement: A History*, (St. Louis: Forum, 1981), 155–158.

25. Philip M. Conti, *The Pennsylvania State Police: A History of Service to the Commonwealth, 1905–to the Present*, (Harrisburg, PA: Stackpole, 1977), 31–46.

The Pennsylvania State Police became a model for other states creating their own state police agencies. Typically, the state police developed in response to the following needs:

1. The necessity of coordinating state and local law enforcement agencies,
2. The need for a uniformity of law enforcement practices,
3. The lack of police protection and services in rural areas,
4. The inability of local law enforcement agencies to cope with crime problems,
5. The hesitancy of local law enforcement to enforce laws that were unpopular,
6. The lack of coordination in controlling crimes involving mobility,
7. The need to counteract political pressures on local law enforcement,
8. The mismanagement, corruption, and inefficiency characterizing many local departments,
9. The increase of the volume of automobiles and traffic accidents.[26]

Momentum for establishing state police agencies began in 1915, and between 1915 and 1921, twenty-three states organized some form of state police agency. Tennessee and Iowa created state police agencies in 1915, New York in 1917, Alabama and Nebraska in 1919, and Wyoming in 1921.[27] State police agencies usually have full police power to enforce all state laws and to investigate any crime anywhere in the state. The state police can arrest for any crime committed in their presence and they have the authority to execute search warrants. They patrol state highways enforcing state traffic laws and they have investigative powers to investigate crimes. State Police agencies—the Pennsylvania State Police, for example—may have the added responsibility of maintaining state criminal-history records, maintaining fingerprint files, keeping state crime statistics, overseeing local policing training, and investigating criminal complaints against local police officers and agencies. One of the pri-

---

26. George T. Felkenes, *The Criminal Justice System: Its Functions and Personnel*, (Englewood Cliffs, NJ: Prentice-Hall, 1973), 41.
27. H. Kenneth Bechtel, *State Police in the United States: A Social-Historical Analysis*, (Westport, CT: Greenwood, 1995), 39–40.

mary functions of the state police is preventing and controlling crime in the rural areas of the state. States that have state police with general law enforcement responsibilities are New York, Michigan, and Pennsylvania.

In the 1920s a number of states began to establish another form of state police known as the *Highway Patrol* who had as their primary responsibility the "enforcing of traffic laws" on state highways and state laws adjacent to state highway property. States that have Highways Patrols are Kansas, Georgia, Ohio, California, and Florida.

Those states that have Highway Patrol agencies have created general investigative agencies to investigate crimes occurring in rural areas or to assist local police agencies that lack the manpower to investigate sophisticated crime. States that have created elite investigative agencies are Kansas (the Kansas Bureau of Investigation) and Georgia (the Georgia Bureau of Investigation). Many of these agencies, the Georgia Bureau of Investigation for example, maintain a crime laboratory, an Automatic Fingerprint Identification System (AFIS), criminal history files, and they perform undercover drug investigations.

Miscellaneous Agencies

Within any state there are numerous agencies with law enforcement powers that do not receive a great deal of publicity. All states have laws controlling, examining, licensing, inspecting, and investigating matters related to specific types of professionals such as barbers, pharmacists, social workers, doctors, and lawyers. Generally, these agencies are not known to the public and often police officers are unaware of them.

Liquid Control Boards

States usually have an agency assigned the responsibility of regulating the alcohol industry. This agency has the responsibility of granting state liquor licenses to sell or serve alcoholic beverages. The agency can also revoke licenses and investigate complaints against establishments violating state liquor laws.

The Fish and Game Commission

Most states have created fish and game commissions to license and regulate the fish and game laws of the state. Fish and game wardens are concerned with crimes like poaching—killing wildlife out of season for private use.

The Racing Commission

States that allow gambling have a commission that sees that the state gambling laws are being followed. A racing commission typically investigates complaints of improprieties against gambling institutions.

The Conservation Commission

The conservation commission is responsible for conserving and protecting the state's natural resources. These include state parks, beaches, hiking and riding trails, and historical landmarks.

Traffic

States also enforce their own laws regulating trucking and ports—including maritime, freshwater, and airports.

Federal Law Enforcement

Prior to the twentieth century, the federal government had a restricted role in law enforcement. The emphasis of federal law enforcement was on safeguarding the country's revenues and protecting the mail. Postal inspectors protected the mails while Secret Service agents protected the country's currencies. It was not until the early part of the twentieth century that the federal government began to increase its role in law enforcement.

In 1908 the Attorney General of the United States created the Bureau of Investigation—the present day Federal Bureau of Investigation—to investigate corruption and violations of business law. With the passage of the Harrison Act, designed to regulate the importing, manufacturing, and dispensing of drugs, Congress established the Bureau of Internal Revenue within the Treasury Department to enforce the Harrison Act.

The federal government's role in law enforcement has evolved in the twentieth century. Until the 1960s the federal government had emphasized that federal law enforcement agencies should concentrate on enforcing federal laws. However, with the passage of the Omnibus Crime Control and Safe Streets Act of 1968, Congress provided resources for local agencies for equipment, training, and man-power. In the 1970s, Strike programs were initiated by the Attorney General of the Nixon Administration. The Strike programs instituted various federal law enforcement agencies to combat organized crime.[28] Today, local police officers are often incorporated into federal task forces for the DEA and the FBI. For example, in Wichita, Kansas, police officers from the Wichita Police Department and the county sheriff's department are members of an FBI Task Force investigating commercial robberies.

There are, however, approximately fifty federal law enforcement agencies and to discuss each one individually would be too cumbersome for any book on policing. Most federal agencies have limited powers and their investigative powers are narrow in scope. Federal law enforcement agencies can be found in the Department of Justice, the Department of Treasury, the Department of State, the Department of Agriculture, the Department of Transportation, Department of Interior, Department of Education, and the U.S. Post Office.

There are approximately 69,000 full-time personnel employed by the federal government who are authorized to make arrests and carry firearms.

The Department of Justice

About half of all federal officers authorized to carry firearms and make arrests are employed by law enforcement agencies located in the Department of Justice.[29] The Department of Justice conducts investigations and coordinates investigations of other departments and deals specifically with organized crime. The Justice Department is also responsible for civil rights violations and investigates complaints

---

28. Johnson, 167–182.

29. Brian A. Reaves, *Federal Law Enforcement Officers, 1993,* (Washington, DC: Bureau of Justice Statistics, U.S. Department of Justice, 1994), 1.

in this area. The Attorney General, one member of the Department of Justice, is the chief legal officer of the United States Government.

The Federal Bureau of Investigation

There are approximately 10,000 special agents in the FBI. The FBI has broad investigative responsibilities covering more than 250 crimes. The Federal Bureau of Investigation also has concurrent jurisdiction with the Drug Enforcement Administration (DEA) over drug crimes under the Federal Controlled Substance Act.[30] It has jurisdiction over crimes that include: bank robbery; interstate crimes, such as kidnapping; auto theft; fraud against the government; civil rights violations; organized crime; and internal security, which includes espionage. The Federal Bureau of Investigation also operates the FBI Academy for law enforcement officers, it operates a crime laboratory, it issues the Uniform Crime Reports, and it issues the FBI *Law Enforcement Bulletin*. Recently FBI field officers established "task forces" working with local law enforcement to handle a specific crime problems in local communities. The FBI office in Wichita, Kansas, works closely with local police to investigate commercial robberies.

The Immigration and Naturalization Service

The Immigration and Naturalization Service (INS) is an agency within the Justice Department. It maintains records on naturalization—the names of witnesses to naturalization proceedings, accounts of deportation proceedings, financial statements of aliens, and details on persons sponsoring the entry of aliens. It also maintains lists of passengers and crews on ships from foreign ports, passenger manifests, and declarations, such as information pertaining to the ship and its date and point of entry into the United States.

The INS employs approximately 9,500 employees with about 3,000 immigration inspectors with law enforcement responsibilities at ports of entry and about 1,500 criminal investigators to investigate crimes within the INS. In addition, the INS employs about 1,100 detention and deportation officers.[31]

---

30. Brian A. Reaves, *Federal Law Enforcement Officers, 1993,* (Washington, DC: Bureau of Justice Statistics, U.S. Department of Justice, 1994), 1–2.
31. Reaves, 2–3.

The *Border Patrol* is a component of the Immigration and Naturalization Service. The Border Patrol is a uniformed police agency whose mission is to prevent the smuggling of illegal aliens into the United States. They are also authorized to detect, apprehend, and initiate deportation of illegal aliens already residing in the United States. The Border Patrol officers are generally deployed along America's borders with Mexico and Canada and along United States coastal shores, but Border Patrol officers may also be assigned to any area of the country where illegal aliens may seek employment. The various patrol strategies used by Border Patrol officers include aircraft, horse, foot patrol, and automobiles.

The Drug Enforcement Administration (DEA)

The Drug Enforcement Administration (DEA) traces its roots to 1917 and the passage of the Harrison Narcotic Act. The Harrison Act was a tax law and the responsibility of collecting that tax was given to the Treasury Department. During the 1920s Congress passed additional laws increasing the authority of Treasury agents. In 1930, the Bureau of Narcotics was established within the Treasury Department. It had an excellent reputation in the law enforcement community when it was reorganized into the Bureau of Narcotics and Dangerous Drugs in 1968. In 1973, the Drug Enforcement Administration agency was created out of four agencies involved in federal drug law enforcement. These drug organizations were the Bureau of Narcotics and Dangerous Drugs (BNDD), the Office of National Narcotics Intelligence (ONNI), the Office of Drug Abuse and Law Enforcement (ODALE), and a contingent of 700 U.S. Custom Service narcotics agents and support personnel transferred.[32] The DEA is responsible for investigating major narcotics violators, for enforcing regulations governing the manufacture and sale of drugs, and for performing a myriad of other activities that support drug trafficking prevention and control. There are approximately 2,800 DEA agents.

---

32. Patricia Rachel, *Federal Narcotics Enforcement: Reorganization and Reform*, (Boston: Auburn House, 1982), 131.

U.S. Marshals

The U.S. Marshals are officers of the federal court. They have a variety of duties that include executing warrants and orders issued by the federal court, conducting fugitive investigations, arresting dangerous fugitives, maintaining custody of federal pre-trial detainees, transporting federal prisoners, escorting missile convoys, managing the asset seizure and forfeiture program of the Department of Justice, providing security for the federal courts and judges, managing the Federal Witness Protection Program, and suppressing riots on federal lands and in federal prisons.

The Department of Treasury

Approximately one quarter of federal law enforcement officers work for the various departments of the Department of Treasury—like the U.S. Customs Service, the Secret Service, the BATF, and the Intelligence Division of the Internal Revenue Service.

The U.S. Customs Service

The U.S. Customs Service maintains records of importers, exporters, custom house brokers, and custom house truckers, as well as a list of smuggling suspects. The Customs Service is responsible for insuring that the federal government receives tariffs on incoming goods and that smuggled drugs and other contraband are not allowed to reach the shores of the United States.

U.S. Secret Service

The Secret Service is best known for its role in protecting the President of the United States, but it is also involved in enforcing laws pertaining to counterfeiting, forgery, and U.S. security violations. The Secret Service maintains records on individuals who threaten the President, Vice-President, and former Presidents. It also has handwriting specimens of known forgers and is often called upon to compare handwriting samples with specimens on file for the purpose of identification. The Secret Service is also responsible for investigating credit card fraud and fraud committed through the use of the computer.

A sub-component of the Secret Service is the *Uniformed Division*, initially called the White House Police. In 1922, President Warren

Harding established the White House Police to give protection to the Executive Mansion complex. Currently—in addition to protecting the White House Complex—the Uniformed Police afford security to foreign diplomatic missions throughout the United States, to the residence of the Vice-President, and to the main Treasury building.

The Bureau of Alcohol, Tobacco, and Firearms (BATF)

The Bureau of Alcohol, Tobacco and Firearms (BATF) has the authority to investigative the criminal use of firearms and explosives. The BATF investigators are trained to investigate bombings and arson. Essentially, the BATF is responsible for two things. First, it can trace any firearm from manufacturer or importer to retailer if the weapon was manufactured or imported after 1968, and toward that end, it maintains complete lists of all federal license holders and federal explosive license holders, including manufactures, importers, and dealers. Second, it keeps records of distillers, brewers, and persons or firms who manufacture or handle alcohol, in addition to keeping inventories of retail liquor dealers, names of suppliers, and names records of bootleggers.

The Intelligence Division of the Internal Revenue Service

Intelligence Agents of the Internal Revenue Service investigate cases involving tax fraud and federal criminal law violations. They also investigate any improprieties within the Internal Revenue Service.

Other Agencies[33]

In addition to the Department of Justice and the Department of Treasury, the U.S. Postal Service and the Administrative Office of the U.S. Courts are two of the federal government's largest employers. The U.S. Courts have about 3,800 employees who are responsible for supervising criminal offenders on probation or parole. The Postal Service employs approximately 2,100 in criminal investigation and law enforcement. They employ an additional 1,500 to provide security for employees, facilities, and assets.

---

33. Reaves, 3-4.

The *National Park Service* employs about 2,000 employees with arrest and firearm authority. This total includes 600 *U.S. Park Police* who provide police service along with 1,500 *Park Rangers* who are commissioned as law enforcement officers. The *U.S. Capitol Police* employ about 1,100 police officers who provide security and protection or police response and patrol service for the U.S. Capital grounds and buildings.

The *Tennessee Valley Authority* (TVA) employs approximately 750 police officers with about one half performing security and protection duties for nuclear plants and about one half performing police response and patrol duties. The *U.S. Forest Service* has about 730 police officers who perform police and investigative services for the National forests and their users. The *General Service Administration* employs about 730 police officers who provide patrol and investigative services for federal buildings and property. The *U.S. Fish and Wildlife Service* has about 620 police officers who also have law enforcement responsibilities. Finally, the *U.S. Supreme Court Police* provide security protection for Supreme Court Justices, and employees of the Supreme Court. Congress made the Supreme Court Police powers effective on December 29, 1982.

Summary

The structure of American law enforcement has its historical roots in Anglo-Saxon England. When the British colonists settled on the eastern shores of the present United States, they brought the English system of law enforcement with them. Like the English system, the American law enforcement system was decentralized. Law enforcement was primarily a local responsibility. This philosophy of policing still holds true in contemporary America.

The structure of law enforcement can be divided into three levels: the federal, the state, and the local. Modern America has law enforcement officers at all three levels. Local law enforcement officers include any police officer working for villages, towns, townships, cities, and counties. Small communities comprise the majority of police agencies in America. These small police agencies usually employ ten or fewer officers. The primary mission of creating policing agencies at the local level has always been to maintain social order. Today, municipal police departments are accepted as an important element of city government. The police mission has been defined as the "maintenance of social order within carefully pre-scribed ethical and constitutional restrictions."

The police are assigned to a wide variety of functions usually without any degree of government planning. The priorities or ob-jectives of the police functions are not specified. The police operate in a broad mission with broad functions. When government officials don't know whom to assign to a specific task, the task usually goes to the police. The police function by responding to specific inci-dents—what the police refer to as reactive policing (a citizen calls the police and the police react to the citizen's complaint). But the current trend is a move toward proactive policing in which the po-lice initiate a specific action—a drug buy, for example—for the pur-pose of making an arrest.

Policing in America has a big city focus. The entertainment in-dustry and the news media play up the big city angle. For instance, big city crime news is emphasized over suburban or rural crime news and action-packed police dramas are usually set in Los Ange-les, San Francisco, New York, Chicago, or Miami.

In addition to big-city and small-town police forces, there are county sheriffs' departments and county police departments. County police frequently exist when the Sheriff's Office provides limited service. County police generally provide police service in the unin-corporated areas of the county. As an elected official, the county sheriff is unique in policing. The Sheriff's duties can vary from county to county and from state to state, though they generally re-quire him to be a tax collector, a coroner, an assessor, or to oversee the maintenance of the county highways. Normally, the Sheriff's office has charge of a detention facility and it usually has the task of executing criminal warrants and serving civil papers. Another func-tion of the Sheriff's Department includes the security of the county courthouse. The full-service sheriff's office provides patrol, courts, and correctional services.

All states, except Hawaii, have some form of state police agency. The first modern state police agency was established in 1905 by the Commonwealth of Pennsylvania. The Pennsylvania State Police be-came the model for other state police departments. Momentum for establishing state police agencies began in 1915, and between 1915 and 1921, twenty-three states organized some form of state police agency. The state police patrol state highways enforcing state traffic laws and they also have investigative powers. Many state police agencies are responsible for maintaining criminal history records, fingerprint files, and state crime statistics. They also investigate criminal complaints against local police officers and agencies. In the 1920s, many states established another form of state police known as the "Highway Patrol" who are responsible, primarily, for enforcing traffic laws on state highways and state-highway property. Those states that have Highway Patrol agencies have created general investigative agencies to investigate crimes occurring in rural areas or to assist local police that lack the manpower to investigate sophisticated crime.

At the state level there are numerous miscellaneous agencies such as Liquor Control Boards, Fish and Game Commissions, and Racing Commissions that have specific law enforcement authority.

There are approximately fifty federal law enforcement agencies. Most federal agencies have limited powers and their investigative powers are narrow in scope. The best-known of the federal agencies is the Federal Bureau of Investigation which has jurisdiction over interstate crimes, bank robberies, and internal security. The Drug Enforcement Administration is responsible for investigating major narcotics violators, enforcing regulations governing the manufacture and selling of drugs, and performing a myriad of other activities. The U.S. Marshals' duties include executing warrants, conducting fugitive investigations, transporting federal prisoners, and managing asset seizure and forfeiture programs. Other well-known federal law enforcement agencies are the Secret Service, which protects the President and Vice-President, and the Bureau of Alcohol, Tobacco and Firearms which investigates the criminal use of firearms and explosives.

Key Terms

BATF
big-city focus
Big Six Cities
county police
county sheriff
constable
coroner
DEA

medical examiner
municipal police
Pennsylvania State Police
police mission
proactive policing
reactive policing
rural police
state police

FBI   U.S. Customs
highway patrol   U.S. Marshals
INS   U.S. Secret Service

Review Questions

1. What kind of policing system does the United States have?
2. Describe the three levels of law enforcement in the United States?
3. What is the police mission?
4. Describe the police functions?
5. Describe the Big City Focus of policing?
6. Describe the duties of the county sheriff?
7. Describe the duties of the state police?
8. Describe the duties of the FBI?

References

American Bar Association. *The Urban Police Function*. New York: American Bar Association, 1973.

Bechtel, H. Kenneth. *State Police in the United States: A Social-Historical Analysis*. Westport, CT: Greenwood Press, 1995.

The Big Six, Washington: Police Foundation, 1991.

Brown, Lee P. "The Role of the Sheriff." *The Future of Policing*. Edited by Alvin W. Cohn. Beverley Hills: Sage, 1978.

Conti, Philip M. *The Pennsylvania State Police: A History of Service to the Commonwealth, 1905 to the Present*. Harrisburg, PA: Stackpole Books, 1977.

Dictionary of Criminal Justice Data Technology. 2d ed. Washington: U.S. Department of Justice, Bureau of Justice Statistics, 1981.

Eastman, George D., Ed. *Municipal Police Administration*. Washington: International City Management Association, 1972.

Felkenes, George T. *The Criminal Justice System: Its Functions and Personnel*. Englewood Cliffs, NJ: Prentice-Hall, 1973.

Gladwin, I. *The Sheriff: The Man and His Office*. London: Victor Gollanez, 1974.

Goldstein, Herman. *Policing A Free Society*. Cambridge, MA: Ballinger, 1977.

Johnson, David R. *American Law Enforcement: A History*. St. Louis: Forum Press, 1981.

Kansas. *State Medical Examination Act* (1968): sec. 52: 17B- 78.

Maguire, Branden, et al. "Rural Police Job Function," *Police Studies* 14: 4.

McCann, S. Anthony. *County-Wide Law Enforcement: A Report on a Survey of Central Police Services in 97 Counties*. New York: National Association of Counties Research Foundation, 1975.

"Police Departments in Large Cities, 1987." *Bureau of Justice Statistics: Special Report*. Washington: U.S. Department of Justice, Office of Programs, 1987.

Rachel, Patricia. *Federal Narcotics Enforcement: Reorganization and Reform*. Boston: Auburn House, 1982.

Reaves, Brian A. *Federal Law Enforcement Officers, 1993*. Washington: Bureau of Justice Statistics, Department of Justice, 1994.

———. "Sheriffs' Departments 1990." *A LEMAS Report*. 1991.

———. "State and Local Police Departments, 1990." *A LEMAS Report*. Washington: U.S. Department of Justice, Office of Justice Programs, Bureau of Statistics, 1992.

Sopher, Irwin M. and William C. Masemore. "The Police Officer and the Medical Examiner, *Police* 16, (1971): 3.

Walker, Samuel. *A Critical History of Police Reform*. Lexington, MA: Lexington Books, 1977.

CHAPTER 3

The Police and Constitutional Law

Major Issues

1. What is the importance of the Supreme Court's role in policing?
2. What are the important issues of the Fourth Amendment?
4. What are the important issues of the Fifth Amendment?
5. What are the important issues of the Sixth Amendment?

Introduction

The United States is governed by laws that are grounded in the United States Constitution. In enforcing the laws of his or her individual state, the police officer's role is ultimately determined by the Constitution.

Our founding fathers adopted the federal Constitution in 1789 establishing our present form of government and its three branches: the legislative, the judicial, and the executive. Prior to the adoption of the Constitution as the supreme law of the land, a controversy existed between supporters of the Constitution and its opponents. The main disagreement was that the Constitution lacked a section guaranteeing individual rights to the citizens of the country. As a means of gaining support for the adoption of the Constitution, an agreement was made that the Constitution would include a Bill of Rights. In 1791, the first ten amendments to the constitution—the Bill of Rights, which secured the rights of individuals—were adopted. Supporters of the Bill of Rights insisted that a guarantee of individual rights was needed to protect Americans from potential abuses by the national government.

Initially, the Bill of Rights was intended to protect the American citizen from possible abuses by the federal government It did nothing to curtail states' abuse of personal freedoms. However, the adoption of the Fourteenth Amendment in 1868 and the United States Supreme Court's interpretation that the "due process clause" of the Fourteenth Amendment makes the Bill of Rights applicable to the states led to the nationalization of the Bill of Rights. Since a state cannot abuse a citizen's individual rights and a police officer functions as an agent of the state—enforcing state laws—the actions of police officers come under federal scrutiny.

It is the job of the United States Supreme Court to decide how the United States Constitution is to be interpreted. The Supreme Court functions as the court of last resort, it serves as the last stop in the judicial interpretation of a law or an action that challenges our understanding of the Constitution.

In this century, numerous police actions have been interpreted as being in conflict with the Bill of Rights. Primarily, the Fourth, Fifth, and Sixth Amendments of the Constitution dictate the limits of police behavior in matters of a citizen's individual rights.

In 1803 the Supreme Court under Chief Justice John Marshall in the *Marbury v. Madison*[1] case decided that the Supreme Court had the power of judicial review to determine the legality of the laws and the actions of the legislative and executive branches of government. The *Marbury v. Madison* case determined that the judges were responsible for protecting the rights of individuals.

The Fourth Amendment

The Fourth Amendment has important implications for the police officer. Police activity such as arrest, due process, probable cause, search and seizure, warrants, line-ups, and hot pursuit are some areas that come under the purview of the Fourth Amendment. The Fourth Amendment states:

> The right of the people to be secure in their persons, houses, papers, and effects, against unreasonable searches and seizures, shall not be violated, and no Warrants shall issue, but upon probable cause, supported by Oath or affirmation, and particularly describing the place to be searched, and the person or things to be seized.

Arrest

An arrest can be defined as "taking an adult or juvenile into physical custody by authority of law, for the purpose of charging the person with a criminal offense or a delinquent act or status offense, terminating with the recording of a specific offense."[2] Al-

---

1. 1 Stat. 4 (1978)
2. Frank Schmalleger, *Criminal Justice Today: An Introductory Text for the 21st*

The Bill of Rights

Amendment I

Congress shall make no law respecting an establishment of religion, or prohibiting the free exercise thereof; or abridging the freedom of speech, or of the press, or the right of the people peaceably to assemble, and to petition the Government for a redress of grievances.

Amendment II

A well regulated Militia, being necessary to the security of a free State, the right of the people to keep and bear Arms, shall not be infringed.

Amendment III

No Soldier shall, in time of peace be quartered in any house, without the consent of the Owner, nor in time of war, but in a manner to be prescribed by law.

Amendment IV

The right of the people to be secure in their persons, houses, papers, and effects, against unreasonable searches and seizures, shall not be violated, and no Warrants shall issue, but upon probable cause, supported by Oath or affirmation, and particularly describing the place to be searched, and the persons or things to be seized.

Amendment V

No person shall be held to answer for a capital, or otherwise infamous crime, unless on a presentment or indictment of a Grand Jury, except in cases arising in the land or naval forces, or in the Militia, when in actual service in time of War or public danger; nor shall any person be subject for the same offense to be twice put in jeopardy of life or limb, nor shall be compelled in any criminal case to be a witness against himself, nor be deprived of life, liberty, or property, without due process of law; nor shall private property be taken for public use without just compensation.

Amendment VI

In all criminal prosecutions, the accused shall enjoy the right to a speedy and public trial, by an impartial jury of the State and district wherein the crime shall have been committed; which district shall have been previously ascertained by law, and to be informed of the nature and cause of the accusation; to be confronted with the witnesses against him; to have compulsory process for obtaining witnesses in his favor, and to have the assistance of counsel for his defense.

Amendment VII

In Suite at common law, where the value in controversy shall exceed twenty dollars, the right of trial by jury shall be preserved, and no fact tried by a jury shall be otherwise re-examined in any Court of the United States, than according to the rules of the common law.

Amendment VIII

Excessive bail shall not be required, nor excessive fines imposed, nor cruel and unusual punishments inflicted.

Amendment IX

The enumeration in the Constitution of certain rights shall not be construed to deny or disparage others retained by the people.

Amendment X

The powers not delegated to the United States by the Constitution, nor prohibited by it to the States, are reserved to the States respectively, or to the people.

Amendment XIV

Section 1. All persons born or naturalized in the United States and subject to the jurisdiction thereof, are citizens of the United States and subject to the jurisdiction thereof, are citizens of the United States and of the State wherein they reside. No State shall make or enforce any law which shall abridge the privileges or immunities of citizens of the United States; nor shall any State deprive any person of life, liberty, or property, without due process of law; nor deny to any person within its jurisdiction the equal protection of the laws.

Section 2. Representatives shall be apportioned among the several States according to their respective numbers, counting the whole number of persons in each State, excluding Indians not taxed. But when the right to vote at any election for the choice of electors for President and Vice President of the United States, Representatives in Congress, the Executive and Judicial officers of a State, or the members of the Legislature thereof, is denied to any of the male inhabitants of such State, being twenty-one years of age, and citizens of the United States, or in any way abridged, except for participation in rebellion, or other crime, the basis of representation therein shall be reduced in the proportion which the number of such male citizens shall bear to the whole number of male citizens twenty-one years of age in such State.

Section 3. No person shall be a Senator or Representative in Congress, or elector of President and Vice President, or hold any office, civil or military, under the United States, or under any State, who, having previously taken an oath, as a member of congress, or as an officer of the United States, or as a member of any State legislature, or as an executive or judicial officer of any State, to support the Constitution of the United States, shall have engaged in insurrection or rebellion against the same, or given aid or comfort to the enemies thereof. But Congress may by a vote of two-thirds of each House, remove such disability.

Section 4. The validity of the public debt of the United States, authorized by law, including debts incurred for payment of pensions and bounties for services in suppressing insurrection or rebellion, shall not be questioned. But neither the United States nor any State shall assume or pay any debt or obligation incurred in aid of insurrection or rebellion against the United States, or any claim for the loss or emancipation of any slave; but all such debts, obligations and claims shall be held illegal and void.

Section 5. The Congress shall have power to enforce, by appropriate legislation, the provisions of this article.

though police officers are government employees with formal authority to make arrests, there are times when arrests by private citizens are permissible.

Generally, a *private citizen* may arrest someone who commits a crime in his presence. In most states this is applicable whether the crime is a misdemeanor or a felony. A private citizen can also make an arrest when a felony has been committed or is being committed and the private citizen has probable cause to believe that the individual being arrested is the person who committed the felony. However, the author suggests that a private citizen take caution in making an arrest, since most private citizens are not familiar with criminal law. Occasionally, what appears to be an illegal act may not be. Even if a crime is being committed, the private citizen who takes action may be putting himself or another individual in harm's way. Criminal offenders often will not cooperate with the police; they will generally cooperate less with a private citizen.

A police officer can make a lawful arrest when he has an arrest warrant. An arrest warrant provides the police officer with legal protection, and a police officer should make an arrest with an arrest warrant whenever possible. A police officer can also arrest a suspect if he has probable cause to believe that an arrest warrant has been issued. Any police officer who has probable cause to believe that an individual has committed or is committing a felony or a misdemeanor and believes that:

1. The person will not be apprehended or evidence of the crime will be irretrievably lost unless the person is immediately arrested;
2. The person may cause injury to self or others or damage to property unless immediately arrested;
3. The person has intentionally inflicted bodily harm to another person; or
4. Any crime except a traffic infraction has been or is being committed by the person in the officer's view.[3]

Since a police officer must have *probable cause* before making an arrest, the term needs to be clearly defined. The term probable cause means "A set of facts and circumstances that would induce a

---

Century, 3rd ed., (Engelwood Cliffs, NJ: Prentice-Hall, 1995), 714.
  3. Kansas Statutes Annotated 24 (1988), 353.

reasonably intelligent and prudent person to believe that a particular person had committed a specific crime; [or] reasonable grounds to make or believe an accusation."[4] In *Dunway v. New York*[5] the United States Supreme Court ruled that the police-station detention of a suspect without probable cause constitutes an illegal arrest.

The Fourth Amendment also protects individuals against unreasonable *searches and seizures* of property and possessions. A warrant can be issued for the arrest, search, and seizure of persons or objects—providing that probable cause exists. Typically, most arrests outside the home are made without arrest warrants, while arrests made in the home are made with arrest warrants. The Fourth Amendment protects people, places, and things from physical intrusion from police officers. To meet the guidelines established by the Fourth Amendment it is best to obtain a search warrant to search private property, but there are several exceptions when a search warrant may not be required to conduct a search, including: searches incident to arrest; consent searches; stop-and-frisk searches; vehicle searches; inventory searches, and open-field and plain-view searches.

The Fourth Amendment permits a *search incident to lawful arrest*. A police officer making an arrest can legally search an arrested person for a concealed weapon in order to protect himself and other police officers and to prevent the arrestee from escaping or destroying evidence. A search warrant does not necessarily have to be obtained for a search incident to a lawful arrest. In *Chimel v. California*[6] the United States Supreme Court stated that the police may search the locality under the immediate control of an arrestee when making a valid arrest, regardless of whether the arrest has been made with or without a warrant. The Supreme Court defines immediate control as "the area from within which [one] might gain possession of a weapon or destructible evidence."

The *exclusionary rule*, with few exceptions, excludes any evidence obtained illegally in violation of the Fourth, Fifth, and Sixth Amendment. In 1914 the Supreme Court, in *Weeks v. United States*,[7] decided that illegally obtained evidence seized by federal law enforcement officers can not be admissible as evidence in a federal

---

4. Frank Schmalleger, *Criminal Justice Today*, 3rd ed., (Englewood Cliffs, NJ: Prentice-Hall, 1995), 731.
5. 442 U.S. 200 (1979)
6. 395 U.S. 752 (1969)
7. 232 U.S. 383 (1914)

court. At the time, the exclusionary rule as outlined by the Weeks case did not apply to state law enforcement officers. It was not until 1961 in *Mapp v. Ohio*[8] that the Supreme Court applied the exclusionary rule to state law enforcement officers. *Mapp* disallowed the use of illegally obtained evidence to be used in state courts. Since the *Mapp* decision the Supreme Court has rendered a number of important decisions on the exclusionary rule. In *Nix v. Williams*[9] the Supreme Court decided that illegally obtained evidence could be admissible as evidence provided that the police discovered the evidence through lawful means. The Supreme Court in *United States v. Leon*[10] found that evidence obtained illegally could be admissible as evidence if the police officer—acting in good faith—believes that the search warrant issued by a magistrate is valid.

Police officers may search without warrants and without reasonable suspicion of a crime if they receive the voluntary permission of the person who has the right to give *consent*. A consent search has to be voluntary and the person giving the consent for the search has to have the authority to give consent for the search. The Supreme Court ruled that "Voluntariness is a question of fact to be determined from all the circumstances, and while the subject's knowledge of a right is a factor to be taken into account, the prosecutor is not required to demonstrate such knowledge as a perquisite to establishing voluntary consent."[11] In *Florida v. Royer*[12] the Supreme Court decided that if consent is given after an illegal act by the police then the search is invalid since the consent has been tainted.

Stop and Frisk Searches allow the police to stop and frisk an individual who they suspect of being involved in a criminal activity and who may be considered dangerous. In *Terry v. Ohio*[13] the Supreme Court ruled that the police could detain an individual without probable cause for questioning. The stopping of a person is permitted and does not constitute an arrest when unusual behavior has been observed leading to the reasonable suspicion that a criminal act may be likely. It should be noted, however, that reasonable suspicion is not as strictly defined as probable cause. The police officer can se-

---

8. 367 U.S. 643 (1961)
9. 467 U.S. 431 (1984)
10. 468 v. 897 (1984)
11. Schneckloth v. Bustamonte 412 U.S. 218 (1973)
12. 460 U.S. 491 (1983)
13. 392 U.S. 1 (1968)

lect specific facts to justify his suspicion. Therefore, a police officer may frisk a person if he believes the suspect may be dangerous, but he may search only for weapons and not for evidence. The Supreme Court ruled that

> Where a police officer observers unusual conduct which leads him reasonably to conclude in light of his experience that criminal activity may be afoot...he identifies himself as a policeman and makes reasonable inquiries,...he is entitled for the protection of himself and others in the area to conduct a carefully limited search of the outer clothing in an attempt to discover weapons which might be used to assault him.

The Supreme Court decided in the 1920s that *vehicle searches* could be made without requiring a search warrant. Originally, searching vehicles without a warrant was a practice reserved for motor vehicles stopped on a highway. It was thought that the vehicle might be gone before a search warrant could be obtained. The 1925 case of *Carrol v. United States*[14] established a precedent allowing automobiles to be searched without a search warrant. The court felt that the automobile might be taken out of the jurisdiction, or that evidence could be destroyed, and that it was appropriate for the police to search a vehicle without a warrant provided they had probable cause. In a 1981[15] case, the Supreme Court ruled that the police, in a warrantless search of an automobile, can search the passenger compartment and any containers found in the passenger compartment—a container being any object capable of holding another object, including glove compartments, bags, luggage, boxes, and clothing.

In *United States v. Ross*[16] the Supreme Court indicated that when the police had probable cause for a warrantless search of a vehicle that they could search the entire vehicle, including the trunk, and open any packages or luggage found that could reasonably contain items in question.

Police officers arresting a suspect are allowed to perform an *inventory* search of the suspect and of his possessions. A search warrant is not required. An inventory search is "an incidental administrative

---

14. 267 U.S. 132 (1925)
15. New York v. Belton 453 U.S. 454 (1981)
16. 456 U.S. 798 (1982)

step following arrest and preceding incarceration."[17] The Supreme Court in *Illinois v. Lafayette*[18] indicated that inventory searches do not rest on probable cause. The court further claimed that it was not in a position to second-guess police administrative methods that would best deter theft and false claims by its employees and that would best preserve the security of the police station. The court further stated in *Illinois v. Lafayette* that it is not " 'unreasonable' for police, as part of the routine procedure incident to incarcerating an arrested person, to search any container or article in his possession, in accordance with established inventory procedures."

To summarize, an inventory search can be made without a warrant for very practical reasons. The arrestee's property has to be protected while in police custody. Furthermore police personnel have to be protected from false claims of damaged, lost, or stolen property. Finally, the police are responsible for protecting themselves from danger.

The *plain view doctrine* allows a police officer to search and seize contraband and illegal items, such as cocaine or stolen goods, that happen to be in his or her presence. In other words, if the police officer has a legal right to be where the contraband is, a warrant to seize the contraband does not have to be obtained. There are four basic elements of the "plain view" doctrine:

1. Awareness of the item must be gained solely through the sense of sight;
2. The officer must be legally present in the place from which he or she sees the item;
3. Discovery of the items must be inadvertent; and
4. The items must be immediately recognized as being subject to seizure.[19]

The Fourth Amendment protects persons and not places. Under the *open field* doctrine, police officers can enter and search undeveloped land and fields that are in public view. Since open fields are accessible to the public, either physically or visually, privacy cannot be expected; therefore, police officers do not have to obtain a search

---

17. Deleware v. Pouse, 440 U.S. 648, 654 (1979)

18. 462 U.S. 640 (1983)

19. Rolando V. del Carmen and Jeffery Walker, *Briefs of 100 Leading Cases in Law Enforcement*, (Cincinnati: Anderson, 1991), 112.

warrant to search them. However, a police officer must obtain a search warrant when searching a *curtilage*—the grounds and buildings adjacent to a dwelling. A curtilage is not considered an open field and a warrantless search of a curtilage will generally be considered an unreasonable search.

In 1928 the Supreme Court heard the first case dealing with *electronic surveillance*. The case of *Olmstead v. United States*[20] ruled that wiretapping was not a violation of search and seizure under the Fourth Amendment unless there exists an invasion of privacy of an area constitutionally protected. In 1967 the Supreme Court reversed the *Olmstead v. United States* decision. The case of *Katz v. United States* raised two major constitutional questions[21]:

1. Whether a public telephone booth is a constitutionally protected area so that evidence obtained by attaching an electronic listening recording device to the top of such a booth is obtained in violation of the right to privacy of the user of the booth.
2. Whether physical penetration of a constitutionally protected area is necessary before a search and seizure violates the Fourth Amendment.

The *Katz* decision has become the legal standard by which search and seizure cases are reviewed. Electronic surveillance—including wiretapping—comes under the purview of search and seizure of the Fourth Amendment which protects a citizen's right to a "reasonable expectation of privacy." The Fourth Amendment protects people—and not areas—against unreasonable searches. Therefore, the Fourth Amendment's protection travels with the individual. The court stated, "electronically listening to and recording the petitioner's words violated the privacy upon which he justifiably relied while using the telephone booth and [that it] thus constitutes a "search and seizure" within the meaning of the Fourth Amendment." The Supreme Court holds that the Fourth Amendment includes not only seizure of tangible items but extends to oral statements.

20. 277 U.S. 438 (1928)
21. 399 U.S. 347 (1967)

The Fifth Amendment

> ...nor shall [he] be compelled in any criminal case to be a witness against himself, nor be deprived of life, liberty, or property, without due process of law....

The Fifth Amendment of the Bill of Rights protects individuals accused of a crime against self-incrimination. It assures that no individual can be compelled to answer any question if the answer could help convict him of a crime. The cornerstone of the American accusatorial system is the freedom from self-incrimination. American policing in its attempts to solve crime has not always recognized the "self-incriminating" clause of the Fifth Amendment. For example, in the 1936 *Brown v. Mississippi*[22] case, a confession for murder was used that was obtained after the defendant was beaten by a deputy sheriff. Brown was told he would be beaten until he confessed. During the trial, Brown claimed that his confession was false, and the deputy sheriff performing the brutality—which left marks on Brown's back—did not deny that a confession was forced from Brown. Thus, it was determined that Brown's due-process rights guaranteed by the Fourteenth Amendment were denied and his confession was held to be inadmissable.

In *Miranda v. Arizona*[23] the Supreme Court declared that the police must inform a suspect—who is the subject of a custodial interrogation—of his constitutional rights involving self-incrimination and of his right to be represented by an attorney. Therefore, it is now standard practice to inform a suspect of his constitutional rights before he can be questioned by the police. These rights are as follows:

1. You have the right to remain silent. You do not have to answer any questions or make any statements unless you want to.
2. If you make any statement it can be used and will be used in a court of law.
3. You have the right to have an attorney present during any questioning.
4. If you cannot afford an attorney, one will be appointed for you prior to questioning.

---

22. 297 U.S. 278 (1936)
23. 384 U.S. 436 (1966)

The *Miranda* decision is over thirty years old and there are legal scholars who are claiming that the original intent of *Miranda* is eroding. There are several cases that address this erosion of *Miranda*. For example, the "public safety" exception to the *Miranda* warnings. When the police are legitimately concerned about public safety, the questions they ask a suspect may be admissible in court.[24] Further, voluntary statements made by suspects who are mentally disoriented and to whom the police give the *Miranda* warning can be admissible as evidence in court.[25] Oral confessions, the Supreme Court has ruled, are admissible in court if the suspect voluntarily agrees to talk to police.[26]

The Sixth Amendment

> In all criminal prosecutions, the accused shall...be informed of the nature and cause of the accusation;...be confronted with the witnesses against him;...have compulsory process for obtaining witnesses in his favor, and...have the assistance of counsel in his favor.

One of the most important issues pertaining to the Sixth Amendment—as it applies to police investigation—is the *lineup*. The lineup is one technique the police use to identify the potential suspect of a crime. The police place several suspects in a line for the express purpose of having either the victim or a witness identify the suspect as being the criminal. Once a suspect has been formally charged with a crime, the Supreme Court considers a lineup to be a "critical stage of the proceedings" which requires counsel to be present.[27] Ultimately, whenever the police use a lineup it must be conducted in a fair manner and be free from bias. For example, the individuals in the lineup should be of the same sex, they should be approximately the same age and height, they should have similar skin texture and hair color, and they should be wearing similar clothes.

---

24. New York v. Quarles 467 U.S. 649 (1984)
25. Colorado v. Connelly 479 U.S. 157 (1986)
26. Connecticut v. Barrett 479 U.S. 523 (1987)
27. United States v. Wade 388 U.S. 218 (1967)

In *Powell v. Alabama*[28] nine young black males were accused or raping two white girls on a train in Alabama. The young men were illiterate and were not represented by an attorney. They were tried and convicted in one day and given the death penalty. The Supreme Court found that the young men were denied due process of law and the equal protection of the law as guaranteed by the Fourteenth Amendment. The court specifically addressed the following:

1. They were not given a fair, impartial, and deliberate trial;
2. They were denied the right to counsel, with the accustomed incidents of consultation and opportunity to prepare for trial; and
3. They were tried before juries from which qualified members of their own race were systematically excluded.

The Supreme Court delineated that defendants are presumed innocent until they are convicted of a crime. Furthermore, a defendant should be afforded the opportunity to obtain an attorney of his choice, or else it is the duty of the trial judge to appoint counsel for the accused when he is unable to employ counsel. Additionally, the Supreme Court claimed that "the failure of the trial court to give them [the defendants] reasonable time and opportunity to secure counsel was a clear denial of due process."

The Supreme Court extended the right to an attorney in all felony cases in *Gideon v. Wainwright*;[29] prior to this, the right to attorney existed for capital cases, as required in the *Powell* case. The *Argersinger* case, decided by the Supreme Court in 1972, extended the right to be represented by an attorney to defendants in misdemeanor cases in which the possibility of incarceration exists.

Another decision of importance to police officers was a result of the case of *Escobedo v. Illinois*.[30] Escobedo was arrested without a warrant and accused of killing his brother-in-law. During the interrogation process, Escobedo made numerous requests to confer with his lawyer. Also, Escobedo's attorney made numerous requests to confer with his client. The requests by both Escobedo and his attorney were ignored. The Supreme Court wrote "We have learned the lesson of history, ancient and modern, that a system of criminal law enforcement which comes to depend on the 'confession' will, in the

28. 287 U.S. 45 (1932)
29. 372 U.S. 335 (1963)
30. 378 v. 478 (1964)

long run, be less reliable and more subject to abuses than a system which depends on extrinsic evidence independently secured through skillful investigation." The court ruled that Escobedo had the right to confer with his attorney and that this denial violated his Sixth Amendment rights that are made obligatory by the Fourteenth Amendment.

Summary

The United States is governed by laws that are grounded in the United States Constitution. In enforcing the laws of his or her individual state, the police officer's role is ultimately determined by the Constitution.

The United States Supreme Court is responsible for interpreting the Constitution, thereby establishing guidelines that the police at all levels of government are required to follow.

The Fourth, Fifth, and Sixth Amendments have especially important implications for the police. Arrests, due process, probable cause, search and seizure, warrants, and line-ups are all under the purview of the Fourth Amendment. The Fifth Amendment protects accused individuals against self-incrimination. It assures that no individual can be compelled to answer any questions if the answers could help convict him of a crime. The Sixth Amendment gives a citizen the right to an attorney when he or she is accused of a crime. This right exists not only during trial, but also during police interrogations, during arraignment, and during a line-up.

Key Terms

arrest
consent searches
curtilage
electronic surveillance
exclusionary rule
Fifth Amendment
Fourth Amendment
inventory search
lineup

open field
plain view
probable cause
Sixth Amendment
Supreme Court
search and seizure
stop and frisk
vehicle search

Review Questions

1. What influence does the United States Supreme Court have on policing?
2. What is the Bill of Rights?
3. What are the key elements of the Fourth Amendment?
4. What are the key elements of the Fifth Amendment?
5. What are the key elements of the Sixth Amendment?

References

Argersinger v. Hamlin 407 U.S. 25 (1972)
Brown v. Mississippi 297 U.S. 278 (1936)
Carrol v. United States 267 U.S. 132 (1925)
Chimel v. California 395 U.S. 752 (1969)
Colorado v. Connelly 479 U.S. 649 (1984)
Connecticut v. Barrett 479 U.S. 523 (1987)
del Carmen, Rolando V. and Jeffery Walker. *Briefs of 100 Leading Cases in Law Enforcement.* Cincinnati: Anderson Publishing Company, 1991.
Delaware v. Pouse 440 U.S. 648 (1979)
Escobedo v. Illinois 378 U.S. 478 (1964)
Florida v. Royer 392 U.S. 1 (1968)
Gideon v. Wainwright 372 U.S. 335 (1963)
Illinois v. Lafayette 462 U.S. 640 (1983)
Kansas Statutes Annotated, Volume 24, 1988.
Katz v. United States 399 U.S. 347 (1967)
Mapp v. Ohio 367 U.S.643 (1961)
Miranda v. Arizona 384 U.S. 436 (1966)
New York v. Belton 453 U.S. 454 (1981)
New York v. Quarles 467 U.S. 649 (1984)
Nix v. Williams 467 U.S. 431 (1984)
Olmstead v. United States 277 U.S. 438 (1928)
Payton v. New York 445 U.S. 573 (1980)
Powell v. Alabama 287 U.S. 45 (1932)
Schmalleger, Frank. *Criminal Justice Today: An Introductory Text for the 21st Century.* 3d ed. Englewood Cliffs, NJ: Prentice-Hall, 1985.
Schneckloth v. Bustamonte 412 U.S. 218 (1973)
Terry v. Ohio 392 U.S. 1 (1968)
United States v. Leon 468 U.S.533 (1988)
United States v. Ross 456 U.S. 798 (1982)
United States v. Wade 388 U.S. 218 (1967)
Weeks v. United States 232 U.S. 383 (1914)

CHAPTER **4**

Private Security

1. Why is the private security industry important to crime prevention and control in our society?
2. Why is it important that public police agencies and the private security field develop a partnership?
3. Private security personnel should assume many of the functions currently being carried out by police officers.

Introduction

Traditionally the police force has been society's principal means of controlling and preventing crime. However, as we get closer to the twenty-first century, scholars who study crime prevention and crime control recognize that the police agencies in America, without the assistance of the general public, other units of government, and the private sector, will not be able to control and prevent crime effectively. The police and the other criminal justice components—the judiciary and the corrections field—will find it extremely difficult to prevent criminality.

Currently, in the United States, two policing systems exist: the public police, who are under governmental control and who are supported by public funds, and the private police—usually referred to as private security—who are employed and supported by private individuals and companies. It has been advocated by private security specialists that the private security industry can reduce the work load of police personnel and that sophisticated alarms systems, armored trucks, security consultants, and crime prevention professionals can provide an immense amount of assistance to public police agencies.

Research indicates that with 1.5 million persons employed in private security, compared with 600,000 public police officers, the private security industry plays a vital role in our country's crime prevention and crime controlling strategies. The private security industry out-spends public police agencies by seventy-three percent. The annual spending for private security is $52 billion a year versus $30 billion per year for public law enforcement. In 1980, the National Institute of Justice found that the private security industry had expenditures larger than public law enforcement. A 1990 study, spon-

Private Security and Law Enforcement Employment

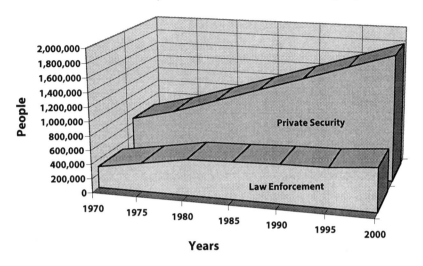

Private Security and Law Enforcement Spending

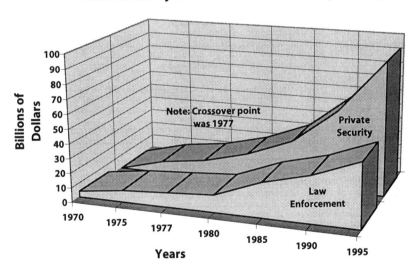

Source: William C. Cunningham, John J. Strauchs, and Clifford W. Van Meter.
"Private Security: Patterns and Trends," *National Institute of Justice*, 1991, p. 3

sored by the National Institute of Justice, for the years 1970 to 2000,
confirmed the trend that the private sector spends more money on
crime prevention and control than public law enforcement agencies.[1]

---

1. William C. Cunningham, John J. Strauchs, and Clifford W. Van Meter,

A Brief History of Private Security

The concern for security can be traced to ancient times. Guards were used by nomadic tribes to protect their flocks and themselves from raiding tribes and wild animals. Ancient rulers used guards for personal protection. For example, the Romans used the Praetorian Guards and the Egyptians used the Mamelukes. Security forces were used in Europe and England during the Middle Ages.

It should be noted that modern policing developed in the nineteenth century, but prior to the advent of a formalized public police agency, security was conducted by the military or by private citizens.

During the last century, private security received wide recognition through the efforts of Allan Pinkerton. Pinkerton established the National Detective Agency, the most successful investigative agency during the nineteenth century in America. Pinkerton provided service for the U.S. Post Office and various railroad companies and he provided protection to President Lincoln en route from Springfield, Illinois, to Washington, D.C., to be sworn in as President. Pinkerton collected intelligence data for the Union Army during the Civil War, and he provided information about workers to steel barons. According to James D. Horan, Pinkerton initiated the modern day investigative agency:

> They were the nineteenth-century prototype of the present Federal Bureau of Investigation and a forerunner of Interpol. By 1872, they had established a liaison with the important police organizations of Europe, for the exchange of information about international crime and criminals, and most of the frontier sheriffs and heads of metropolitan police in the United States sought their assistance. Through it is a little-known fact, the Pinkerton's pioneering Rogues' Gallery formed a basis for the modern FBI's Criminal Identification Bureau, the largest in the world.[2]

Pinkerton's first major competitor was William J. Burns who established the Burns Detective Agency in 1909. Burns received pub-

---

"Private Security: Patterns and Trends," *National Institute of Justice: Research in Brief*, (Washington, DC: U.S. Department of Justice, Office of Justice Programs, 1991), 1.

2. James D. Horan, *The Pinkertons: The Detective Dynasty that Made History*, (New York: Crown, 1967), x.

licity for his work involving the investigation of municipal corruption for the United States Secret Service. The Burns agency represented the American Bankers Association and the American Hotel Association.[3]

The *armored car industry* was also created in response to the crime control problem of the nineteenth century. Valuable assets such as money, securities, and jewelry needed protection and often required transportation across legal jurisdictions. Since law enforcement lacked some sophistication, a private model of security was needed. Thieves could move from jurisdiction to jurisdiction free from apprehension, and so the security of valuable assets depended upon secrecy, speed, and physical protection.

In Chicago in 1859 Washington Perry Brink launched a parcel delivery service. Others during this period who established similar services were Henry Wells, William Fargo, and Alvin Adams. In 1850 Wells, with partners, initiated the American Express Company. Wells, with Fargo, established the Wells Fargo and Company in 1852. Adams, with several associates, organized the Adams Express Company in 1854. All these companies transported valuable assets.

The Brinks company in 1881 transported the first payroll for the Western Electric Company. The first recorded delivery of bank funds by an armored car company occurred in 1900 by Brinks. The first regular contract from the Federal Reserve Bank took place in Cleveland in 1949.

Today, there are three large armored car companies: Brinks, Loomis Armored, and Wells Fargo. There are approximately 125 total armored car companies of various sizes in our country.[4]

The *guard industry* can trace its roots to Allan Pinkerton who in 1855 was given $10,000 by six Midwestern railroad companies to organize the *North West Police Agency* to provide guard and patrol service for the railroads.[5] From this period the guard industry has grown into a multi-million-dollar industry.

---

3. Milton Lipson, "Private Security: A Retrospective," in *The Annals* 498, "The Private Security Industry: Issues and Trends," Ira A. Lipman, Special Editor (1988), 21.

4. Robert D. McCrie, "The Development of the U.S. Security Industry," in *The Annals* 498, "The Private Security Industry: Issues and Trends, Ira A. Lipman, Special Editor (1988), 27–29.

5. James D. Horan, *The Pinkertons,* (New York: Bonanza, 1962), 31.

The *burglar alarm* as a security device can be traced to 1852 when August R. Pope used electricity to sound a continuous alarm when a door or window was opened without approval. It is not known if Pope marketed the burglar alarm system, but by 1900 there were several burglar alarm companies in New York City. The telegraph companies in the early part of the twentieth century provided fire, police, and messenger signals. Today, burglar alarms are a billion-dollar industry providing security not only to affluent Americans but to the middle-class as well.[6]

Defining Private Security

What does the term private security mean? Does it have the same meaning to the various segments of the American population? The issue of the meaning of private security was addressed by the *Private Security Task Force* of the mid-1970s. It was concluded that "A universally acceptable and explicit definition is difficult to construct because private security is not only identified with the performance of certain functions and activities of a public nature, but also encompasses many activities of a private nature."[7] Private security should have as one of its motivating factors the ensuring of security for lives and property. In their classic text on security, Richard Post and Arthur Kingsbury define the concept of security as "those means, active or passive, which serve to protect and preserve an environment which allows for the conduct of activities within the organization of society without disruption."[8]

The Post-Kingsbury definition of security provides for a condition that is equally as important to other governmental units such as fire departments, police departments, and the national guard. The *Private Security Task Force* postulates that a definition of private security should portray the mission and roles as it applies to security standards and goals. The *Private Security Task Force* formulated a

---

6. Robert D. McCrie, 24–27.

7. Arthur J. Bilek, Task Force Chairman, *Private Security: Standards and Goals—From the Official Private Security Task Force Report,* (Cincinnati: Anderson, 1970), 3.

8. Richard S. Post and Arthur A. Kingsbury, *Security Administration: An Introduction,* (Springfield, Ill: Charles C. Thomas, 1970), 5.

working definition that they deemed appropriate for establishing such standards and goals. Their definition of private security seems more inclusive for the private security field than the Post-Kingsbury definition and others. The Task Force stipulated that

> Private security includes those self-employed individuals and privately funded business entities and organizations providing security-related services to specific clientele for a fee, for the individual or entity that retains or employs them, or for themselves, in order to protect their persons, private property, or interests from various hazards.[9]

There are countless types of *hazards* that can interfere with or severely limit personal security and protection of property. Hazards to individuals and property include:

> Crime; fire and attendant risks, such as explosion; accidents, disasters; espionage; sabotage; subversion; civil disturbance; bombing (both actual and threatened); and, in some systems (of protection), attack by external enemies. Most security and protection systems emphasize certain hazards more than others.[10]

Hazards fall into two categories: *man-made* and *natural*. Natural disasters such as floods, hurricanes, fires and black-outs are not caused by man and are generally uncontrollable. Man-made disasters are caused by people and often are controllable. Man-made hazards include the following:

1. Accidents
2. Theft and pilferage
3. Fraud
4. Employee disloyalty
5. Subversion
6. Sabotage
7. Strikes
8. Riots

---

9. Arthur J. Bilek, *Private Security: Standards and Goals—From the Official Private Security Task Force Report,* (Cincinnati: Anderson, 1977), 4,
10. *Encyclopedia Britannica,* s.v. "security and protection systems."

**Figure 3. Common Objectives of Private Security
and Public Law Enforcement**

Source: Arthur J. Bilek. *Private Security: Standards and Goals—From the Official Private Security Task Force Report*, Anderson, 1977, p. 6.

9. Demonstrations
10. Violent crime[11]

The Contrast Between Public
and Private Security

Public and private security can be distinguished by the clientele they serve. The clientele for the private security field are concerned with prevention, deterrence, and crime detection against private

---

11. *D. Paine, Principles of Industrial Security*, (Madison, WI: Oak Security Publications, 1972), 36.

Security Continuum

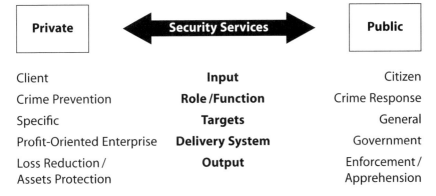

Private	Security Services	Public
Client	**Input**	Citizen
Crime Prevention	**Role/Function**	Crime Response
Specific	**Targets**	General
Profit-Oriented Enterprise	**Delivery System**	Government
Loss Reduction/ Assets Protection	**Output**	Enforcement/ Apprehension

Private Security Standards and Goals, Anderson, 1977, p. 7

property of individuals or companies. The public police are attentive to law enforcement activities, traffic control, criminal investigation, and the prevention and control of predatory crime. However, as chart 2 indicates, common objectives such as crime prevention, crime reduction, and order maintenance can apply to both the public police and the private security field.

The Private Security Task Force believed that it was important that the differences between public and private security be comprehended. The Task Force viewed security as having characteristics common to both the protection and detection services (See Figure 3). The following levels mark the contrast between the fields of private security and public policing:

1. *Input*—the manner in which the service is initiated (citizen or client)
2. *Role or Function*—predominant activity or purpose (crime response or crime prevention)
3. *Targets*—the beneficiaries or objectives to which service is directed (general public or specific client)
4. *Delivery System*—the mechanism through which services are provided (government agencies or profit-oriented enterprises)
5. *Output*—the end product of services performed (law enforcement/criminal apprehension or loss reduction/asset protection)[12]

---

12. Bilek, 6.

Major Private Security Components

Because of the sophistication of crimes based on modern technologies, society currently cannot expect the police to protect against and investigate crimes related to computers, fraud, employee theft, and various other economic crimes. Private individuals and companies cannot expect the police to patrol apartment or office buildings, computer facilities, or parking lots.

The complexity of the private security industry can be better understood by dividing it into nine categories:

1. Proprietary (in-house) Security,
2. Guard and Patrol Services,
3. Private Investigations,
4. Armored Car Services,
5. Manufacturers of Security Equipment,
7. Locksmiths,
8. Security Consultants and Engineers,
9. Other (which include categories such as drug testing, forensic analysis, and honesty testing.)[13]

Proprietary Security

There are two types of private security organizations: the proprietary security segment which is housed within the corporation and *contract security firms.*

The *Hallcrest Report II* reports that an emerging trend places security within an organization's "risk management" program that not only includes security but also internal audit, safety, fire prevention, and facility management.[14] Most large money-making organizations have established an internal security component. Proprietary security divisions that operate exclusively in-house—in which all security personnel are employees of the commercial company—tend to have large security forces.

13. William C. Cunningham, John J. Strauchs, and Clifford W. Van Meter, *The Hallcrest Report: Private Security Trends 1970–2000,* (Butterworth-Heinemann, 1990), 127.

14. *The Hallcrest Report II,* 128.

Contract security firms are hired by private companies to provide specific security services. The services that contract security companies can provide include either temporary or long term guarding, investigative services, armored-car services, polygraph testing, and various other kinds of protective services. The decision to employ contract security services often depends upon the cost, the needs of the commercial company, the qualifications of the contract personnel, and the reputation of the contract security firm. A growing number of profit-making corporations have a director of security who employs an external contract security firm. This in-house security operation is usually small with its main functions being to

1. Ensure that contract firms are supplying the type and quality of services desired,
2. Investigate (or hire external personnel to investigate) internal security losses and problems,
3. Conduct security surveys and other assessments of security threats,
4. Advise top management on security-related matters, and
5. Serve as the corporation's principal liaison for any security-related problems that occur.[15]

Guard and Patrol Services

The general public often equates private security with security guards. Typically, guards are uniformed security personnel assigned to stationary posts like gates, doors, or other specific locations to protect valuable merchandise, or they are assigned to monitor videos. Guards can also be assigned to motorized or foot patrols to monitor specific geographical areas. Guard and patrol services are provided to almost every segment of American industry. For instance, factories, banks, transportation companies, and retail companies all use guard and patrol services. Even the federal government uses guard services for federal office buildings.

The *body guard*, a special category of guard that provides *personal protection*, is responsible for protecting a specific individual or group of individuals. Generally, these guards wear appropriate street

---

15. Howard W. Timm and Kenneth E. Christen, *Introduction to Private Security*, (Belmont, CA: Brooks/Cole, 1991), 242.

Table 1. Advantages and Disadvantages of Contract and Proprietary Guard Services

Advantages

Contract	Proprietary
1. *Selectivity*—employer retains only those personnel personally approved	1. *Loyalty to the employer*—as opposed to loyalty the contracting firm
2. *Flexibility*—more or fewer personnel, as required	2. *Incentive*—promotion possibilities within the entire company
3. *Absenteeism*—replacement of absentees on short notice	3. *Knowledge*—of operation, products, personnel due to permanent position with one host firm
4. *Supervision*—supplied at no cost to the client	4. *Courtesy*—can render courtesies to VIPs because of familiarity with company personnel
5. *Training*—supplied at no cost to client; may be superior to in-house training	5. *Tenure*—less turnover than found with contract guards
6. *Objectivity*—judgment not clouded by personalities	6. *Morale*—a hoped-for state maintained by the in-house security manager
7. *Cost*—20% less than in-house, not counting administrative savings (e.g., social security, insurance, medical care, retirement, etc.)	7. *Control*—stays inside company structure
8. *Quality*—may be of higher caliber than in-house guards	8. *Supervision*—stays inside the company structure
9. *Administration and budgeting*—brunt borne by the guard company	9. *Training*—can be specifically geared to the job to be performed
10. *Unions*—very little problem, because security contract guards are seldom unionized	10. *Company image*—may be a status symbol
11. *Variety of services and equipment*—may specialize in skills or equipment not available to in-house security	11. *Better law enforcement liaison*—security managers can informally develop law enforcement liaison with fewer conflicts of interest developing
12. *Hiring and screening costs*—borne by guard service	12. *Selection*—company selection procedures can be applied
13. *Better local law enforcement contacts*—may know more law enforcement officers	13. *Better communication*—more direct
14. *Sharing expertise and knowledge*—may have developed skills on certain jobs that can be shared with new clients	

Disadvantages

Contract	Proprietary
1. *Turnover*—extremely high industry-wide	1. *Unions*—may go out with the company union, refuse to cross picket lines, and so forth
2. *Divided loyalties*—serving two masters at the same time quandaries	2. *Familiarity*—may become too familiar with personnel to be effective on the job
3. *Moonlighting*—low salary for guards may force them into second jobs, resulting in tired unalert personnel	3. *Cost*—expensive (salary, benefits, worker compensation, social security, liability insurance, work space, equipment, training
4. *Reassignment*—some agencies send in the best employees initially, then replace them with poorer quality ones as new contracts open	4. *Administrative burdens*—must develop an upper-level staff to handle the administrative needs of these personnel
5. *Screening standards*—may be inadequate	5. *Inflexibility*—hard to replace absent personnel
6. *Insurance*—difficulties determining liability and ensuring individual guards are bonded and insured	

NOTE: From Private Security: Report of the Task Force on Private Security by the National Advisory Commission on Criminal Justice Standards and Goals, 1976, Washington, DC: U.S. Government Printing Office. Private Security Standards and Goals, Anderson, 1977, pg 145-146.

clothes, depending upon the occasion, to blend in with the general public. Personal protection specialists should be as inconspicuous as possible. Bodyguards have the obligation of detecting and investigating any possible threats to the welfare of their clients. They perform this function by taking evasive action, stopping the source of the threat, and if necessary, obtaining medical treatment for their client.[16]

The primary services that guard and patrol services provide are

1. The prevention and/or detection of unauthorized entry or activity,
2. The prevention and/or detection of fire, theft, and losses,
3. The control and regulation of traffic—either vehicular, or pedestrian—
4. The protection of individuals from bodily harm, and
5. The enforcement of rules, regulations, and policies related to asset protection[17]

Alarm Services

The alarm-services industry has been a growing private security service for several decades. Alarm systems have been used for decades by commercial establishments. In the 1990s, alarms systems are affordable by most middle-class individuals and families.

Generally, before alarm systems are installed onto premises, alternative physical protective devices should be considered including fences, locks, and safes. To justify an alarm system for a facility, a security survey should be conducted and a review of unauthorized entry and prior crimes on the premises should be conducted. The following questions should be asked before setting up an alarm system:

1. Who can respond to an alarm system fastest and most effectively?
2. What are the costs of such responses as opposed to responses of somewhat lesser efficiency?
3. What is the comparable predicted loss factor between these alternatives?[18]

16. Howard W. Timm and Kenneth E. Christian, 6.
17. *The Hallcrest Report II,* 128.
18. Robert J. Fischer and Gion Green, *Introduction to Security,* 5th ed., (Boston: Butterworth- Heinemann, 1992), 246.

The purpose of an alarm is to alert a security company and neighbors that an intruder has entered an area where he does not belong.

There are various types of alarm systems, but all have three basic elements in common:

1. An *alarm sensor*—a device that is designed to respond to a certain changes in conditions such as the opening of a door, movement within a room, or a rapid rise in heat;
2. A *circuit or sending device*—a device that sends a signal from the alarm sensor to some other location. This may be done via an electrical circuit that transmits the alarm signal over a telephone, fiber optic lines, or through air waves;
3. An *enunciator or sounding device*—a sounding device, which is used to alert someone that the sensor has detected a change in conditions. The device may be a light, a bell, a horn, a self-dialing phone, or a punch tape.[19]

There are six alarm monitoring systems available to commercial and private individuals: 1) the *central system* monitors fire and intrusion—generally, the monitoring alarm system is centrally located to service a large number of clients simultaneously; when an alarm sounds private security officers are sent to the alarm scene and the police department is notified; 2) the *proprietary system* is an in-house alarm- monitoring system that is operated and manned by the facility; 3) the *Local alarm system* utilizes a sensor that activates a circuit that, in turn, activates a siren or some other audio, sound, or lighting device—only area-specific security personnel can hear the alarm and respond; 4) *auxiliary systems* are installation circuits that run into the police department; 5) the *local alarm-by-chance-system* is a local alarm system that has a bell that sounds but it has no guarantee of response; 6) the *dial alarm system* is set to dial a predetermined telephone number when the alarm is activated.[20]

Private Investigators

Private Investigators or (PI's) are usually plainclothes personnel who are licensed by the state to obtain information for their employers. The private investigation field requires that investigators

---

19. Ibid., 246.
20. Ibid., 258.

know the law and possess excellent interviewing and interrogation techniques. They must also have good verbal, written, and analytical skills. The private investigator's work can entail the use of surveillance techniques and undercover investigations. Many law firms and insurance companies use private investigative services on a continuous basis. Private investigative services can be retained for the following services:

- To perform background investigations including credit checks on personnel applicants,
- To conduct the investigation of internal theft or other employee crimes,
- To conduct undercover drug investigations,
- To locate or recover stolen property, and
- To secure evidence to be used before investigating committees, boards, or in civil or criminal trials[21]

Armored Car Service

Armored car services are used to provide protection for the transfer of valuable goods like currency, coins, jewelry, credit cards, works of art, and other items of economic and cultural value. The principle purpose of the armored car industry is to transport payrolls, cash supplies, and cash receipts, but the primary responsibility of armored car security personnel has been confined to the safe delivery of the item to be delivered and not to the security of the premises where the item has been delivered.

Locksmiths

Locks are probably the most commonly used form of physical device used to safeguard facilities and property. Locks are delaying devices for entry and not foolproof deterrence mechanisms. There are an estimated 70,000 locksmiths in the United States who sell, install, and repair locking devices, safes, and vaults. Private and public organizations need to establish lock and key procedures to maintain the quality of security for a facility.

Maintaining effective lock control requires the following procedures: a system should be established for the use of locks as a secu-

---

21. *The Hallcrest Report II.*, 129.

rity device, responsibility should be specifically assigned for lock and key control, and individuals assigned keys and locks should be held accountable for following the lock and key procedures.[22]

Security Consultant Services

Many corporations currently obtain assistance from private security consultant firms that provide an expertise that public law enforcement cannot provide. Consultants are specialized professionals who are paid for their services. The *Hallcrest II* study reports that there are four areas that comprise security consultant services: (1) engineering-related, (2) security management, (3) executive protection, and (4) computer security. According to *Hallcrest II* engineering-related security consultants are usually involved in the design of security systems. Security management consultants conduct security surveys, develop security awareness programs, evaluate specific loss problems, and structure asset protection programs with budget and staffing plans. Executive management consultants are immersed in planning the protection of corporate executives and facilities. Because of the fear of terrorism, the executive protection services have grown substantially. The computer security consultant develops programs to protect trade secrets and computer-based information.[23]

Manufacturers and Distributors

There are over 2,500 companies who manufacture and/or distribute security equipment. The major types of equipment manufacturers included in the technological component of private security include the following:

- Access control
- Closed-circuit television
- Alarms
- Bomb detection systems
- Metal detection
- Electronic article surveillance devices
- Computer security shielding
- Telephone security

---

22. Howard Timm and Kenneth Christian, 176.
23. *The Hallcrest Report II,* 130–131.

- Security lighting
- Security fencing
- Safes and vaults
- Security locks[24]

Other Services

The Hallcrest Report II claims that there are over twenty miscella-neous segments of the private security industry, separate from the previously mentioned components. These miscellaneous compo-nents include the following segments:

- Guard dogs
- Drug testing
- Forensic analysis
- Security insurance underwriting
- Security market research
- Security publishing
- Security storage
- Security training
- Shopping (honesty) services
- Honesty testing
- Uniform rentals/sales[25]

Cooperation Between Public Law Enforcement and Private Security[26]

Can crime be prevented or controlled? For over the last one hun-dred years this onerous task has fallen to public policing in America. Yet, can American society expect public policing to either prevent or control crime without public or private cooperation? The Presi-dent's Crime Commission found that a hostile public can and does have a bearing on public operations. The Commission stated that "People hostile to the police are not so likely to report violations of law, even when they are the victims. They are not so likely to report

24. Ibid., 132.
25. Ibid., 132.
26. Michael J. Palmiotto, *"The Law Enforcement-Security Connection: Equal Status For Crime Prevention and Control,"* Journal of Security Administration 12, No. 1, (1989), 37–47.

suspicious persons or incidents, to testify as witnesses voluntarily, or to come forward and provide information."[27]

In the 1960s and 1970s police agency administrators recognized the importance of community support and cooperation. This has been reflected in the implementation of police/community relations programs and crime prevention.

The latest buzz word for the police in the 1990s has been *community policing*. The purpose of community policing is for the police to develop a close relationship with the community.

Traditionally, law enforcement agencies have neglected to perceive the importance and the value of developing a cooperative relationship with private police/security agencies. In the 1970s *The Rand Report* indicated that a dichotomy existed between policing and the private security field. However, upon reviewing the objectives of policing and those of private security, it can be readily observed that the police and private security have similar goals and functions.

In a study entitled *Private Security in the United States*, Kakalik and Wildhorn came to the conclusion that public policing and private security shared the same common goal—"the maintenance of order."[28] In a 1980 study pertaining to contract security in Canada, researchers supported the concept that both public policing and private security are responsible for maintaining order.[29] Post and Kingsbury suggest ten functions that both policing and private security perform: prevention, protection, enforcement, detection, investigation, deterrence, emergency services, reporting, inspection, and general services.[30]

The public police and private security are both concerned with crime prevention (known as loss prevention by the private security fields). Both the police and private security perform similar functions

27. The President's Commission on Law Enforcement and Administration of Justice, *Task Report: The Police*, (Washington, DC: Government Printing Office, 1967), 144.

28. J. S. Kakalik and S. Wildhorn, *Private Security in the United States*, Vol. 3, *The Private Police Industry: Its Nature and Extent*, (Santa Monica, CA: Rand Corporation, 1971).

29. Clifford Shearing, Margaret B. Farnell, and Philip C. Stenning, *Contract Security in Ontario*, (Toronto: Centre of Criminology, University of Toronto), 180.

30. Richard S. Post and Arthur A. Kingsbury, *Security Administration: An Introduction*, (Springfield, IL: Charles C. Thomas, 1977), 473.

for the same individuals and organizations to prevent and control crime. In specific instances the police are assigned to protect threatened individuals, to escort merchants to banks, and to respond to burglar alarms, and the same functions are typically performed by private security. Also, the police perform routine patrol functions which include checking the external premises of retail establishments and manufacturing facilities, and one of the major functions of private security has been the patrol function. Additionally, the right to use violence is shared by both public police officers and private security personnel for self-protection or apprehension when appropriate.

Generally, private security personnel have three types of legal authority: "citizen's arrests and search authority; deputization of commissioning from a public law enforcement agency; and limited peace officer status."[31]

Most states allow private citizens to arrest if an offense is committed in their presence or if they have immediate knowledge of a crime. Some states allow private persons to arrest when a felony offender is escaping. In the private sector the power of citizen's arrest has great significance, since security personnel protect property. The following can be said about arrests by security officers:

> The arrest power is valid only where the purpose of such arrest is to turn the subject over to proper authorities as soon as practicable. The arrest power does not allow for other purposes (such as to obtain a confession) and liability is imposed if there is unreasonable delay in turning the suspect over to the authorities.[32]

Public police officers are protected from civil liability for false arrest when officers have *probable cause* that a crime has been committed. The private sector personnel must be certain that a crime was committed if they are to make an arrest; otherwise, they will be liable if a crime did not occur. When private security personnel are compared with police officers, parallels of negligence are often found in both systems of policing. A delineation of security negligence liability follows:

---

31. Robert J. Meadows, "Private Security and Public Safety: Development and Issues," *Journal of Security Administration* 7, No. 2, (1984), 55.

32. James S. Kakalik and Sorrel Wildhorn, *The Law and Private Police, Volume VI,* (Santa Monica, CA: Rand Corporation, 1971), 107.

1. As in policing, liability can be imposed on security operations, their agents or both,

2. Under the doctrine of Respondent Superior, security employers can be held liable for the actions of their officers if such acts were done during the scope of employment,

3. When security officers detain someone unlawfully, for example, employers would most likely be held responsible for the negligent acts of the guard,

4. The negligent hiring theory considers the employer's duty to provide safe employees because a dangerous employee is as dangerous as a defective machine,

5. Security officers can be held liable under the Federal Civil Rights Act.[33]

Public Police Functioning as Private Police / Security Officers

Private security personnel are usually not considered to be on a par with public police officers in the areas of training and arrest powers. Because private security personnel have a lower professional status than public police officers, private companies have employed "moonlighting" police officers as security officers. When this occurs it raises a variety of questions. Are the moonlighting police officers security personnel or are they police officers? Who is liable for their behavior, their public employer or their private employer? It seems the courts have not yet made a final determination. Many police departments like Savannah, Georgia's, will permit their officers to "moonlight" provided the private employer obtains the approval of the Police Chief and provided the officers follow the Police Department's Standard Operation Procedure. Under the Savannah Police Department's policy, the private employee assumes liability for any actions by the moonlighting police officer. Incidentally, no Savannah police officer has been sued since working as a private security officer. However, one Savannah police officer was murdered while employed as a private security officer.

Since the 1950s there have been three primary reasons why police officers accepted employment as private security officers. The first reason is the demand by police officers for increased compensa-

---

33. Robert J. Meadows, "Negligence in the Private Guard Industry," *Journal of Security Administration* 10, No. 2, (1987), 13.

tion. With the growth of police unions as bargaining agents, cities had to find a way to increase the salaries of police officers. One way was to allow off-duty officers to work for private companies. Another way was to change the concept of police responsibility to include the duty to provide service to both public and private events. Traditionally, police departments have provided services for major public and quasi-public events ranging from traffic control for funerals to security at public sporting events. Thirdly, private demand for police involvement in private events increased. Because of the escalation of the crime rate in the 1960s and 1970s there was an increased demand for protecting property and people in retail establishments and at public events. Municipal governments had no aversion to allowing off-duty police officers to be employed as private security officers. By allowing off-duty work, city governments met the demand for an increased income for officers and provided a service that the private sector was willing to pay for.[34]

The demand for off-duty police officers can vary from community to community. Generally, there are a number of circumstances in which a uniformed police officer may be needed:

For traffic control and pedestrian safety—road construction and repair, access to utility lines under public thoroughfares, and construction sites all pose problems of control of traffic and pedestrian movement. In some States, one or more officers must be stationed at such sites. Traffic control may be required for funerals, business operations, and other private events;

For crowd control—major private events that attract large paid audiences or public ones sponsored by nonprofit organizations pose problems of crowd control. Some, such as rock concerts and jazz festivals, many require large numbers of officers to prevent disorder as well as to ensure the orderly behavior of the crowd. Others, such as local religious or neighborhood festivals ordinarily require far fewer officers. County and municipal sports arenas, concert halls, and public and private school events likewise demand these services;

For private security and protection of life and property—many private businesses and well as other public authorities demand uniformed officers as visible deterrents of crime. They may per-

34. Albert J. Reiss, Jr., *Private Employment of Public Police,* (Washington, DC: U.S. Department of Justice, National Institute of Justice, 1988), 7–8.

form duties that are commonly performed by private security officers but with the additional expectation that they will enforce the laws by arrest, if necessary;

For routine law enforcement for public authorities—in large cities, the scale of public authorities such as housing, airport, and parks usually leads to their employing a separate enforcement staff with full police powers. But in small municipalities such police service may be obtained on contract basis with the city police department for extra-duty employees;

For plainclothes assignments—none of the departments (surveyed) reported a heavy demand for plainclothes police officers, although several reported some demand.[35]

Police Services Provided by Private Security

Municipalities usually do not provide all services to their communities. Police and sheriffs' agencies for years have contracted with the private sector for such services as repairing communications, data processing, and maintaining vehicles.

Police tasks that can be performed by private contractors include:

- Fingerprinting prisoners or applicants for various licenses or security clearances,
- Conducting sobriety tests,
- Escorting funerals, and oversized vehicles,
- Investigating embezzlement through electronic fund transfer,
- Checking whether warrants have been issued for arrest,
- Serving subpoenas,
- Verifying vehicle titles,
- Conducting background checks on applicants,
- Dispatching police vehicles,
- Enforcing weed abatement or similar ordinances,
- Securing and controlling access to sensitive records,
- Diagraming the scene of a motor-vehicle accident,
- Reviewing records and pictures to identify suspects,
- Comparing records of reported crimes to determine which ones appear to have a similar *modus operandi* or method of operation,
- Securing and patrolling disaster areas,
- Protecting storage areas for parades,

---

35. Ibid., 17.

Table 2
Examples of Government Installations Protected
by Private Security

Federal:	U.S. Department of Energy sites
	Nuclear test sites
	Veterans' libraries
	Presidential libraries
State:	State administration buildings
	University buildings and campuses
	Departments of transportation—parking lots
	Welfare center
	Unemployment offices
County:	Courts
	Medical centers
Municipal:	Public sports areas
	Welfare centers
	Public shelters
	Public housing projects
	Parking lots for municipal vehicles and towed cars
	Airports

Source: Marcia Chaiken and Jan Chaiken. *Public Policing- Privately Provided*, Washington, DC: U.S Department of Justice, National Institute of Justice, 1987, p. 9.

- Enforcing parking regulations,
- Controlling traffic, and
- Protecting parking lots at government facilities, or where towed vehicles are stored.[36]

Conflicts Between Law Enforcement and Private Security

The National Advisory Committee on Criminal Justice Standards, in their *Task Force on Private Security*, stated that "public law enforcement and private security agencies should work together because their respective roles are complementary in the effort to con-

---

36. Marcia Chaiken and Jan Chaiken, *Public Policing-Privately Provided,* (Washington, DC: U.S. Department of Justice, National Institute of Justice, 1987), 8.

trol crime. Indeed the magnitude of the nation's crime problem should preclude any form of competition between the two."[37]

Although the objectives of law enforcement and private security are similar and both groups can compliment each other, there are at times negative contacts. According to Fischer, the relationship between the two groups are strained because of

1. A lack of mutual respect;
2. A lack of communication;
3. A lack of law enforcement knowledge by private security;
4. Perceived competition;
5. A lack of standards for private security personnel;
6. A perceived corruption of police;
7. Jurisdictional conflicts, especially when private problems (i.e., corporate theft and arson) are involved;
8. Confusion of identifying and the issues flowing from it, such as arming and training of private police;
9. Mutual image and communications problems;
10. Provision of services in borderline or overlapping areas or responsibility and interest (i.e., provision of security during strikes, traffic control, shared use of municipal and private firefighting personnel);
11. Moonlighting policies for public police and issues stemming from them;
12. Differences in legal powers, which can lead to concerns about abuse of power, and so on (i.e., police officers working off duty may now be private citizens subject to rules of citizens's arrests);
13. False alarm rates (police resent responding to false alarms) which in some communities are over 90% of all alarm incidents.[38]

Cooperation Between Public and Private Security

Although conflict has existed between law enforcement and private security there has been movement toward cooperation between both groups. As early as 1964, Deputy Chief Thad F. Brown of the Los Angeles Police Department listed forty different ways private security could provide assistance to public policing. During the

---

37. Report of the *Task Force on Private Security*, 19.

38. Robert J. Fischer and Gion Green, *Introduction to Security,* 4th ed., (Boston: Butterworth- Heineman, 1987), 61.

1980s, the International Association of Chiefs of Police (IACP) and the American Society for Industrial Security (ASIS) had committees on public policing and private security cooperation and liaison. These organizations, with the National Sheriffs' Association (NSA) and with financial support from the National Institute of Justice, established a Joint Council of Law Enforcement and Private Security Associations to improve communication and cooperation between the two groups. The Joint Council identified fifteen areas for cooperative efforts. The needed programs and topics in order of importance to the Joint Council members are as follows:

1. Developing public law enforcement and private security protocols or guidelines for cooperation;
2. Cataloging and publishing success stories;
3. Making criminal history information available to the private sector;
4. Exchanging expertise, training, and technology between the private/public sectors;
5. Enhancing working relationships between both sectors in crime prevention;
6. Setting selection and training standards for private security;
7. Suppressing drugs in the workplace;
8. Improving an understanding of the private security role by law enforcement;
9. Privatizing selected law enforcement functions;
10. Conducting joint public/private operations (e.g., VIP protection, hazardous material transport, oversees threat information);
11. Providing cooperation and honesty in background checks;
12. Improving public/private sector operational communications;
13. Reviewing polygraph legislation;
14. Developing guidelines for police moonlighting in the private sector; and
15. Reducing false alarms[39]

Since the publication of the fifteen points by the Joint Council on Law Enforcement and Private Security Association there have been numerous cooperative efforts between the public police and private security. Cooperation between these two groups has occurred in such areas as product tampering, drugs, and telecommuni-

39. *The Hallcrest Report II.*, 246–247.

cations fraud. Both the public police and private security need to recognize how they both play an important role in crime prevention and control. They must cooperate and interact with one another to curtail crime. Public police and private security leaders need to sell to their respective professions the importance of recognizing each other's professionalism.

Summary

Currently, the United States has two policing systems: public and private police. The public police are under public control and are supported by governmental funds and private police are police supported by private individuals and companies. There are twice as many private police officers as there are public police personnel. The private security industry substantially outspends public police agencies and this trend is expected to continue until the year 2000.

The concern for security can be traced to ancient times. Guards were used by nomadic tribes to protect their flocks and themselves from raiding tribes and wild animals. During the nineteenth century, private security received wide recognition. The Pinkerton and the Wells-Fargo companies can trace their company roots to the last century.

Public and private security can be distinguished by the clientele they serve. The clientele for the private sector are concerned with prevention, deterrence, and detection of crime against the private property of individuals or companies. The public police are attentive to law enforcement activities, traffic control, criminal investigation, and prevention and control of predatory crime. The major private security components include: proprietary (in-house) security, guard-and-patrol services, private investigations, armored-car services, manufacturing of security equipment, locksmithing, security consulting, and other areas such as drug testing, and guard-dog services.

In the 1970s it was recognized that public policing and the private security field had similar goals and functions. Both the public police and private security have as a common goal "the maintenance of order." In specific instances, the police are assigned to protect threatened individuals, to escort merchants to banks, and to respond to burglar alarms. These same functions are performed by private security.

Private security personnel are usually not considered to be on a par with public police officers in the areas of training and arrest powers. Because private security personnel have a lower professional status than public police officers, private companies have employed "moonlighting" police officers as security officers. When this occurs it raises a variety of questions. On the one hand, are the moonlighting police officers security personnel or are they police officers? On the other hand, who is liable for their behavior, their public employer or their private employer?

Although conflict has existed between law enforcement and private security, there has been a movement toward cooperation between the two groups. The International Association of Chiefs of Police (IACP) and the American Society for Industrial Security (ASIS) have committees on public policing and private security cooperation and liaison. These organizations, with the National Sheriffs' Association (NSA) and with financial support from the National Institute of Justice, established a Joint Council of Law Enforcement and Private Security Associations to improve communication and cooperation between the two groups.

Key Terms

Allan Pinkerton	private investigator
armored-car service	Private Security Task Force
contract security	proprietary security
guard service	*Rand Report*
locksmith	security consultants
man-made hazards	William Burns
natural hazards	Washington Perry Brink
Northwest Police Agency	Wells Fargo

Review Questions

1. Explain the differences between public policing and private police/security?
2. Explain the similarities between public policing and private police/security?

3. What are the major components of the private security field?
4. Discuss the development of private security in the nineteenth century.
5. Why is the private security field held in lower regard than public law enforcement?

References

Bilek, Arthur J., Task Force Chairman. *Private Security: Standards and Goals—From the Official Private Security Task Force Report*. Cincinnati: Anderson Publishing Company, 1970.

Chaiken, Marcia and Jan Chaiken. *Public Policy-Privately Provided*. Washington: U.S. Department of Justice, National Institute of Justice, 1987.

Cunningham, William C., John J. Strauchs, and Clifford W. Van Meter. *The Hallcrest Report II: Private Security Trends, 1970–2000*. Boston: Butterworth-Heinemann, 1990.

Cunningham, William C., John J. Strauchs, and Clifford W. Van Meter. "Private Security: Patterns and Trends." *National Institute of Justice: Research in Brief*. Washington: U.S. Department of Justice, Office of Justice Programs.

Fischer, Robert J. and Gion Green. *Introduction to Security*. 5th ed. Boston: Butterworth-Heinemann, 1992.

Horan, James D. *The Pinkertons: The Detective Dynasty that Made History*. New York: Crown Publishers, 1967.

Kakalik, J.S. and S. Wildhorn. *The Law and the Private Police*. Vol. VI. Santa Monica, CA: Rand Corporation, 1971.

Kakalik, J.S. and S. Wildhorn. *Private Security in the United States*. Vol. 3, *The Private Police Industry: Its Nature and Extent*. Santa Monica, CA: Rand Corporation, 1971.

Lipson, Milton. "Private Security: A Retrospective." in Vol. 498 of *Annals*. "The Private Security Industry: Issues and Trends" Ira A. Lippman, Special Editor. 1988.

McCrie, Robert. "The Development of the U.S. Security Industry." in Vol. 498 of *Annals*. "The Private Security Industry: Issues and Trends." Ira A. Lippman, Special Editor, 1988.

Meadows, Robert J. "Negligence in the Private Guard Industry" *Journal of Security Administration* 10, no.2 (1987).

Meadows, Robert J. "Private Security and Public Safety: Development and Issues." *Journal of Security Administration* 7, no. 2 (1984).

Paine, D. *Principles of Industrial Security*, Madison, WI: Oak Security Publications, 1972.

Palmiotto, Michael J. "The Law Enforcement-Security Connection: Equal Status For Crime Prevention and Control." *Journal of Security Administration* 12, no. 1 (1989).

Post, Richard S. and Arthur A. Kingsbury. *Security Administration: An Introduction*, Springfield, IL: Charles C. Thomas, 1970.

President's Commission on Law Enforcement and Administration of Justice. *Task Force Report: The Police*. Washington: Government Printing Office, 1967.

Reiss, Albert J. Jr. *Private Employment of Public Police*, Washington: U.S. Department of Justice, National Institute of Justice, 1988.

Shearing, Clifford, Margaret B. Farnell and Philip C. Stenning. *Contract Security in Ontario, Toronto*, Toronto: Centre of Criminology, University of Toronto.

Timm, Howard W. and Kenneth E. Christian. *Introduction to Private Security*, Belmont, CA: Brooks/Cole Publishing Company, 1991.

Weaver, Leon. "Security and Protection Systems," *Encyclopedia Britannica*. Vol. 16. 1975.

CHAPTER 5

Administration and Organization

1. Are the scientific management concept and the bureaucracy of police departments outdated?
2. Are the principles of organization appropriate for the modern police agency?
3. Are the basic functions of administration applied appropriately by the current crop of police chief executives?
4. Are most police administrations aware of the roles defined for them by Mintzberg?
5. How can police organizations change with the numerous administrative barriers that are currently in place?
6. Why will Quality Policing be the wave of the future in police organization?

Introduction

Police departments are, simply, organizations that are managed by administrators. But understanding the organizational structure of police departments and the role of their administrators is crucial to comprehending how policing works in America, how it responds to its mission, and how it will reach its goals. The work of policing is subject to a wide variety of pressures, but effective policing begins with a sound organizational structure.

America is an organizational society. As Americans we are born in organizations and are a part of organizations throughout our lives—our lives begin in a hospital, we are educated in a school and then a university, we work for a company or two, we get married in a church, and eventually return there for our funeral.

Amitai Etzioni defines modern organizations as "social units (or human groupings) deliberately constructed and reconstructed to seek specific goals."[1] Organizations include armies, corporations, hospitals, churches, and fraternal clubs. Etzioni further asserts that organizations are characterized by:

---

1. Amitai Etzioni, *Modern Organizations,* (Englewood Cliffs, NJ: Prentice-Hall, 1964), 3.

1. The division of labor, power and communication responsibilities, divisions which are random or traditionally patterned, but deliberately planned to enhance the realization of specific goals;
2. The presence of one or more power centers which control the concerted efforts of the organization and direct them toward its goals; these power centers also must review continuously the organization's performance and re-pattern its structure, where necessary, to increase its efficiency;
3. The substitution of personnel, i.e., unsatisfactory persons can be removed and others assigned their tasks. The organization can also recombine its personnel through transfer and promotion.[2]

Organizational Theory

Police work is an organizational effort. The successes and failures of a police department are usually dependent upon the overall effectiveness of the organization.

There are a variety of organizational theories that can be applied to police agencies. Traditional organizational theory—which has been used by many governmental institutions, non-profit organizations, and private businesses—can be divided into three types of theory: scientific management, bureaucratic, and administrative.

Scientific Management

"Classical" organizational theory has two lines of development. The first is Frederick W. Taylor's *Scientific Management* theory, which focuses upon the basic physical activities involved in the production process, and is typified by time study and methods study. Taylor's Scientific Management concept was tested and applied in a factory environment where physical and temporal effects are more observable than they would be in a police agency. Taylor concludes that supervision should be divided according to tasks and that a subordinate should report to a number of different supervisors who are each responsible for the various tasks the subordinate performs. A worker could have, ultimately, four, five, or more bosses. For example, a patrol officer who performs a variety of tasks could find

---

2. Ibid.

himself reporting to a Traffic Sergeant, a Records Sergeant, an Investigative Sergeant, and a Patrol Sergeant. But can a patrol officer successfully function working for four bosses?

The scientific management approach is oriented toward achieving the following results:

1. Replacing rules of thumb with science (organized knowledge);
2. Obtaining harmony in group action, rather than discord;
3. Achieving the cooperation of human beings, rather than a chaotic individualism;
4. Working for maximum output, rather than restricted output;
5. Developing all workers to the fullest extent possible for their own and their company's highest prosperity.[3]

The second theory, based on the works of Gulick and Urwick concerns the organizational problems of the departmental division of work and coordination. This theory, known as the "administrative management theory," addresses the following:

> Given a general purpose of an organization, we can identify the unit tasks necessary to achieve that purpose. These tasks will normally include basic productive activities, service activities, coordinating activities, supervisory activities etc. The problem is to group these tasks into individual jobs, to group the jobs into administrative units, and finally to establish the top level departments—and to make these groupings in such a way as to minimize the total cost of carrying out all the activities. In the organizing process each department is viewed as a definite collection of tasks to be allocated among, and performed by, the employees of the department. To understand the formal theory, it is important to recognize that the total set of tasks is regarded as given in advance.[4]

Essentially, the objective of the administrative management approach is to, first, define the objectives or tasks of an organization and, then, to organize units of individuals to accomplish each task as efficiently as possible.

3. Harold Koontz, Cyril O'Donnell, and Heinz Weihrich, *Essentials of Management*, 4th ed., (New York: McGraw-Hill, 1986), 10.

4. James March and Herbert Simon, *Organizations,* 2nd ed., (Cambridge, MA: Blackwell, 1993), 41.

Bureaucracy

Organizations in modern society are *bureaucracies*. Both private companies and public institutions function as bureaucracies. Max Weber, the German sociologist, developed the bureaucratic model based upon the Prussian Army.

We can only understand how police departments operate in our contemporary society when we have an understanding of how bureaucracy works.

To many Americans a bureaucracy means red-tape, waste, inefficiency, and at times, corruption; however, the purpose of the bureaucratic organization is simply to develop lines of legitimate authority, to delineate effective divisions of labor, and to create productive workers and job efficiency. According to Weber's concept of "rational legal authority,"

1. Any given legal norm may be established by agreement or by imposition, on grounds of expediency or rational values or both, with a claim to obedience at least on the part of the members of the corporate group;
2. Every body of law consists essentially in a consistent system of abstract rules which have normally been intentionally established;
3. The typical person in authority occupies an "office." In the action associated with his status, including the commands he issues to others, he is subject to an impersonal order to which his actions are oriented;
4. The person who obeys authority does so, as it is usually stated, in his capacity as a 'member' of the corporate group and what he obeys is only 'the law';
5. The members of the corporate group, in so far as they obey a person in authority, do not owe this obedience to him as an individual, but to the impersonal order. Hence, it follows that there is an obligation to obedience only within the sphere of the rationally delimited authority which, in the order, has been conferred upon him.

Thus, it may be said that the following are characteristic of rational legal authority:

1. A continuous organization of official functions bound by rules;
2. A specified sphere of competence;

3. The organization of offices follow[ing] the principle of hierarchy; that is, each lower office is under the control and supervision of a higher one. There is a right of appeal and of statement of grievances from lower to the higher;
4. A set of rules that regulate the conduct of an office may be technical or norms. In both cases, if their application is to be fully rational then training is necessary;
5. A situation in which the members of the administrative staff should not be completely separated from ownership of the means of production or administration;
6. A complete absence of appropriation of his official position by the incumbent;
7. Administrative acts, decisions, and rules formulated and recorded in writing, even in cases where oral discussion is the rule or even mandatory;
8. Legal authority in a wide variety of different forms which will be distinguished.[5]

Weber's own studies illustrate how a bureaucracy works in a hospital, in the army, and in private clinics. He explains that an ideal bureaucratic administration exhibits efficiency, calculability, substantive rationality, technical competence, knowledgeability, formalistic impersonality, and universality.[6]

But the bureaucratic model has its flaws. It has a tendency to be resistant to change; it has been criticized for stifling employees' creativity, skills, abilities, and potential; and it tends to isolate managers from both their clientele and their employees.

The Administrative Theory

An administrative concept developed in the 1930s by Luther Gulick and often embraced by police administrators is known by the acronym **POSDCORB**. The acronym POSDCORB stands for:

5. Talcott Parsons, Ed., *Max Weber: The Theory of Social and Economic Organizations,* (New York: Free Press, 1947), 229–333.
6. David L. Clark, "Emerging Paradigms of the Paradigmatic Shift," *Organizational Theory and Inquiry,* Yvonna S. Lincoln, Ed., (Beverley Hills: Sage Publication, 1985), 49–50.

P Planning, that is, working out in broad outline the things that need to be done and the methods for doing them to accomplish the purpose of the enterprise;

O Organizing, that is, the establishment of the formal structure of authority through which work subdivisions are arranged, defined, and coordinated for the defined objective;

S Staffing, that is, the whole personnel function of bringing in and training the staff and maintaining favorable conditions of work;

D Directing, that is, the continuous task of making decisions and embodying them for specific and general orders and instructions and serving as the leader of the enterprise;

CO Coordinating, that is, the all important duty of interrelating the various parts of the work;

R Reporting, that is, keeping those to whom the executive is responsible informed as to what is going on, which thus includes keeping himself and his subordinates informed through records, research, and inspections;

B Budgeting, with all that goes with budgeting in the form of fiscal planning, accounting, and control.[7]

Principles of Organization

There are numerous organizational principles that support police organizations and create the basis for a functioning department, namely

1. Sound and clear cut allocation of responsibilities;
2. Equitable distribution of work loads among elements and individuals;
3. Clear and unequivocal lines of authority;
4. Authority adequate to discharge assigned responsibilities;
5. Reasonable spans of control for administrative, command, and supervisory officers;
6. Unity of command;
7. Coordination of effort;

---

7. Luther Gulick, "Notes on the Theory of Organization," *Papers on the Science of Administration*, Luther Gulick and L. Urwick, Ed.s, (1937; reprint, New York: August M. Kelly, 1969), 13.

Table 1
Police Division of Tasks

Operations	Staff	Auxiliary
Patrol	Personnel	Records
Traffic	Training	Communications
Investigations	Planning	Property
Vice	Budget	Laboratory
Organized Crime	Legal Assistance	Lockup
Youth Services	Public Affairs	Identification
Crime Prevention	Clerical/Secretarial	Equipment
Community Relations	Inspections	Maintenance

8. Administrative control.[8]

Since a police department functions as a goal-oriented organization it classifies those components of the police agency that challenge police goals as *line* operations. *Primary* line activities are performed by the *patrol* unit. *Secondary* line activities are performed by traffic units, investigative units, and vice units. Essentially, if the primary line unit is completely successful, there is no need for secondary line units.[9]

A police department has numerous functions that do not fall into line functions, but these functions are, nevertheless, important to the success of the organization. Non-line activities are usually classified as either *staff* services or *auxiliary* services. Staff services are activities that assist the organization in developing better personnel. These include recruitment, selection, promotion, and planning. Auxiliary services provide technical, supportive, and facility services for the organization. These include records, detention, and evidence.[10]

A police department, depending upon the size of the agency, will usually be divided into the following sections: *operations, staff,* and *auxiliary* services. Generally, the operations sections include the primary line units of patrol, the secondary units of investigations, and

---

8. Luther Gulick, "Notes on the Theory of Organization," *Papers on the Science of Administration,* Luther Gulick and L. Urwick, Ed.s, (New York: Institute of Public Administration, 1937), 97.

9. George D. Eastman, *Municipal Police Administration,* 7th ed., (Washington, D.C.: International City Management Association, 1971), 18.

10. Ibid., 18.

the youth bureau. Staff services include those activities that help the department accomplish its mission through such activities as training and planning, while auxiliary services provide technical support that includes records and communications. However, there are some police activities, like community relations, that do not clearly fall into any specific category.

Functions and tasks that are grouped together are referred to as *divisions of work*. In middle-sized and large departments a division of work will be needed in order to have an efficiently performing police department. There are five methods of dividing the work among members of the organization—by *purpose*, by *process* or *method*, by *clientele*, by *time*, or by *area*. Usually, because of the nature of police work, the "purpose" method will be the most common. For instance, a large police department will need to divide even investigative work into various types or "purposes" like traffic reconstruction, vice, property crimes, and crimes against persons. The process or method approach to dividing work can be of major importance in departments of substantial size. In this approach a variety of tasks that form a "process" are grouped together. Motorized patrol offers, for example, often function in this way. Units that receive their division of work based on clientele include detention or traffic units. Dividing work according to "time of day" is also a common feature of policing. Police agencies usually have three or four shifts. Normally, departments have an 8 a.m. to 4 p.m. shift, a 4 p.m. to 12 a.m. shift, and a 12 a.m. to 8 a.m. shift. Some departments have either an 6 p.m. to 2 a.m. shift or an 8 p.m. to 4 a.m. shift. There are some departments that have overlapping shifts in order to make certain that there are always officers available to respond to a call. Work in police departments can also be organized according to geographical "area." The areas are generally designed according to citizen complaints or crime data and not necessarily according to the geographical size of the area.

The *delineation of responsibility or delegation of authority* requires that the functions and assignments of individuals be explicitly clarified. The police organizations should have clear and definite lines of authority. Every individual should know where he fits into the organization and to whom he is responsible and who is responsible to him.

Many organizations are hierarchical in nature. An hierarchical organization has a *chain of command* or *lines of authority* which allow communications to flow upwards and downward through the various levels of authority.

Pyramid / Hierarchy of Authority

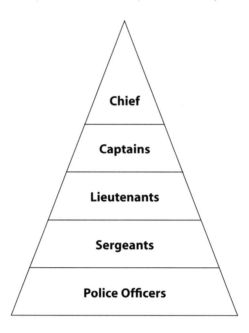

Authority flows downward in the police department.
This chart shows different levels of authority.

Police officers, supervisors, and administrators should possess *authority commensurate with responsibility*. Responsibilities have to be fixed before authority can be delegated. Organizational members should be given only the authority that will be necessary to carry out their duties. The *span of control* principle recognizes that there is a limit to the number of subordinates that a supervisor can effectively oversee. The *unity of command* principle refers to the reality that a subordinate should report to one and only one superior. The subordinate cannot effectively please two bosses. Contradictions exist when a subordinate has more than one superior.

Policing in large metropolitan organizations is complex, and specialized units are created to deal with specific crime problems or to achieve organizational objectives. Examples of specialized units include the traffic unit, the juvenile bureau, the fraud unit, the training unit, and the homicide investigation unit. But in small police departments police officers have to be generalists—they have to be able to perform a wide variety of tasks. The small police agency

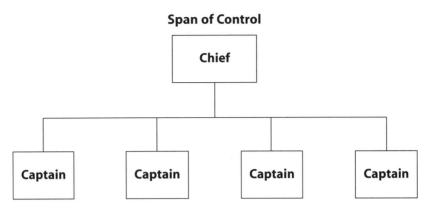

Span of Control

The span of control for this chart is four. Only four captains report directly to the Chief.

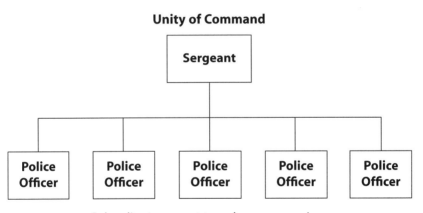

Unity of Command

Subordinates report to only one supervisor.
These five patrol officers have only one boss.

cannot afford the luxury of specialization. If a specialist is required for a specific job, like homicide investigation, then the small department usually calls in a homicide investigator from the District Attorney's office or the state investigative agency. There are a number of advantages to establishing specialized units, namely

- *The placement of responsibility*—definite fixing of responsibility is the first rule of effective operation;
- *The development of experts*—personnel qualified by training;
- *The improvement of training*—persons assigned to a specialized field may be given more intensive training;

- *The promotion of esprit de corps*—a small group which is made responsible for the performance of specific task tends to form a cohesive unit with high morale and pride in its accomplishment;
- *The stimulation of special police interest*—because of their definite responsibility, specialized personnel develop a proprietary interest in department operations that relate to their field;
- *The arousal of public interest*—specialized units arouse and organize public interest and support of police activities.[11]

Although there are advantages to police agencies having specialization there are also disadvantages. These disadvantages include a *limitation of usefulness, restrictions of general public interest*, the *complication of tasks of command*, the *creation of administrative problems*, the *hampering of the development of well-rounded police programs*, and the *diminishing of territorial coverage*[12]. Specialization can sometimes lead to confusion when responsibilities are divided between the patrol and a specialized unit, such as a traffic unit. Police officers may also lose interest in performing certain functions, or they may simply feel that it is not their job to perform a task that may be the primary responsibility of a specialized unit. For example, officers may not feel compelled to issue traffic citations when a traffic unit has this as their primary duty. Ultimately, if there is too much emphasis on specialization, then the department may not develop well-rounded officers. Before a police department creates a specialized unit, a careful evaluation should be conducted to determine if such a need exists.

What are the determining elements for a police department to create a specialized unit? There are several factors that could assist the police agency in establishing the need for a specialized unit: first, the *quality of personnel*, the higher the quality of personnel the less need for a specialized unit; second, the *need for special skill and ability*; third, the *importance of the job*, if the importance of the job is great enough to warrant the use of a specialized unit; fourth, the *amount of work to be done*, if a particular kind of work requires an inordinate amount of time; fifth, the *need for readily available services*, if a unit must be available around the clock, like crime scene technicians; sixth, the *intermittent emergency needs*, if a unit must be ready to be

---

11. O.W. Wilson and Roy McLaren, *Police Administration,* 4th ed., (New York: McGraw-Hill, 1977), 93–94.
12. Ibid., 94–95.

Table 2
Police Organizational Terms

Department	Primary organizational unit within a government structure.
Bureau	The largest unit within a police department.
Division	A subdivision of a bureau.
Section	A subdivision of a division.
Unit	A subdivision of a section.
Detail	Personnel assigned to a specific detail.
Zones	Also called commands or regions. A geographical subdivision of an area.
Precinct	Also called District. A geographical area of a city usually under the command of a police Captain.
Watch	Also called a platoon or shift. Three or more watches which a specific number of officers work.
Beat	A geographical area of a city for patrol purposes.
Post	An assigned geographical area for a police officer.

called upon for emergency situations, like hostage negotiations; sixth, the *need for maintaining skill*, if it is necessary to keep personnel with special technical skills, like photography, available; seventh, the *need for planning and control*, if there is a substantial need for a unit with specific functions, like traffic control; eighth, the *dissimilarity of tasks to other duties*, if there is a need for skills that are outside of the normal responsibilities of first-line officers, like credit card fraud investigation; ninth, the *attitude of personnel toward their tasks*, if police officers display an uncooperative attitude toward specific responsibilities, like not giving out traffic citations for speeding; tenth, the *interference with usual duties*, if a particular job interferes with normal responsibilities, for example when officers are unable to respond to citizens' complaints if they have to perform criminal investigations; eleventh, the *size of the force and area of jurisdiction*, small agencies usually cannot justify specialized units, but, as the department increases in size, specialized units may be justified.[13]

---

13. Ibid., 95–97.

Administration

Administrative practice requires a *systems* approach for managing an organization. A system can be either physical or theoretical, and is "essentially a set or assemblage of interconnected, interdependent things that form a complex whole."[14]

It is also important to remember that an organization does not function in a vacuum and is, to some extent, influenced by its external environment.

All organizations can be characterized as being either *open systems* or *closed systems*, though they are never completely either one or the other. An open system is one that is subject to a great deal of influence by its environment, while environment has only a limited effect on the closed system.

The organization, as a system, receives *inputs*, in the form of people, money, or administrative skills. Administrative functions, in turn, transform inputs into *outputs*. Outputs can vary with the organization but they generally include services or "satisfactions" or they can serve to integrate the goals of various interest groups within an organization. If an organization hopes to retain and elicit contributions from its members, then "satisfactions" must be provided. These "satisfactions" can include material needs such as money and job security, but they can also include the need for affiliation, esteem, and acceptance. Another systems output is known as goal integration. Different interests groups within the organization often have opposing objectives. The administrator is responsible for resolving conflicts and integrating the goals of the organization. In the systems model of operational administration output can, in turn, become input. Employee satisfaction must be considered an important human input.[15]

There are a number of implications that police administrators should recognize in the systems approach:

1. For an organization to be effective, it must constantly adapt to its environment;
2. As an organization adapts to the environment by changing its goals, objectives, and procedures, it also changes its relationship to its environment;

---

14. Koontz, O'Donnell and Weihrich, 13.
15. Ibid., 13–17.

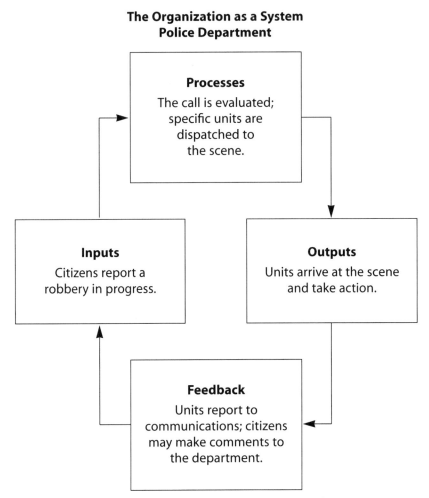

The Organization as a System
Police Department

Processes

The call is evaluated; specific units are dispatched to the scene.

Inputs

Citizens report a robbery in progress.

Outputs

Units arrive at the scene and take action.

Feedback

Units report to communications; citizens may make comments to the department.

Source: David A. Tansik and James F. Elliott. Managing Police Organizations, Belmont, CA: Duxbury, 1981, p.3.

3. Organizations are composed of numerous interdependent units. A change in one unit will, in turn, cause changes in others;
4. Communications are necessary both within the organization and with environment components so as to facilitate more effective adaptation.[16]

---

16. David A. Tansik and James F. Elliott, *Managing Police Organizations,* (Belmont, CA: Duxbury, 1981), 3–4.

The Functions of Administrators[17]

Understanding the functions of administrators provides a framework for organizing administrative awareness. The basic functional areas of administration include planning, organizing, staffing, leading, and controlling.

Planning entails decision making; it involves selecting a route that an organization will follow. There are various types of plans, ranging from the detailed to the broadly defined plan for getting organizational goals on track. Planning asks the basic questions, *What* to do? *How* to do it? *When* to do it? and *Who* will do it? Planning brings an organization's present situation in line with its goals for the future. Most importantly, members of an organization need to be aware of these objectives and goals in order to effectively accomplish the organization's mission.

Organizing involves the establishment of roles for workers within the organization. Providing a worker with a role suggests that he has a specific purpose or objective to perform within the organization. Organizing involves: determining what activities are necessary to achieve goals; grouping activities into sections; assigning administrators to specific tasks; delegating the authority to administrators to carry out their tasks; and preparing for coordinating communication and tasks. The intention of organizing is to create an environment where workers can be successful at performing their jobs.

Staffing consists of hiring and maintaining positions for the organization. In addition to establishing the requirements and responsibilities of particular positions, the staffing function includes recruiting, evaluating, and choosing candidates for positions. Staffing includes the training of personnel so that they perform their jobs efficiently.

Leading is the means by which administrators influence people to strive willingly to achieve organizational goals. Administrators need people skills in order to motivate employees to perform effectively and efficiently.

Controlling measures the employee's performance and corrects any deficiencies of the performance of the worker. The activities of the organization are controlled to obtain organizational goals and objectives.

---

17. Koontz, O'Donnell, and Weihrich, 35–38.

Administrative experts consider the coordination of activities to be an important function of operating an organization. When workers understand how their positions contribute to the organization, good coordination of organizational activities is occurring.

The Administrator's Roles

An administrator can be defined as a "person in charge of an organization or one of its subunits."[18] This description, for instance, could include a police chief who is given formal authority over an organization. From formal authority comes status, which leads to interpersonal relations, and from interpersonal relations comes admittance to information. Information, usually allows the administrator to make decisions and to develop strategies for the organization.[19]

Henry Mintzberg[20] outlines what the administrator actually does on the job. He claims that three of the manager's roles arise from formal authority and involve basic interpersonal relations. The three *interpersonal roles* that Mintzberg defines for the administrator are the *figurehead*, the *leader*, and the *liaison*. As a figurehead, the administrator performs ceremonial duties, such as meeting dignitaries. As a leader, the administrator takes action in situations requiring leadership. As a liaison, the administrator makes contacts outside his organization.

The administrator, because of his personal contacts both within and outside the organization, has an *informational role*. In the informational role, the administrator is either a *monitor*, a *disseminator*, or a *spokesman*. As a monitor, the administrator scans his contacts for information. This information comes as gossip, hearsay, and sometimes as pure speculation. As a disseminator, the administrator passes on information to his subordinates. As a spokesmen, the administrator forwards information to parties outside his organization.

In addition to his interpersonal roles and informational roles the administrator has *decisional roles*. Only the administrator can commit the organization to a plan of action. There are four roles that

---

18. Henry Mintzberg, "The Manager's Job: Folklore and Fact, *Harvard Business Review* (July-August, 1975), 54.

19. Ibid., 54.

20. Mintzberg, 54–59.

define the administrator's decision-making functions—the *entrepreneur*, the *disturbance handler*, the *resource allocator*, and the *negotiator*. As an entrepreneur the administrator aims to improve the organization. This includes being on the lookout for good ideas. As a disturbance handler, the administrator responds to pressure situations. As a resource allocator, the administrator is responsible for deciding who gets what in the organization. Finally, as a negotiator, the administrator works at all levels within the organization to maintain a smoothly operating organization. Negotiations may be routine for the administrator.

Mintzberg believes that the ten roles of administrators are all integrated into the administrator's job. By understanding these ten roles the administrator should have a better understanding of his job and should function more effectively and with more efficiency.

Table of Organization

The structure of an organization is usually depicted by a *table of organization* or organizational charts. "A table of organization is a chart that shows all the positions in an organization and the relationship of authority and responsibility by which they are connected."[21] Such a chart illustrates the structure of an organization with horizontal and vertical lines connecting boxes that represent the various positions that exist within the organization. The distance a position, or box, is from the top of the chart provides a good indication of that position's power, authority, and status. Formal communication and reporting channels are indicated by the lines connecting the positions or boxes.

A good table of organization assists the organization in functioning more efficiently. Administrators must determine if an organization operates more efficiently under a centralized or decentralized organizational structure, and under democratic or authoritarian administration. Poorly operated organizations need more direction, more centralization, more decentralization, and more participatory administration, all at the same time.[22]

21. Theodore Caplow, *Managing the Organization,* 2nd ed., (New York: Holt, Rinehart and Winston, 1983), 15.

22. Ibid., 16.

Table of Organization

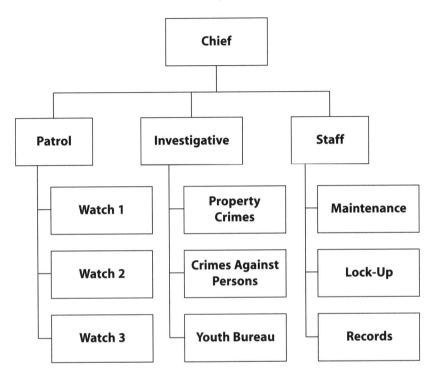

Tables of organization do have limitations. The charts do not provide information about relationships between individuals within the organization who have no authority over or no responsibility to each other. Neither are "informal norms," like seniority, found in organizational charts—situations in which certain positions and individuals have more inherent authority than others. Organizational charts do not illustrate interaction between equal positions or show alliances, coalitions, or personal preferences.

Although tables of organization are not perfect, they are organizational instruments delineating specific, detailed, and valuable information about the operations of an organization. They should be considered a starting point and they need to be used with caution and with a knowledge of their limitations. Tables of organization are valuable tools for the police administrator.

Administrative Barriers

Although the police are generally organized according to a paramilitary model for the sake of efficiency, efficiency has not been the result. Traditionally, police organizations have been under the authority of police chiefs, and typically, such organizations have suffered from barriers to their organizational effectiveness, their communications, and their morale, and good community relations. For the most part, American police have been influenced by Taylor's "scientific management" theory and have adopted the paramilitary bureaucratic organizational model, and as a result of this influence, police administrators normally observe no differences between their roles as administrators and their roles as leaders.[23]

For the last several decades much has been written about changing the organizational structure of policing. Alvin Toffler, over a quarter of a century ago, claimed that bureaucracies did not respond to human needs or the mission of an organization.[24] Reiss,[25] Munro,[26] Roberg[27] contend that the bureaucratic structure of policing interferes with developing police-community relations, that too much emphasis is placed on span of control, and that the turbulent environment that the police work in does not fit into a bureaucratic structure. Consequently, new models are being developed and put in use for police organizations, and eventually, police organizations are going to change.

Observers of current affairs will recognize that since the late 1980s the fundamental nature of corporate America has been changing. Corporations have been downsizing, flattening the organizational structure, eliminating middle managers, and doing more with less. Organizations are losing their paternalism. No longer are

---

23. Norman H. Stamper, *Removing Managerial Barriers: To Effective Police Leadership,* (Washington, DC: Police Executive Research Forum, 1992), 4.

24. Alvin Toffler, *Future Shock,* (New York: Random House, 1970).

25. Albert J. Reiss, "Shaping and Serving the Community: The Role of the Police Chief Executive," *Police Leadership in America: Crisis and Opportunity,* William A. Geller, Ed., (1985), 62.

26. Jim L. Munro, *Administrative Behavior and Police Organization,* (Chicago: University of Chicago Press, 1974), 76–77.

27. Roy R. Roberg, *Police Management and Organizational Behavior: A Contingency Approach,* (St. Paul, Minnesota: West, 1979), 314.

incompetent employees guaranteed a job and corporations are slowly decreasing or eliminating benefits such as pensions and health insurance. In America, corporations are the leaders of innovation in administrative structuring and organization. For example, the Federal Government, along with many state governments, is now following the corporate model in downsizing its own work forces. Governmental agencies are also looking closely at employee benefits and looking for new ways to save money for the taxpayer.

Model of a Healthy Organization[28]

There are seven components of a healthy organization, all of which are coordinated by the chief executive officer. This model holds that the head police administrator functions not only as an administrator or manager but also as a leader.

A Clear and Common Purpose

It is a necessary function of leadership to have a clear and common purpose—to make clear what the organization stands for, what it plans to do, and where its leaders are taking it. Police administrators need to get away from their paperwork to lead. They have to stop putting out fires. Police departments require enthusiastic leadership that motivates individuals to perform satisfactorily.

A Sound Structure

The semi-military police bureaucracy with its emphasis on specialization and its numerous layers of supervisors and managers makes it difficult for the police to perform their job. Too often police chiefs don't get the information they should have. The officer on the street all too often has to read about what's going on in the department in the newspapers. Cliques develop instead of team work. Communications are stifled or distorted. Ultimately, the steep hierarchical structure of many police departments often makes them dysfunctional. Police organizations have to be restructured to become more efficient, more effective, and more responsive to the

---

28. Norman H. Stamper, *Removing Managerial Barriers: To Effective Police Leadership,* (Washington, DC: Police Executive Research Forum, 1992), 131–144.

Model of a Healthy Organization

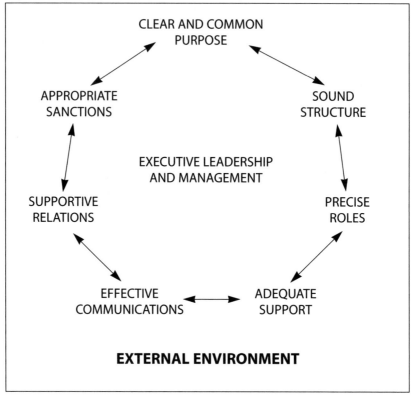

CLEAR AND COMMON
PURPOSE

APPROPRIATE
SANCTIONS

SOUND
STRUCTURE

EXECUTIVE LEADERSHIP
AND MANAGEMENT

SUPPORTIVE
RELATIONS

PRECISE
ROLES

EFFECTIVE
COMMUNICATIONS

ADEQUATE
SUPPORT

EXTERNAL ENVIRONMENT

Source: Stamper, Norman H. (1992) Removing Managerial Barriers to Effective Police Leadership. Washington, DC: Police Executive Research Forum, p. 132.

community. The police structure needs to be flattened and the specialization trend curtailed.

Precise Roles

To function effectively in a police organization, the roles of all personnel need to be defined precisely. Obscure lines of authority between positions create confusion and resentment over duties and responsibilities. The police chief needs to be a leader, not desk-bound. Change will occur within the police organizations when the police chief leads creatively and does not function as an administrator who simply wants to maintain the status quo.

Adequate Support

Police work in American cities requires adequate personnel support in order for the police job to be safe and successful. The number-one priority of the police force has to be safety. Police administrators need to strive to reduce the risk associated with police work. All police employees are entitled to a healthy work environment, to an equitable and fair system of compensation, and to education and training. Competent administration and leadership is fundamental to ensuring adequate support for the police organization.

Effective Communication

Effective communication can be defined as "a timely and satisfying exchange of relevant, mutually understood information."[29] Communication in the police organization occurs between investigators and patrol officers and between sworn personnel and civilians. Communication occurs both internally, throughout the organization, and it also occurs externally, outside the organization, with politicians, interest groups, and with the general public. The police chief is responsible for organizing and overseeing an organization's communication. Information is absolutely necessary for the police organization's effort to pursue a common purpose. How the police chief handles "confidential," and "need-to-know," information can go a long way in developing trust in the organization. Furthermore, administrators must listen to their followers if they are to have their trust. Ultimately, good administrators know what their followers think about organizational issues; this information is a source of the administrator's power.

Supportive Relations

The police administrator has to expect that there will be harmony within the police organization and that personnel will support one another. Petty bickering cannot be tolerated. When interpersonal feuds occur, the police administrator needs to find out why they are happening. Interpersonal competence should be required at all levels of police work.

---

29. Ibid., 138.

Appropriate Sanctions

Police employees need to know when their performance is satisfactory, and police employees performing unsatisfactorily have to be informed and should be expected to come up to par. The performance evaluation system has be fair and equitable.

The police in America work for the public. The police must be concerned with their *external public* and the police structure should be geared to providing *service* to the community. Police departments should have a service orientation and this philosophy should be espoused throughout the entire police agency—including police department personnel who interact directly with the public as well as those who have limited or no contact with the public. The police chief should be a powerful influence who works to develop cooperation between the community and the police department. To have good cooperation between the community and the police, the organizational structure of the police department should reflect job satisfaction, efficiency, and effectiveness.

Total Quality Management

Since the early 1980s American businesses and governmental institutions have been examining and adopting the "Total Quality Management" concept of operating a company or agency. Administrative practices in America, as previously mentioned, have emphasized the "scientific management" of Frederick Taylor which emphasizes rigid rules and autocratic managing—a system that is unresponsive to both employees and to customers. With such an approach, authority and power rest with the head of the organization and change is difficult to effect. To combat the stagnation of American-operated businesses and governmental institutions, Dr. W. Edwards Deming devised a system called Total Quality Management (TQM). TQM has been adopted by many companies such as the Ford Motor Company and the Florida Power and Light Company. Total Quality Management has also been adopted by colleges and universities, the military, and even by police departments. The Deming Method includes **Fourteen Points** that are the basis for improving the administration of an organization:

1. **Create constancy of purpose for improvement of product and service.** Dr. Deming suggests a radical new definition of a company's role: rather than to make money, it is to stay in business and provide jobs through innovation, research, constant improvement and maintenance.
2. **Adopt the new philosophy.** Americans are too tolerant of poor workmanship and sullen service. We need a new religion in which mistakes and negativism are unacceptable.
3. **Cease dependence on mass inspection.** American firms typically inspect a product as it comes off the assembly line or at major stages along the way; defective products are either thrown out or reworked. Both practices are unnecessarily expensive. In effect, a company is paying workers to make defects and then to correct them. Quality comes not from inspections but from improvements of the process. With instruction, workers can be enlisted in this improvement.
4. **End the practice of awarding business on the price tag alone.** Purchasing departments customarily operate on orders to seek the lowest-priced vendor. Frequently, this leads to supplies of low quality. Instead, buyers should seek the best quality in a long-term relationship with a single supplier for any one item.
5. **Improve constantly and forever the system of production and service.** Improvement is not a one- time effort. Management is obligated to continually look for ways to reduce waste and improve quality.
6. **Institute training.** Too often, workers, have learned their job from another worker who was never trained properly. They are forced to follow unintelligible instructions. They can't do their jobs well because no one tells them how to do them.
7. **Institute leadership.** The job of a supervisor is not to tell people what to do nor to punish them but to lead. Leading consists of helping people do a better job of learning by objectives methods who is in need of individual help.
8. **Drive out fear.** Many employees are afraid to ask questions or to take a position, even when they do not understand what their job is or what is right or wrong. They will continue to do things the wrong way, or not do them at all. The economic losses from fear are appalling. To assure better quality and productivity, it is necessary that people feel secure.
9. **Break down barriers between staff areas.** Often a company's departments or units are competing with each other or

have goals that conflict. They do not work as a team so they can solve or foresee problems. Worse, one department's goals may cause trouble for another.

10. **Eliminate slogans, exhortations and targets for the work force.** They never help anybody do a good job. Let workers formulate their own slogans.

11. **Eliminate numerical quotas.** Quotas take into account only numbers, not quality or methods. They are usually a guarantee of inefficiency and high cost. A person, to hold a job, meets a quota at any cost, without regard to damage to his company.

12. **Remove barriers to pride of workmanship.** People are eager to do a good job and distressed when they cannot. Too often, misguided supervisors, faulty equipment and defective materials stand in the way of a good performance. These barriers must be removed.

13. **Institute a vigorous program of education and retraining.** Both management and their work force will have to be educated in the new methods, including team work and statistical techniques.

14. **Take action to accomplish the transformation.** It will require a special top management team with a plan of action to carry out the quality mission. Workers cannot do it on their own, nor can managers. A critical mass of people must understand the Fourteen Points....[30]

Although Deming's Fourteen Points appear to be geared toward the private sector, the major premises can be applied by police administrators. Total Quality Management can be translated as "Quality Policing." Like the "Model of a Healthy Organization," the concept of "Quality Policing" considers administration and leadership to be one and the same. The new police strategies of problem-oriented policing and community-oriented policing (to be described in chapter 9) fit into the TQM concept.

The Madison, Wisconsin, Police Department has adopted "Quality Policing" as their administrative style to change the structure of their police department. When establishing "Quality Policing" (QP) the Madison Police Department established five points to focus its attention:

30. Mary Walton, *Deming Management at Work,* (New York: Perigee, 1990), 17–19.

The Mission Statement of the Madison Police Department

We believe in the DIGNITY and WORTH of ALL PEOPLE.
We are committed to:
PROVIDING HIGH-QUALITY, COMMUNITY-ORIENTED POLICE SERVICES
WITH SENSITIVITY
PROTECTING CONSTITUTIONAL RIGHTS
PROBLEM-SOLVING
TEAM WORK
OPENNESS
CONTINUOUS IMPROVEMENT
PROVIDING LEADERSHIP TO THE POLICE PROFESSION
We are proud of the DIVERSITY of our workforce
which permits us to GROW and which RESPECTS each of us as individuals
and we strive for a HEALTHFUL workplace.

Source: David C. Couper and Sabine H. Lobitz, *Quality Policing: The Madison Experience*, Washington, DC: Police Executive Research Forum, 1990, p. 23.

- A clear and understandable mission statement;
- A commitment to engaging in teamwork and problem- solving in each and every unit;
- The creation of a community orientation and customer focus on the part of each and every employee;
- The full utilization of the important resources of the organization by recognizing employee worth and the untapped resources and potential of employees; and
- An overall focus on quality[31]

It is readily observed by closely reviewing the five points outlined by the Madison Police Department that they are based upon Deming's Fourteen Points. Not only did the Madison Police Department establish a five point focus to change their organization, but they also focused on carrying out these points. For example, they rewrote their mission statement to reflect "Quality Policing." In addition, the Madison Police Department established the Neighborhood Patrol Bureau to "get closer to the people they serve."[32] The

---

31. David C. Couper and Sabine H. Lobitz, *Quality Policing: The Madison Experience,* (Washington, DC: Police Executive Research Forum, 1991), 64.
32. Ibid., 25.

Madison Police Department
Principles of Quality Leadership

---

1. Believe in, foster, and support **TEAMWORK**.
2. Be committed to the **PROBLEM-SOLVING** process: use it, and let **DATA**, not emotions, drive decisions.
3. Seek employees' **INPUT** before you make key decisions.
4. Believe that the best way to improve the quality of work or service is to **ASK** and **LISTEN** to employees who are doing the work.
5. Strive to develop mutual **RESPECT** and **TRUST** among employees.
6. Have a **CUSTOMER** orientation and focus toward employees and citizens.
7. Manage on the **BEHAVIOR** of 95 percent of employees, and not on the 5 percent who cause problems. Deal with the 5 percent **PROMPTLY** and **FAIRLY**.
8. Improve **SYSTEMS** and examine **PROCESSES** before placing blame on people.
9. Avoid "top-down," **POWER-ORIENTED** decision making whenever possible.
10. Encourage **CREATIVITY** through **RISK-TAKING**, and be **TOLERANT** of honest **MISTAKES**.
11. Be a **FACILITATOR** and **COACH**. Develop an **OPEN** atmosphere that encourages providing and accepting **FEEDBACK**.
12. With **TEAM-WORK**, develop with employees agreed upon **GOALS** and a **PLAN** to achieve them.

Source: Couper, David C., and Lobitz Sabine H. (1991) *Quality Policing: The Madison Experience*. Washington, DC: Police Executive Research Forum, p. 48.

department developed "Principles of Quality Leadership" to reflect the concept of "Quality Policing" and they have integrated the concept of "Quality Policing" into the entire department.

The experience of the Madison Police Department illustrates several key ingredients in organizational change:

- A strong vision of the future;
- A strong unyielding commitment from the chief executive;
- A commitment to developing the skills and abilities of leaders as well as employees in the organization and continually training them; and

- A patient and persistent focus on the long-term operations of the organization.[33]

Summary

Police departments function as organizations that are managed by administrators. An understanding of organizational structure and the importance of administration is necessary for understanding policing in America, its mission, and its goals. Our daily lives are directly influenced by organizations. We work, play, and pray in organizations.

Organizational theory plays an important part in police departments. Scientific Management concepts, developed in the early part of the twentieth century, have been implemented by police administrators. These concepts focus on obtaining harmony in group action and obtaining the maximum work output. American police organizations are considered semi-military bureaucracies that resist change, stifle the creativity of police personnel, and isolate administrators from their clientele and other police personnel.

There are numerous organizational principles that form the basis of a functioning department. The police department's functions can be divided into line, staff, and auxiliary categories. Line functions, the prevention and control of crime, are the reason for the police department's existence. Patrol officers and the investigators perform this function. Staff services are activities that assist the organization in developing better personnel, these include recruitment, selection, and planning. Auxiliary services provide technical, supportive, and facility services for the police department.

Policing in large metropolitan organizations is a complex operation and specialized units are created to deal with specific crime problems or to achieve organizational objectives. Specialized units include juvenile bureaus, fraud units, or homicide units. Generally, small police agencies do not have the personnel to create specialized units. There are both positive and negative aspects to specialized police units. For example, specialization could lead to bickering between police officers or units. On the other hand, it could lead to the development of expertise in a high crime field—i.e., homicide investigations.

---

33. Ibid., 87.

Administrative practice requires a systems approach for managing an organization. The organization receives input, like people and financial resources, and by means of administrative functions it produces output. To achieve output the police administrator has five functional areas: planning, organizing, staffing, leading, and controlling. These major functions assist the police administrator in achieving the mission of the organization.

To perform his job, the police administrator has several interpersonal roles as a figurehead, a leader, and a liaison; several informational roles as a monitor, a disseminator, and a spokesman; and several decisional roles as an entrepreneur, a disturbance handler, a resource allocator, and a negotiator. Police executives who understand their roles as administrators are usually more effective and efficient.

The structure of the police organization is usually depicted by a table of organization. A good table of organization assists the organization in functioning more efficiently. Tables of organization should be considered a starting point for defining the organization and its goals and they need to be used with caution and knowledge of their limitations.

Although the police have been organized according to a paramilitary structure for the sake of efficiency, efficiency has not always been the result, but police organizations are changing. The "Healthy Organization," which has seven components and is coordinated by the police chief, has been proposed as one model to make the police organization more efficient and effective. Quality Policing, which has been implemented by the Madison, Wisconsin, Police Department, has also been proposed as an administrative strategy to improve the organizational structure of police departments. Both of these concepts are service oriented and empower police personnel to be decision-makers. Some aspects of these philosophies are expected to be adopted by police agencies.

Key Terms

auxiliary	outputs
bureaucracy	POSDCORB
chain of command	primary line
decisional roles	Quality Policing
delegation of authority	secondary line

division of work	staff
hierarchical authority	scientific management
informational roles	systems
inputs	Total Quality Management
interpersonal roles	unity of command

Review Questions

1. Describe scientific management.
2. Describe a bureaucracy.
3. What does the acronym POSDCORB stand for?
4. Discuss the differences between line, staff, and auxiliary functions of an organization.
5. Describe the administrator's roles.
6. What is the value of the Table of Organization to a police department?
7. Discuss administrative barriers to effective police administration.
8. Discuss Total Quality Management.

References

Caplow, Theodore. *Managing the Organization.* 2d ed. New York: Holt, Rinehart and Winston, 1983.

Clark, David L. "Emerging Paradigms in Organizational Theory and Research." *Organizational Theory and Inquiry.* Edited by Yvonna S. Lincoln. Beverley Hills: Sage, 1985.

Couper, David C. and Sabine H. Lobitz. *Quality Policing: The Madison Experience.* Washington: Police Executive Research Forum, 1991.

Eastman, George, Ed. *Municipal Police Administration,* 7th ed. Washington, 1971.

Etzioni, Amitai. *Modern Organizations.* Englewood Cliffs: NJ: Prentice Hall, 1964.

Gulick, Luther. "Notes on the Theory of Organization," *Papers on the Science of Administration.* Edited by Luther Gulick and L. Urwick. 1937. Reprint, New York: August M. Kelly, 1969.

Koontz, Harold, Cyril O'Donnell, and Heinz Weihrich. *Essentials of Management,* 4th ed. New York: McGraw-Hill, 1986.

March, John, and Herber Simon. *Organizations.* 2d ed. Cambridge: Blackwell Publishers, 1993.

Mintzberg, Henry. "The Manager's Job: Folklore and Fact." *Harvard Business Review* (July-August 1975).

Munro, Jim L. *Administrative Behavior and Police Organization.* Chicago: University of Chicago Press, 1974.

Parsons, Talcott, Ed. *Max Weber: The Theory of Social and Economic Organizations.* New York: Free Press, 1947.

Reiss, Albert J. "Shaping and Serving the Community: The Role of the Police Chief Executive." *Police Leadership in America: Crisis and Opportunity.* Edited by William A. Geller. 1985.

Royberg, Roy R. *Police Management and Organizational Behavior: A Contingency Approach.* St. Paul, MN: West Publishing Company, 1979.

Stamper, Norman H. *Removing Managerial Barriers: To Effective Police Leadership.* Washington: Police Executive Forum, 1992.

Tansik, David A. and James F. *Managing Police Organizations.* Belmont, CA: Duxbury, 1981.

Toffler, Alvin. *Future Shock.* New York: Random House, 1970.

Walton, Mary. *Deming Management at Work.* New York: Perigree, 1990.

Wilson, O.W. and Roy McLaren. *Police Administration.* 4th ed. New York: McGraw-Hill, 1977.

CHAPTER **6**

Patrol

Major Issues

1. Is patrol still relevant as we approach the twenty-first century?
2. Is there one specific type of patrol method that would play a greater role in public support and at the same time prevent and control crime?
3. Do we know enough about patrol strategies to determine if they actually prevent and control crime?
4. Which of the three policing styles—watchman, legalistic, or service—are the most appropriate for the twenty-first century?
5. Should patrol officers be involved in traffic operations?

Introduction

Patrol has often been called the *backbone of the police department.* Generally, other services provided by the police department evolve from the work of the patrol division. The patrol units are the primary line units that have as their mission the preventing and controlling of criminal conduct. If the aphorism "thin blue line" is to be considered accurate, then it has to be applied to the patrol force. The patrol force, more than any other police operations unit, provides the first line of defense against the street criminal and against predatory crimes. The delivery of police service to the community by the patrol force has become expected by the community. Most police-citizen contacts occur at the patrol level.

Patrol, as a means of protection, can be traced to ancient times when tribal people selected a group of individuals to protect the entire group by forming a patrol segment. The Greeks, Egyptians, and Romans all used patrol units as a method of controlling the people. During the Middle Ages, the Normans established patrols to maintain public safety. The Normans, after invading England in 1066, introduced the system of patrol to the English. During the Industrial Revolution of the early nineteenth century in England when violence was at an all-time high in London and its metropolitan areas, citizens formed vigilante patrols to combat crime. The concept of patrolling city streets was brought to America by the English colonists. Initially, patrolling was a night function, and the patrolling of city streets did not take place during daylight hours. It was not until 1833 that this country's first daytime patrol was formed in Philadelphia.[1]

In 1846 New York City established the first big-city police department in the United States. Unlike the London Metropolitan Police, the New York City Police did not wear *uniforms*. The London police wore blue uniforms, copper buttons, and top hats, and it was not until 1864 that the London force adopted the helmet that became their symbol.[2] Initially, the American police would not consent to wearing uniforms because they considered them a symbol of servility. The New York state law creating the New York City Police Department did not require officers to wear uniforms, only badges were required to identify police officers.

The use of uniforms for police officers was an important issue, since one of the purposes of having patrol officers was to deter crime. It was believed that the presence of a uniformed officer could both deter criminals from committing crime and could assist victims in identifying patrol officers when there were crimes to report. Additionally, supporters of uniforms concluded that patrol officers would be more likely to perform their duty, since they could be readily identified by their uniforms. In 1853, the New York City Police Commissioners required all police officers to wear uniforms. Later, Boston adopted uniforms, in 1858, and then Chicago, in 1861.[3]

In our modern era, we take it for granted that police officers wear uniforms and we would find it strange if a patrol officer did not wear some type of uniform. Some states require patrol officers to be in uniform when issuing traffic citations. Georgia is one state that has this legal requirement.

Initially, both the Metropolitan London Police and the American patrol officers were *not armed*. During the 1840s and 1850s, however, there was a sharp increase in the use of firearms in America, and newspapers began to report that police officers were being killed in the line of duty. Consequently, the police officer in the 1850s began arming himself for the first time without formal authorization. Slowly patrol officers were given official approval to

1. Nathan F. Iannone, *Principles of Police Patrol,* (New York: McGraw-Hill, 1975), 2–5.
2. Thomas A. Reppetto, *The Blue Line,* (New York: Free Press, 1978), 18.
3. David R. Johnson, *American Law Enforcement: A History,* (St. Louis: Forum Press, 1981), 29.

carry firearms. In contemporary society, we expect patrol officers to be armed and most Americans would not support taking firearms away from the patrol officers.

Approximately one-half of police personnel are assigned to the patrol force. The uniformed patrol officer functions as a generalist whose time has traditionally been devoted to responding to service calls and to the patrol of his beat. The patrol officer usually performs a *reactive* function—he reacts to citizens' complaints by responding to 911 calls. Even in the late 1990s, with community policing, citizens want the patrol officer to respond to their complaints. Like it or not, the 911 number will not go away, and the patrol officer will continue to be dispatched to handle nuisance calls. Citizens want the police to handle noise disturbances, barking dogs, rowdy neighbors, and the numerous other annoying incidents, and though police departments are capable of taking police reports from citizens over the telephone (the Wichita Police Department takes stolen automobile reports over the telephone) citizens still tend to insist that patrol officers respond to their complaints in person.

Dorothy Guyot, in reviewing the variation in the handling of incidents, has drawn four conclusions underscoring the variety of police work:

1. Within every category there is a tremendous range in the time that officers spend on a call—from less than a minute to more than three hours for violent crimes, nonviolent crimes and traffic problems. Officers have considerable control over how long they will spend in handling each incident. Even to matters usually requiring only two minutes, such as a request for information, officers have chosen on rare occasions to devote more than thirty minutes;

2. Officers spend little time on most calls, resulting in median times of less than twenty-four minutes for each type of incident. Situations involving disputes, dependent persons, and medical emergencies are often complex yet are usually handled in about fifteen minutes, so quickly as to raise doubts concerning the adequacy of the police response. The last two columns of Table 1 show the percentage of each type of incident in which officers gave assistance and in which they used coercion;

3. Both giving assistance and using coercion occur within every category. Overall, however, officers give assistance far more often than they resort to coercion, four times as often in non-

Table 1
Variation in Police Handling of Incidents

Type of Incident	% Total Incidents (N=5,688)	Service Time (min.)[a]		% Involving	
		Range	Median	Assist-ance[b]	Coer-cion[c]
Crime Totals	29%			49%	15%
Nonviolent Crime	15	0–224	18	53	9
Suspicion	10	0–157	9	37	17
Violent Crime	3	2–305	23	23	26
Morals Crime	1	1–133	14	37	47
Non-crime Totals	71%			54%	13%
Traffic	24	0–221	9	40	9
Nuisances	11	0–161	10	57	23
Disputes	9	0–149	15	71	30
General Assistance	9	1–161	10	60	4
Administrative	4	0–100	7	23	3
Information Request	4	0–47	2	95	1
Dependent Persons	3	1–142	15	69	14
Information Offer	3	0–61	9	48	1
Medical	2	2–100	16	64	3
Gone on Arrival	2	1–48	7	23	3

Notes:

a. Total number of minutes the officer spent arriving at the scene and handling the incident. The median is shown in the table, rather than the mean, to take full account of the many quick jobs.

b. Includes settling arguments, offering comfort, providing information, finding lost property, providing transportation, giving first aid, and making referrals.

c. Includes all uses of physical force, threats with a weapon, and verbal threats, but not peaceable arrests.

Sources: These data are from the 1977 study of 24 police departments (Mastrofski 1983) and his paper presented to the 1982 annual meeting of the American Society of Criminology. Interviewers recorded the actions, which were later coded into categories. The data were collected by trained observers riding in patrol cars. From Guyot, Dorothy. *Policing as though People Matter*, Temple University Press, Philadelphia, 1991, p. 39.

criminal incidents and three times as often in criminal incidents. Because a call for service initiated the vast majority of encounters over criminal incidents, officers have more opportunity to assist the victim than they have to arrest the suspect;

4. The mix of assistance and coercion in every category suggests the difficulty of culling from the police work load those incidents where law enforcement powers and coercion are not required. This mixture should give pause to those who seek to winnow out for officers the incidents likely to require use of force and to leave all other tasks to personnel with less training and lower salaries.[4]

Patrol officers in urban areas often have little time to perform preventive patrol. They are too busy responding to service calls. In some precincts in New York City, patrol officers spend their eight-hour tour of duty going from service call to service call. However, in suburban communities a patrol officer may get one service call in an eight-hour tour of duty. The suburban-community patrol officer would have ample time to perform preventive patrol in his beat. Traditionally, when patrol officers are not responding to service calls they are expected to patrol their beat doing preventive patrol. The patrol officers are expected to observe any crimes and the suspicious actions of any persons on their beat. The officers are expected to be familiar with businesses, schools, and the habits of individuals who work the busy sections of their beat. Only by knowing a beat can patrol officers recognize any suspicious situations.

The patrol officer's job is complex and in the late 1960s a university research team reported a list of essential behavioral requirements that a patrol officer must possess to be successful. This listing is as valid in the late 1990s as it was thirty years ago. According to the university research team a police officer must

1. Endure long periods of monotony in routine patrol yet react (almost instantaneously) and effectively to problem situations observed on the street or to orders issued by the radio dispatcher (in much the same way that a combat pilot must react to interception or a target opportunity;

2. Gain knowledge of his patrol area, not only of its physical characteristics but also of its normal routine of events and the usual behavior patterns of its residents;

3. Exhibit initiative, problem-solving capacity, effective judgment, and imagination in coping with the numerous complex situa-

---

4. Dorothy Guyot, *Policing as though People Matter,* (Philadelphia: Temple University Press, 1991), 38–39.

tions he is called upon to face, e.g., a family disturbance, a potential suicide, a robbery in progress, an accident, or a disaster. Police officers themselves clearly recognize this requirement and refer to it as "showing street sense";

4. Make prompt and effective decisions, sometimes in life-and-death situations, and be able to size up a situation quickly and take appropriate action;

5. Demonstrate mature judgement, as in deciding whether an arrest is warranted by the circumstances or a warning is sufficient, or in facing a situation where the use of force may be needed;

6. Demonstrate critical awareness in discerning signs of out-of-the-ordinary conditions or circumstances which indicate trouble or a crime in progress;

7. Exhibit a number of complex psychomotor skills, such as driving a vehicle in normal and emergency situations, firing a weapon accurately under extremely varied conditions, maintaining agility, endurance, and strength, and showing facility in self-defense and apprehension, as in taking a person into custody with a minimum of force;

8. Adequately perform the communication and record-keeping functions of the job, including oral reports, preparation of formal case reports, and completion of departmental and court forms;

9. Have the facility to act effectively in extreme divergent interpersonal situations. A police officer constantly confronts persons who are acting in violation of the law, ranging from curfew violators to felons. He is constantly confronted by people who are in trouble or who are victims of crimes. Besides his dealings with criminals, he has contact with para-criminals, informers, and people on the border of criminal behavior. (He must also be 'alley-wise.') At the same time he must relate to the people on his beat—businessmen, residents, school officials, visitors, etc. His interpersonal relations must range up and down a continuum defined by friendliness and persuasion on one end and by firmness and force at the other.

10. Endure verbal and physical abuse from citizens and offenders (as when placing a person under arrest or facing day-in and day-out race prejudice) while using only necessary force in the performance of his function;

11. Exhibit a professional, self-assured presence and a self-confident manner in his conduct when dealing with offenders, the public, and the courts;
12. Be capable of restoring equilibrium to social groups, e.g., restoring order in a family fight, in a disagreement between neighbors, or in a clash between rival youth groups;
13. Be skillful in questioning suspected offenders, victims, and witnesses of crimes;
14. Take charge of situations, e.g., a crime or accident scene, yet not unduly alienate participants or bystanders;
15. Be flexible enough to work under loose supervision in most of his day-to-day patrol activities (either alone or as part of a two-man team) and also under the direct supervision of superiors in situations where large numbers of officers are required;
16. Tolerate less stress in a multitude of forms, such as meeting the violent behavior of a mob, arousing people in a burning building, coping with the pressure of a high-speed chase or a weapon being fired at him, or dealing with a women bearing a child.
17. Exhibit personal courage in the face of dangerous situations which may result in serious injury or death;
18. Maintain objectivity while dealing with a host of "special interest" groups, ranging from relatives of offenders to members of the press;
19. Maintain a balanced perspective in the face of constant exposure to the worst side of human nature;
20. Exhibit a high level of personal integrity and ethical conduct, e.g., refrain from accepting bribes or "favors," provide impartial law enforcement, etc.[5]

Types of Patrol

There are a variety of patrol methods used by police departments, and all of them have advantages and disadvantages. The type of patrol method used by a police agency often depends upon the department's philosophy, the weather conditions, the terrain, economics, political influence, and citizen involvement.

---

5. Charles B. Saunders, Jr., *Upgrading the American Police*, (Washington, DC: Brookings Institution, 1970), 19–21.

Foot Patrol

The oldest procedural method, one that has received much attention and has continued to be proven valuable, is foot patrol. Before the advent of the automobile, foot patrol was the primary means of patrol. When the automobile became popular with police departments as a patrol technique, foot patrol lost favor. Foot patrols are useful for special events such as parades, dignitary protection, and public relations. They are also valuable for patrolling shopping malls, beaches, apartment complexes, schools, and areas where a motorized vehicles cannot gain access.

Officers on foot can observe more than officers in vehicles. By being on the street, an officer's sense of smell and sense of hearing are also improved. Foot patrol officers provide "an effective method of improving face-to-face communication between community residents and police officers. The increased communication often culminates in the exchange of information needed to prevent and solve crime."[6] In addition, foot patrol officers, making personal contact with citizens on their beat, can function as community organizers, as dispute mediators, and as valuable links between social service agencies and the community.[7]

There are several disadvantages to foot patrol. Beat size must be limited, since officers on foot can only be expected to patrol a limited geographical area. Officers must be concerned about the elements—snow, rain, sleet, cold, and heat. Often, because of weather conditions, it is not practical for officers to walk a beat. Furthermore, prisoners cannot be transported by foot patrol officers. Foot patrol officers usually will not be able to come to the assistance of fellow officers, because walking and running is much slower than other means of patrol. Equipment that foot patrol officers take to the field has to be limited, since carrying excessive equipment on their person would limit their mobility. Another major disadvantage of foot patrol is its cost; foot patrol continues to be an expensive method, since officers can only patrol a limited area, which makes their beats smaller than motorized patrol beats.

---

6. Robert C. Trojanowicz, "Foot Patrol: Some Problem Areas," *The Police Chief,* (June, 1984), 49.

7. Ibid., 47.

Automobile Patrol

The most common method of patrol since the 1930s has been the automobile. The greatest advantage patrol vehicles offer is *mobility*. A patrol officer can cover a larger geographical area or beat than a foot patrol or an officer on horseback. Officers in patrol vehicles offer a faster response for emergency situations, and they can carry more emergency equipment, like a fire extinguisher, and police equipment, like a shotgun. They are much more useful for pursuing suspects and can be used to transport prisoners. Officers are protected from the elements snow, rain, sleet, cold, and heat, and they can still patrol their beats, and except for extreme weather conditions, they can still be available for service calls and emergencies. Additionally, response time in a crisis situation is quicker than by most other means.

One key advantage to automobile patrol is the cost, since the patrol officers are a police department's biggest expense. Essentially, it takes fewer officers to cover an area by automobile than it does to cover the same area on foot.

The major disadvantages of vehicular patrols, however, are that

1. Such patrols lack the close, intimate relationships that can develop between a "beat cop" and the local community. Along with this loss is an accompanying increase in mistrust of the police by the public because of the relative remoteness of the patrol unit;
2. Rapid movement through the patrol area requires fast, sharp observation skills;
3. Mobile patrol loses the "eye-and-ears" sensitivity of the foot officer;
4. Sources of information lack depth and are more difficult to develop;
5. Vehicular patrol officers generally do not know their beat very well beyond the portion visible from the street;
6. The ability to "feel" the conditions of the community through interaction with the people on the beat is decreased;
7. The deterrent effect of patrol presence is limited to the period of its visibility in the area; larger patrol areas mean less frequent coverage of the area, which correspondingly decreases the possibility of detection of the criminal;

8. The criminal element is more likely to "read" the patterns of patrol by routine coverage becoming predictable coverage;
9. The priority shifts from the silence of the approach to the swiftness of approach. Rapid response by vehicular patrols often requires use of the lights and/or siren to clear traffic, which announces police presence prematurely.[8]

Bicycle Patrol

Bicycle patrol can be traced to the nineteenth century, but its popularity and practicability has generally been unpredictable. Currently, with the advent of "mountain bikes," bicycle patrols are becoming more acceptable as a means of patrol for many police departments. They are useful for patrolling college campuses, parks, beaches, housing areas, and congested downtown areas. Bicycles offer police officers more speed, mobility, and flexibility than they have on foot. An officer on a bicycle can, for example, travel down alleyways and run down "purse snatchers" more quickly than motorized patrol officers. Police agencies creating bicycle patrols are finding that they are not only a good public relations tool but that they are an effective mechanism for controlling crime in the downtown areas of cities.

Motorcycle Patrol

Motorcycles are traditionally used for traffic enforcement and control. They are also used as an escort service for funerals or for parades. Some cities, like Pittsburgh, Pennsylvania, use three-wheeled motorcycles for traffic control. An advantage of the two-wheeled motorcycle has always been its maneuverability. It can move through crowds of people, between vehicles, and through traffic more easily than patrol vehicles. Disadvantages to motorcycles include the lack of protection from inclement weather, the motorcycle's inability to carry equipment, and a lack of safety (motorcycles offer little protection when they are involved in accidents).

8. Larry D. Nichols, *Law Enforcement Patrol Operations: Police Systems and Practices,* 2nd ed., (Berkeley: McCutchan, 1995), 23.

Horse Patrol

In many of our major cities horse patrol goes back to the last century. Since maintaining horses is expensive and requires a great deal of care, only large departments can afford them. Horses need to be fed, stabled, and at times, they need to be checked by a veterinarian. Mounted patrols are used for crowd control, traffic control, and search-and-rescue missions. These units are excellent public relations tools. Both children and adults are impressed with horse patrol units. In Savannah, Georgia, a citizens' committee was instrumental in establishing a Mounted Patrol unit for that city. In a study of twenty-five cities that had mounted patrol units, the following reasons were given for the existence of mounted units: riot control, visibility (crime repression), community relations, crowd control (the movement and circulation of people), general law enforcement (arrest, citation, etc.), traffic control, and the public demand for the units.[9]

Marine Patrols

Communities near bodies of water often have a marine patrol to control crime. Marine patrols are needed to control water safety violations, for search-and-rescue missions, and for traditional law enforcement functions. In addition to drug smuggling along American's coast lines, predatory crimes also occur on our nation's waterways. Patrol officers assigned to the marine patrol unit are required to have a knowledge of boating, water safety, and emergency management. Maintaining marine patrol boats is expensive for a police agency and many agencies have a marine patrol operation during summer months when waterways are used the most. Depending upon the body of water, cities use different types of boats to patrol the waterways. Anything from speedboats to tugboats or personal watercraft (PWC) are used by marine patrol units.

---

9. William E. Carfield, "Comparative Analysis of Twenty-Five Horse Mounted Police Units in the United States," Eastern Kentucky University, Unpublished publication, (1982), 4.

Aircraft Patrol

For the last several decades aircraft patrol has been growing. It provides assistance to ground patrol units by observing areas that ground units cannot view. Aircraft are valuable for search-and-rescue missions, surveillance, traffic control and enforcement, and pursuit of suspects. As a patrol method, the aircraft patrol is the most expensive and requires highly trained personnel. Police agencies use either the fixed wing or rotary wing aircraft depending upon what best fills the needs of the department.

Special Purpose Vehicles

Police departments in the northern United States and Canada use snowmobiles for patrol of rural areas during winter weather, for controlling snowmobile drivers, and for emergencies. All-terrain vehicles (ATF) are used in rural areas and for locations that are otherwise difficult to reach.

Patrol Concepts and Tactics

The Traditional Patrol Model[10]

The traditional patrol model can be divided into four categories: call-for-service, preventive patrol, officer-initiated activities, and administrative tasks.

Traditionally the patrol officer responds to service calls without analyzing the time necessary to meet the demands of other patrol activities. Call-for-service usually consumes anywhere from twenty-five percent to forty percent of an officer's time.

Preventive patrol is non-committed patrol time. The assumption underlying preventive patrol has been that the deployment of highly visible patrol vehicles serves as a crime prevention and deterrence device. Patrol officers perform preventive patrol between service calls and administrative assignments. Officers assigned patrol duty have the option of deciding how they will use preventive patrol.

---

10. William G. Gay, Theodore H. Schell, and Stephen Schack, *Improving Patrol Productivity Volume 1: Patrol,* (Washington, DC: U.S. Department of Justice, LEAA, 1977), 2–6.

Some police departments assign patrol officers areas of priority or provide crime analysis data to assist the patrol officer in planning his activities.

Officer–initiated activities usually occur as a result of preventive patrol. Often this activity results from a patrol officer's observation of an illegal activity that leads to an arrest. In many instances, officer–initiated activities are linked to citizen contacts and building-security checks. Also, the observation by a patrol officer of a suspicious situation may prevent a crime from occurring. For most patrol officers, officer–initiated activities play a secondary role in their work activity.

Administrative tasks usually account for about twenty-five percent of the patrol officer's workload. These activities include preparing the patrol vehicle, writing reports, appearing in court, and running departmental errands. However, these activities, if monitored, can require very little time.

Proactive Versus Reactive

Patrol officers who patrol their beats aimlessly are not making the most of their time. The emphasis for the patrol unit has been the movement toward forming a closer working relationship with residents and businesses in the patrol area. Police solve crimes when citizens cooperate and provide information about being victims and witnesses. The intelligent patrol officer realizes this and works to gain the cooperation of the people on his beat. The patrol officer who practices proactive patrol knows the trouble spots on his beat. He knows the watering holes, the individuals who create disturbances, and the burglar who operates on his beat. By being a proactive patrol officer, he observes the drinking establishments, making certain intoxicated individuals are not driving. This does not necessarily mean making an arrest, but it could involve having a barkeep call a taxi for someone who has had too much to drink. By acting proactively the patrol officer can prevent automobile accidents. If the patrol officer keeps tabs on the known burglars who work his district, he might be able to make an arrest. Obviously, the patrol officer cannot watch all residents, but the proactive patrol officer can analyze the problem locations of his beat to take a realistic proactive approach to enforcement. He needs to know the times when he can be more effective. When the patrol officer locates the problem areas, then he can spend more time in these locations.

Reactive patrol simply means responding to 911 calls—getting to the scene of an automobile accident or an incident after the fact. As previously mentioned, reactive patrol is a major part of the patrol officer's job.

One Officer Versus Two-Officer Patrol Units

The issue of one-officer patrol units versus two-officer patrol units has been the subject of debate among police officers and researchers for several decades. There is a great deal of speculation pertaining to one-officer versus two-officer patrol units. Two-officer patrol cars are usually preferred to one-officer cars for reasons of safety. Two-officer patrol units take less time to service calls than one-officer patrol units because of the additional manpower available. The two-officer unit does not have to wait for back-up like one-officer units since many calls cannot be handled by one officer. Proponents of two-officer patrol cars claim that the two-officer unit provides a safer work environment and better quality of service.

However, there are many police proponents of one-officer patrol units. Larry Nichols in his patrol operations text states that one-officer patrol units are better than two-officer patrol units for the following reasons:

1. Reliance on a partner becomes a crutch that allows individual performance to suffer;
2. A high degree of admiration by one partner for another can cause the first officer to take unnecessary risks;
3. Resentment, jealousy, or fear of the partner can cause negative conduct by one or both partners;
4. Overzealous activity by one partner can result in the other's withdrawal and ineffectiveness;
5. One partner may cover up for another who is engaged in unethical, immoral, or possibly, illegal activity;
6. It is difficult for supervisors to give credit or blame to the proper partner for good or bad performance;
7. The productivity of a two-person unit is half that of a one-person unit, while the cost of operation is almost doubled;
8. The additional costs of vehicles and their maintenance to provide one-person-unit coverage is offset by the increased productivity;

9. Nine out of ten calls for police service can be effectively handled by one-person units;
10. The one in ten calls requiring more than one officer almost always allows enough time for the second to arrive;
11. One-person units encourage the officer to become observant and subsequently less susceptible to accident or sudden attack;
12. One-person units make quicker, wiser decisions, and the officer assumes more personal responsibility for actions and decisions;
13. More and better care of vehicles and equipment is seen in one-person units;
14. One-person units tend to develop more accurate, detailed investigations and stronger court cases.[11]

Directed Patrol

Preventive or random patrol is often performed in a haphazard, unstructured manner, especially when patrol officers are not provided with information about problems on their beat. With the availability of crime analysis and crime information, patrol activities can be planned. Problems on a patrol officer's beat can be identified and activities can be planned to solve those problems. Directed patrol means that patrol officers plan activities to solve specific problems on their beats rather than simply reacting to problems after the fact. "To be effective directed patrol must be closely linked to crime analysis and must have equal priority with calls for service as a patrol function."[12] The goal of directed patrol is to increase the patrol unit's effectiveness and the productivity of the department. Directed patrol deals with specific crime violations or situations and their time and location of occurrence. For example, patrol officers may be directed to patrol a specific area where there are many automobile accidents or many assaults.

Specialized Patrol

Specialized patrol can be defined as patrol activities in which the patrol officer concentrates on specific crime problems and when the patrol officer does not handle routine service calls. The objectives of

---

11. Larry D. Nichols, *Law Enforcement Patrol Operations: Police Systems and Practices,* 2nd ed., (Berkeley: McCutchan, 1995), 27–28.
12. Ibid., 7.

specialized patrol are to suppress crime and to arrest offenders in the commission of a crime. Specialized patrol operations can involve using saturated patrol of a specific area, using surveillance, and using decoys. These patrol activities can be done by the regular patrol officers or by a specialized patrol unit. Usually, specialized units concentrate on criminal activities such as robberies, rapes, burglaries, and larceny, which are referred to as suppressible crimes.[13]

Cities with populations of fifty thousand or more are more likely to use specialized patrol than those cities with a population under fifty thousand. There are three types of specialized patrol: plainclothes, uniform tactical, and mechanical devices. Visibility will be decreased with plainclothes units, but there is an increase in the opportunities available to make arrests. Uniformed tactical units support the patrol units and are used to saturate a specific geographical area for a specific time period. Mechanical devices consist of such contraptions such as alarm systems and night vision scopes.[14]

Team Policing

Team policing was popular in the 1970s when many large police departments adopted the strategy. The team policing approach was more popular with large police agencies than with medium or small agencies. Team policing has a decentralized structure with decision-making responsibilities given to the lower-level supervisors and line officers who have the authority to plan, investigate, and perform community relations activities. The team-policing patrol officer is usually an experienced generalist who is highly motivated.[15] Usually, team policing units convert specific geographical areas to team policing. "One of the central goals of team policing was to integrate all police service (patrol, investigative, etc.), with team members functioning as 'generalists.'"[16] Team policing faded out of use

---

13. Stephen Schack, Theodore H. Schell, and William G. Gay, *Improving Patrol Productivity Volume II: Specialized Patrol*, (Washington, DC: U.S. Department Of Justice, LEAA, 1977), 1–2.

14. Lawrence J. Szynkowski, "Preventive Patrol: Preventive Patrol Versus Specialized," *Journal of Police Science And Administration,* 9, No.2, (1981), 171.

15. Szynkowski, 176.

16. Samuel Walker, "Does Anyone Remember Team Policing? Lessons of the Team Policing Experience for Community Policing," *American Journal of Police* XII, No. 1, (1993), 40.

in most cities, except for a few cities, like Rochester, New York, where it has been operating successfully since the 1970s.

Saturation

Saturated patrol fills a geographical area with patrol officers. The purpose is to curtail traffic violations and crimes involving narcotics. Large police departments with large numbers of patrol officers have more of an opportunity to use saturated patrol than small police agencies with limited patrol personnel. Generally, saturated patrol is used in specific geographical locations where there is a distinctive crime trend.

Displacement

A large segment of the American population, including the average citizen and politicians, believes that adding more patrol officers to their city streets will prevent and deter crime, and there have been several studies conducted to test this concept. "Operation 25" was one of the first studies to determine whether or not adding more patrol officers to our city streets would curtail crime. This study took place in 1954 in the twenty-fifth precinct of the New York City Police Department. On September 1, 1954, the Police Commissioner doubled the police strength of the twenty-fifth precinct. Prior to "Operation 25" two-thirds of foot posts were unmanned. During the study, no post was left unmanned, the number of foot patrol beats were increased from fifty-five to eighty-nine, and the sizes of the posts were shortened. Operation 25 lasted for four months. During this time frame, serious crime dropped. Street crimes, like muggings, declined substantially while private crimes, like murder increased. One of the flaws of the Operation 25 study, however, was that it made no attempt to determine whether or not crime in the surrounding precincts increased—thereby *displacing* the crime into nearby precincts.[17]

During the mid-1960s, the New York City Rand Institute studied issues that were overlooked in "Operation 25." The Rand Institute considered the theory that reported-crime rates might change for reasons having nothing to do with the adding of additional pa-

---

17. James Q. Wilson, *Thinking About Crime,* Revised ed., (New York: Vintage, 1985), 61–63.

trol officers to a precinct. The Rand Institute studied two precincts that were given additional manpower while the rest of the city maintained the same manpower. In the twentieth precinct, one of the precincts studied, street robberies fell by thirty-three percent per week and grand larcenies and auto thefts by forty-nine percent per week. Crimes such as assaults and burglaries which occur in private places did not decrease. The Rand Study indicated that any reductions in crime were genuine and that crime was not displaced to adjoining precincts, though only changes in reported crimes were observed, not changes in actual crimes committed. With the increase in patrol manpower, however, it may be possible to assume that criminals did not commit crimes for a while or that they went to an adjoining precinct to commit crimes.[18]

A third study done by the New York City Rand Institute focused on the subway robberies of the New York City Transit Authority. Robberies in subways consist of robbing booth clerks or robbing passengers. In the early 1960s the Mayor of New York increased subway patrol officers from twelve hundred to over thirty-one hundred. The main objective for the increase was to place a patrol officer on every subway train and at every subway station. The evaluation of this study occurred over an eight year period, longer than previous studies. Following the increase of patrol coverage in the mid-1960s, there was a short-term decline in subway crime. Subway robberies began to increase within a year and by 1970 there were six times more subway robberies than there were in 1965 when the additional patrol officers were hired. Generally, the additional patrol officers were deployed during the evening hours, and the number of crimes fell during the hours when there were increased patrol officers. But, the number of crimes during the day increased steadily from 1966 onward. The conclusion of the Rand Institute was that increasing patrol officers on subway trains and at train platforms during the night did have a deterrent effect.[19]

Response Time

How fast should a patrol officer respond to a citizen's calls for service? Can a police department afford to have a patrol officer respond to all citizen calls for service? For several decades, response time was

18. Ibid., 64.
19. Ibid., 65.

considered an important element of police productivity and efficiency. The telephone company convinced police departments that 911 would allow for a quicker response time to answer service calls. Is a quick response time necessary for all 911 calls? Are all 911 calls emergencies or crimes in progress? The obvious answer is No. A quick response time does not necessarily prevent or control crime. It makes no sense for a patrol officer to speed to a burglary scene that occurred three days prior. However, if a burglary happens to be in progress, then a quick response time can be important. The burglar has been reported on the premises. Police departments need to prioritize their calls for service according to their importance. All citizen calls for service should not be treated equally. Many police departments, such as Rochester, New York, and Wichita, Kansas, do not send a patrol unit to all calls. Reports are taken over the telephone or citizens are asked to come to police headquarters to complete the reports. In order to prioritize a citizen's call for service, dispatchers need to obtain accurate information that can only be obtained by asking such questions as:

- Has anyone been injured? Is he or she still at the scene?
- What has been stolen? What is its value?
- Is a suspect still at the scene?
- How long ago did the suspect(s) leave the scene? In what direction did they go? How were they traveling? Can they be described?
- Was a weapon involved? What type? How many?
- Are there witnesses? Where are they located?[20]

A Kansas City Study

In 1972 the Police Foundation sponsored the "Kansas City Preventive Patrol Experiment,"[21]—up to this time, the most comprehensive study conducted to analyze the effectiveness of traditional preventive patrol. The patrol experiment took place within Kansas

---

20. Michael T. Farmer, Ed., *Differential Police Strategies,* (Washington, DC: Police Executive Research Forum, 1981), 5.
21. George L. Kelling, Tony Pate, and Durane Dieckman, et al., *The Kansas City Patrol Experiment: A Summary Report,* (Washington DC: Police Foundation, 1974).

City's South Patrol Division within a thirty-two square mile area that included both commercial and residential areas. There were fifteen beats involved in the patrol experiment and they were matched on the basis of their crime data, their number of calls for service, their ethnic composition, their median income, and the transiency of their population. The beats ranged from areas that were seventy-eight percent black to areas that were ninety-nine percent white. The fifteen beats were divided into reactive beats, control beats, and proactive beats.[22]

The reactive beats of the patrol experiment were removed from the beats and were to respond only to calls for service and they were given no preventive patrol responsibilities. When they were not answering calls for service, officers assigned to reactive beats patrolled adjacent proactive beats or patrolled the boundaries of reactive beats. Patrol visibility was withdrawn although it remained available. The control beats maintained the traditional patrol method of using one car per beat. The five proactive beats increased police visibility from two to three times the normal patrol level. Additional patrol-marked vehicles were assigned to proactive beats. No restrictions were placed upon reactive patrol beats other than that they were not to patrol those beats and they were to respond to calls for service. Control and reactive patrol officers were to be involved in the traditional preventive patrol strategy.[23]

The results of the "Kansas City Preventive Patrol Experiment" were that the increase or decrease of preventive patrol had no effect on crime, on the citizens' fear of crime, on community attitudes toward the police, on police response time, or on traffic accidents. The findings of Kansas City Patrol Experiment are as follows:

1. There were no major differences in victimization between the reactive, control, and proactive beats;
2. In reporting crime there were no major differences between the reactive, control, and proactive beats in reporting crime;
3. There were no major differences in crimes citizens and businesses reported between reactive, control, and proactive beats;
4. There were no major differences in police arrests between reactive, control, and proactive beats;

22. Ibid., 8–9.
23. Ibid., 8–9.

5. There were no major differences between citizen fear of crime and changes made in routine preventive patrol;
6. There were no major differences made by citizens taking protective and security measures detected by variations in the level of routine preventive patrol;
7. There were no major differences in the protective and security measures used by businesses as a result of variations in the level of routine preventive patrol;
8. The alternations in the levels of preventive patrol had no affect on citizens attitudes;
9. The changes in the level of routine preventive patrol did not affect the attitude of the business community toward the police;
10. Changes in patrol levels did not affect citizens' attitudes toward the police;
11. Police officers' behavior toward citizens was not affected by the officers' assignment to a reactive, control, or proactive beat;
12. The levels of routine preventive patrol did not affect the amount of time taken by police in answering calls for service; and
13. The various levels of patrol had no effect on traffic accidents.[24]

Policing Styles

What does the patrol officer do? What is his style of patrol? What style of patrolling does the community expect from the patrol unit? If we are to use the entertainment media to help us understand what the patrol officer does, would we get an unrealistic picture of how the patrol officer functions?

The style of patrolling differs from community to community, because communities are not similar in their socio-economical demographics. Ethnic and racial issues, educational levels, and cultural values differ between communities, and so various communities have different expectations of their patrol officers. James Q. Wilson, a criminal justice scholar, was the first researcher to examine the styles of patrolling in communities. Wilson describes "the behavior of patrolmen discharging their routine law-enforcing and order-maintaining functions, to explain how that behavior is determined by the organizational and legal constraints under which the patrol-

---

24. Ibid., 20–38.

Table 2
Police Use of Non-Committed Time

- **Stationary, police related**
  Report writing, waiting for tows, surveillance, traffic ordinance enforcement, etc.
- **Stationary, non-police related**
  Eating, resting, reading, rest calls, girl watching, phone calls, visits, sleeping, watching movies or sporting events, etc.
- **Mobile, police related**
  Looking for suspicious cars, people, stolen autos, traffic violations, training new patrol officers, watching buildings and residences, etc.
- **Mobile, non-police related**
  Driving to relieve boredom, girl watching, personal errands, etc.
- **Contacting personnel in the field, police related**
  Exchanging information about crime suspects, discussing cases, policies, etc.
- **Contacting personnel in the field, non-police related**
  General talk about hunting, cars, sex, vacations, jokes, etc.
- **Residual**
  Traveling to and from station, court, garage, headquarters, repair, etc.

Source: Kelling, G., T. Pate, D. Dieckman, and C. Brown. *The Kansas City Preventive Patrol Experiment: A Summary Report.* Police Foundation, 1974, p. 43. Reprinted with permission of The Police Foundation.

man works."[25] There are three distinctive police styles or strategies described by Wilson: the watchman, the legalistic, and the service style.

The *watchman* style suggests that police officers should be focused on situations that are not "serious" criminal acts and that the principal function of patrol is order maintenance and not law enforcement. In all cities, patrol officers display a watchman style because order maintenance remains one of the patrol officer's functions. The watchman style not only emphasizes order over law enforcement but it also judges infractions by the consequences of the violation and not necessarily by what the law says about the act. In some departments the watchman style becomes the operational standard of

25. James Q. Wilson, *Varieties of Police Behavior,* (Cambridge, MA: Harvard University Press, 1978), 10.

the police department. The watchman style is reinforced by the attitudes, the policies, and the procedures of the department.[26]

The *legalistic* style of patrol emphasizes law enforcement over order maintenance. The patrol officer follows a legal standard and makes an arrest when the law is violated. The patrol officer takes a law enforcement view of his job. The legalistic style, however, does not imply that all laws are given equal status or that they are always enforced. Some crimes are considered serious enough to enforce, while others may not be considered serious enough to enforce. The legalistic-style patrol force will make more arrests, give more citations, and recommend the filing of complaints and prosecutions.[27]

In the *service* style of patrol, the patrol force takes seriously both the law enforcement and order maintenance style of patrol. However, the service-style patrol officer is less likely to make an arrest than the patrol officer practicing a legalistic approach. Public order is emphasized in the service style and this includes keeping unruly teenagers and homeless people under control. Because the community generally expects its patrol officers to be service-oriented—which includes being courteous and making a good appearance—minor infractions of the law are overlooked when possible, while serious crimes such as burglaries and assaults are taken seriously. Suspicious persons are questioned and appropriate action is taken when it is needed.[28]

Problem Solving

In an article published in 1979[29], Herman Goldstein initiated the philosophy of problem-solving for the police. Goldstein claims that traditional police practices are *incident driven*—a citizen calls the police about a specific problem and the police respond, the police then handle the incident and return to their patrol duties. However, the beat patrol officer is often called to handle the same incident over and over again without being able to correct the situation. For example, the patrol unit responds to a husband-and-wife dispute on a weekly basis for months at a time or even years but the problem is

26. Ibid., 140–141.

27. Ibid., 172–173.

28. Ibid., 200–201.

29. Herman Goldstein, "Improving Policing: A Problem-Oriented Approach," *Crime and Delinquency,* 25 (1979), 236–258.

Table 3

Of about 69,000 Federal officers employed full time in Dec. 1993:

40,002 performed duties related to criminal investigation and enforcement

58% ████████████████████████████████████

11,073 worked in corrections, mostly as correctional officers in Federal prisons

16% ████████

7,127 performed duties primarily related to police response and patrol

10% ██████

5,852
performed duties related to court operations

9% ████

3,945 had security and protection responsibilities

6% ██

- The largest employers of Federal officers, accounting for 57% of the total, were the U.S. Customs Service (10,120), the FBI (10,075), the Bureau of Prisons (9,984), and the Immigration and Naturalization Service (9,466).
- The Administrative Office of the U.S. Courts, the U.S. Marshals Service, the FBI, the Drug Enforcement Administration, the Bureau of Alcohol, Tobacco and Firearms, and the IRS employed one or more officers in every State.
- About half of all Federal officers were employed in California (9,006), Texas (7,761), New York (6,305), the District of Columbia (6,133), or Florida (4,362). Fewer than 100 were employed in New Hampshire, Delaware, and Wyoming.
- Nationwide, there were 2.7 Federal officers per 10,000 residents, ranging from 106 per 10,000 residents in the District of Columbia to less than 1 per 10,000 in Arkansas, Mississippi, Ohio, Wisconsin, New Hampshire, and Iowa.

Source: Bureau of Justice Statistics Bulletin, " Federal Law Enforcement Officers, 1993" December 1994.

Figure 1
Problem-Oriented Policing

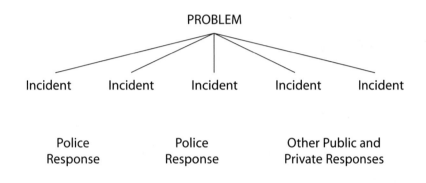

UNDERLYING CONDITIONS

PROBLEM

Incident   Incident   Incident   Incident   Incident

Police   Police   Other Public and
Response   Response   Private Responses

Problem-Solving Process

Source: John E. Eck and William Spelman, *Problem-Solving: Problem-Oriented Policing in Newport News*, Police Executive Research Forum, 1987, p xvii.

never solved. Goldstein's problem–oriented approach, then, would involve making an attempt to eliminate the problem. The solution might involve, in this case, engaging the support of community agencies, both public and private, or bringing in any external entity or resource that could assist in solving the problem. This strategy can be defined as "a department wide strategy aimed at solving persistent community problems. Police identify, analyze, and respond to the underlying circumstances that create incidents."[30]

---

30. John E. Eck and William Spelman, *Problem-Solving: Problem-Oriented Policing in Newport News,* (Washington, DC: Police Executive Research Forum, 1987), xv.

Community Policing

Community policing is being sold as the wave of future. The problem-solving approach to policing has laid the foundation of community policing. The idea that patrol officers are problem solvers has been expanded by the community policing concept. Community policing has been defined as "a philosophy of full-service personalized policing, where the same officer patrols and works in the same area on a permanent basis, from a decentralized place, working in a proactive partnership with citizens to identify and solve problems."[31] The community policing strategy includes the following points:

> *Philosophy.* The community policing philosophy rests on the belief that contemporary challenges require the police to provide full-service policing, proactive and reactive, by involving the community directly as partners in the process of identifying, prioritizing, and solving problems including crime, fear of crime, illicit drugs, social and physical disorder, and neighboring decay. A department-wide commitment implies changes in policies and procedures.
>
> *Personalization.* By providing the community its own community policing officer, community policing breaks down the anonymity on both sides—community policing officers and community residents know each other on a first-name basis.
>
> *Policing.* Community policing maintains a strong law enforcement focus; community policing officers answer calls and make arrests like any other officer, but they also focus on proactive problem solving.
>
> *Patrols.* Community policing officers work and patrol their communities, but the goal is to free them from the isolation of the patrol car, often by having them walk the beat or rely on other modes of transportation, such as bicycles, scooters, or horses.
>
> *Permanence.* Community policing requires assigning community policing officers permanently to defined beats, so that they have the time, opportunity, and continuity to develop the new partnership. Permanence means that community policing

---

31. Robert Trojanowicz and Bonnie Bucqueroux, *Community Policing: How to Get Started,* (Cincinnati: Anderson, 1994), 3.

Table 4
Traditional Versus Community Policing

Question	Traditional	Community Policing
Who are the police?	A government agency principally responsible for law enforcement.	Police are the public and the public are the police; the police officers are those who are paid to give full-time attention to the duties of every citizen.
What is the relationship of the police force to other public service departments?	Priorities often conflict.	The police are one department among many responsible for improving the quality of life.
What is the role of the police?	Focusing on solving crimes.	A broader problem-solving approach.
How is police efficiency measured?	By detection and arrest rates.	By the absence of crime and disorder.
What are the highest priorities?	Crimes that are high value (for example, bank robberies) and those involving violence.	Whatever problems disturb the community most.
What, specifically, do police deal with?	Incidents	Citizens' problems and concerns.
What determines the effectiveness of police?	Response times	Public cooperation.
What view do police take of service calls?	Deal with them only if there is no real police work to do.	Vital function and great opportunity.
What is police professionalism?	Swift effective response to serious crime.	Keeping close to the community.
What kind of intelligence is most important?	Crime intelligence (study of particular crimes or series of crimes).	Criminal intelligence (information about the activities of individuals or groups).
What is the essential nature of police accountability?	Highly centralized; governed by rules, regulations, and policy directives/ accountable to the law.	Emphasis on local accountability of community needs.
What is the role of headquarters?	To provide the necessary rules and policy directives.	To preach organizational values.
What is the role of the press liaison department?	To keep the "heat" off operational officers so they can get on with the job.	To coordinate an essential channel of communication with the community.
How do the police regard prosecutions?	As an important goal	As one tool among many.

Source: Malcolm K. Sparrow. *Implementing Community Policing*, National Institute of Justice (Washington, D.C.: U.S. Department of Justice, 1988), pp 8–9.

officers should not be rotated in and out of their beats, and they should not be used as "fill-ins" for absences and vacations of other personnel.

Place. All jurisdictions, no matter how large, ultimately break down into distinct neighborhoods. Community policing decentralizes police officers often including investigators, so that community policing officers can benefit from "owning" their neighborhood beats in which they can act as a "mini-chief," tailoring the response to the needs and resources of the beat area. Moreover, community policing decentralizes decision making, not only by allowing community policing officers the autonomy and freedom to act, but also by empowering all officers to participate in community-based problem-solving.

Proaction. As part of providing full-service policing, community policing balances reactive responses to crime incidents and emergencies with a proactive focus on preventing problems before they occur or escalate.

Partnership. Community policing encourages a new partnership between people and police, which rests on mutual respect, civility, and support.

Problem Solving. Community policing redefines the mission of the police to focus on solving problems, so that success or failure depends on qualitative outcomes (problems solved) rather than just or quantitative results (arrests made, citations issued—so-called "numbers policing"). Both quantitative and qualitative measures are necessary.[32]

Traffic Patrol

Since the introduction of the automobile to the American highways, the patrol force has been responsible for traffic operations—the rapid and safe movement of automobiles and pedestrians. Overseeing highways, motor vehicles, and pedestrians is the primary responsibility of traffic operations. With approximately 45,000 people killed in traffic fatalities and almost four million injured[33] an-

32. Ibid., 3–4.

33. Thomas D. Larson, *Highway Statistics, 1990*, (Washington, DC: Government Printing Office, 1989), 197.

nually, the traffic patrol unit has the obligation of decreasing high-way fatalities and injuries. The objectives of traffic patrol operations includes the following:

1. To diminish losses from accidents;
2. To determine facts about accident occurrence as a basis for both accident prevention and service to involved citizens who need objective, impartial evidence to obtain justice in civil settlements of accident losses;
3. To assist accident victims by first-aid and by protection of property in vehicles;
4. To assist in obtaining the best possible movement of vehicles and pedestrians consistent with safety;
5. To obtain the compliance of motorists and pedestrians with traffic laws and ordinances and driver license regulations and orders;
6. To assist the traffic engineer and traffic-safety education agencies by providing them with significant information useful in their accident prevention work and, in the case of the engineer, in traffic movement or vehicle parking, as well;
7. To serve as the municipal government's inspection, investigative, and reporting field force to discover problems and propose corrections that will help achieve safer and more efficient motor vehicle and pedestrian travel, and vehicle parking;
8. To plan for traffic routing and directing, removal of vehicles and other traffic hazards, crowd control, and emergency vehicle access for predictable emergencies or catastrophes; and
9. To give information and assistance to motorists and pedestrians.[34]

Patrol officers involved in traffic operations perform a variety of functions to meet the objectives of the traffic operations unit. This can include accident investigation and reconstruction of an accident scene—usually when a fatality occurs. It includes protecting property, having motor vehicles towed from an accident scene, and transporting the injured to the hospital. Traffic patrol officers direct traffic, control parking, provide escort services, and impound abandoned vehicles. Law enforcement actions performed by traffic

34. George D. Eastman and Esther M. Eastman, Ed.s, *Municipal Police Administration,* 7th ed., (Washington, DC: International City Management Association, 1971), 106.

patrol officers include issuing citations for traffic infractions, making arrests for violating motor vehicle laws, preparing cases for court, and appearing as witnesses for the prosecution. Traffic patrol officers provide assistance to motorists, conduct road checks for driver's licenses and for other violations such as drinking while driving, and conduct safety checks for motor vehicles.[35]

Traffic patrol administrators recognize, however, that a traffic unit cannot enforce all the traffic laws and cannot apprehend all traffic violators. *Selective traffic enforcement* allows the traffic officer to concentrate on the specific traffic violations that are the cause of accidents. *Speed limit enforcement* is also a means of providing safer roadways. Collisions of vehicles or vehicles with pedestrians cause serious damages, injuries, and even death. The purpose of controlling speeding, ultimately, is to slow down drivers in order to create safe highways.[36]

Summary

Patrol is the backbone of the police department. Generally, other services provided by the police department evolve from the work of the patrol division. The patrol units are the primary line units that have as their mission the preventing and controlling of criminal conduct. Approximately one half of police personnel are assigned to the patrol force.

The uniformed patrol officer functions as a generalist whose time, traditionally, has been devoted to responding to service calls and to the patrol of his beat. The patrol officer usually performs a reactive function—he reacts to citizen complaints by responding to citizens who call 911.

There are a variety of patrol methods used by police departments. All the patrol methods have advantages and disadvantages. The type of patrol method used by a police agency often depends upon the department's philosophy, the weather conditions, the terrain, economics, political influence, and citizen involvement. The oldest procedural method still considered valuable is foot patrol. When the au-

---

35. Ibid., 106–107.

36. William A. Geller, Ed., *Local Government Police Management,* 3rd. ed., (1991), 169–170.

tomobile became popular with police departments as a patrol technique, foot patrol lost favor, though foot parol is certainly still useful for special events, like parades, dignitary protection, and public relations. The most common patrol method since the 1930s has been by automobile. The greatest advantage that patrol vehicles offer is mobility. A patrol officer in an automobile can cover a large geographical area. Officers in patrol vehicles offer a faster response for emergency situations and they can carry more equipment than other patrol means can.

Bicycle patrol can be traced to the nineteenth century, but its popularity has varied widely. Bicycle patrol is commonly used for patrolling college campuses, parks, beaches, housing areas, and in congested downtown areas. Police agencies that are creating bicycle patrols are finding that they are not only a good public relations tool but that they are an effective mechanism for controlling crime in the downtown areas of cities. Motorcycle patrols are traditionally used for traffic enforcement and control. Horse patrols are used for crowd control, traffic control, and search-and-rescue missions. Communities near bodies of water may often have a marine patrol to control crime. Marine patrols are needed to control water safety violations, search-and-rescue missions, and for other traditional law enforcement functions. For the last several decades the use of aircraft patrol has been growing. Aircraft patrol provides assistance to ground patrol units by observing areas that ground units cannot view. During the winter months police departments in the northern United States use snowmobiles for emergencies and for controlling snowmobilers.

The traditional patrol model can be divided into four categories: call-for-service, preventive patrol, officer initiated activities, and administrative tasks. Traditionally, the patrol officer responds to service calls without analyzing the time needed for other patrol activities. Preventive patrol is non-committed patrol time. Patrol officers perform preventive patrol between service calls and administrative assignments. Officer-initiated activities usually occur as a result of preventive patrol. Administrative tasks include preparing the patrol vehicle, writing reports, making court appearances, and running departmental errands.

During the 1960s James Q. Wilson described three policing styles: the watchman style, the legalistic style, and the service style. The watchman style is focused on situations encountered by the patrol officer that are not "serious" criminal acts—its principal function is order maintenance and not law enforcement. The legalistic style of patrol emphasizes law enforcement over order maintenance. In the service form of patrol the patrol force takes seriously both the law enforcement and order maintenance style of patrol.

Since the inception of the automobile on American highways the patrol force has been responsible for traffic operations. Traffic operations require the rapid and safe movement of automobiles and pedestrians. Patrol officers involved in traffic operations perform a variety of functions to meet the objectives for the traffic operations unit. These can include accident investigation, reconstruction of an accident scene, and transporting the injured to the hospital. Traffic patrol officers direct traffic, control parking, provide escort services, and impound abounded vehicles. Law enforcement actions performed by traffic patrol officers include issuing citations for traffic infractions, making arrests for violating motor vehicle laws, preparing cases for court, and appearing as witnesses for the prosecution.

Key Terms

aircraft	preventive patrol
ATF	proactive
automobile	reactive
bicycle patrol	response time
directed patrol	saturation
displacement	selective traffic enforcement
foot patrol	specialized patrol
horse patrol	speed-limit enforcement
Kansas City study	team policing
legalistic style	traditional policing
marine patrol	reactive
motorcycle patrol	response time
Operation 25	watchman style

Review Questions

1. Provide a brief historical review of police patrol.
2. List the responsibilities of a patrol officer.
3. Describe the various types of patrol.

4. Describe the tradition patrol model.
5. Describe the differences between proactive and reactive patrol.
6. Describe the advantages of one-officer versus two-officer patrol units.
7. Describe directed patrol.
8. Describe specialized patrol.
9. Describe the key elements of the Kansas City study.
10. Describe the role of the traffic patrol officer.

References

Carfield, William E. "Comparative Analysis of Twenty-Five Horse Mounted Police Units in the United States." Working paper, Eastern Kentucky University, 1982.

Eastman, George D. and Esther M. Eastman, Ed.'s. *Municipal Police Administration*. 7th ed. Washington: International City Management Association, 1971.

Eck, John. E, and William Spelman. *Problem Solving: Problem-Oriented Policing in Newport News*. Washington: Police Executive Research Forum, 1987.

Farmer, Michael T., Ed. *Differential Police Strategies*. Washington: Police Executive Research Forum, 1981.

Gay, William G., Theodore H. Schell, and Stephen Schack. *Improving Police Productivity Volume 1: Patrol*. Washington: U.S. Department of Justice, LEAA, 1977.

Geller, William A., Ed. *Local Government Police Management*. 3d ed. 1991.

Goldstein, Herman. "Improving Policing: A Problem-Oriented Approach," *Crime and Delinquency*. Vol. 25. 1979.

Guyot, Dorothy. *Policing as though People Matter*. Philadelphia: Temple University Press, 1991.

Iannone, Nathan F. *Principles of Police Patrol*. New York: McGraw-Hill, 1975.

Johnson, David R. *American Law Enforcement: A History*. St. Louis: Forum Press, 1981.

Kelling, George L. et al. *The Kansas City Preventive Patrol Experiment: A Summary Report*. Washington: Police Foundation, October, 1974.

Larson, Thomas D. *Highway Statistics, 1990*. Washington: U.S. Government Printing Office, 1990.

Nichols, Larry D. *Law Enforcement Patrol Operations: Police Systems and Practices*. 2d ed. Berkeley: McCutchan Publishing Company, 1995.

Reppetto, Thomas A. *The Blue Line*. New York: Free Press, 1978.

Saunders, Jr., Charles B. *Upgrading the American Police*. Washington: The Brookings Institution, 1970.

Schack, Stephen, Theodore H. Schell, and William G. Gay. "Improving Patrol Productivity." Vol. II. *Specialized Patrol*. Washington: U.S. Department of Justice, LEAA, 1977.

Szynkowski, Lawrence J. "Preventive Patrol: Preventive Patrol Versus Specialized." *Journal of Police Science and Administration*. 9, no. 2 (1981).

Trojanowicz, Robert C. and Bonnie Bucqueroux. *Community Policing: How to Get Started*. Cincinnati: Anderson Publishing Company, 1994.

Trojanowicz, Robert C. "Foot Patrol: Some Problem Areas," *The Police Chief* (June 1984).

Walker, Samuel. "Does Anyone Remember Team Policing? Lessons of the Team Policing Experience for Community Policing." *American Journal of Police* XII, no.1 (1993).

Wilson, James Q. *Thinking About Crime*. rev. ed. New York: Vintage Press, 1985.

Wilson, James Q. *Varieties of Police Behavior*. Cambridge: Harvard University Press, 1978.

CHAPTER 7

Criminal Investigation and Specialized Units

Major Issues

1. Modern criminal investigations place more emphasis on eye-witness testimony than on scientific evidence to solve a crime.
2. Specialized criminal investigative units supplement general investigative units.
3. Specialized police units assist the police department in functioning more effectively and efficiently.

Introduction

The idea of police officers performing criminal investigative work has its roots in the "New Police" of Metropolitan London. Initially, the police officer was to walk a beat simply to prevent crime. The concept of the criminal investigator or detective didn't develop until the second half of the nineteenth century. Prior to the formal organization of the London police in 1829 and for several decades after its formation, the investigation of crime was a private business. The private investigator would be paid when he recovered stolen property or when he solved a crime. Because of the profit motive, private investigators were often unscrupulous. For example, some would steal merchandise and then receive a monetary commission for recovering the property.

In 1842, the investigative division of the London police was created, and eight patrol officers were appointed as detectives, but it was not until 1878 that the detective division began to grow. By 1885 there were 800 detectives and all serious crimes were being investigated at the state's expense.[1]

The New York Detective

Although the history of the New York City police department indicates that there were police detectives even prior to the formal

---

1. Carl B. Klockars, *The Idea of Police,* (Newbury Park, CA: Sage Publication, 1985), 74–76.

establishment of the New York City Police Department in 1845, it was not until 1857 that the New York City Police Board adopted a resolution establishing that twenty police officers be designated as detectives. The detectives were divided into squads and each squad was assigned to investigate a specific category of crime, like shop-lifting or pick-pocketing.[2] However, it was not until 1882 that the New York state legislature passed a law authorizing the New York City Board of Police to establish a *Central Office Bureau of Detectives* with a maximum of forty detectives who would receive the same salary as sergeants.[3] With the creation of the Detective Bureau the police Inspection of the Bureau centralized all detectives under his command; prior to that, detectives came under the authority of precinct captains and were assigned to Wall Street.

The Municipal Police Detective

Jack Kuykendall, in a study of the municipal police detective in the United States, identifies several stages of development in the detective's role: the detective as secretive rogue, 1850s to 1920s; the detective as inquisitor, 1890s to 1960s; and the detective as bureau-crat, 1940s to 1980s.[4] The criminal investigator in the "detective as secretive rogue" role used *stool pigeons* to obtain information about crimes. Crimes by stool pigeons were usually tolerated in order to obtain more important criminal information. During this period, the identity of the detective was kept secret and investigative work was considered to be a clandestine exercise. Detectives were con-cerned with crimes such as pick-pocketing, gambling, and nuisance crimes.

The "detective as inquisitor" became concerned with scientific evidence. The scientific laboratory was developed during this pe-riod. Physical evidence began to be recognized as important at crime scenes. They began to use the *Bertillon System* of identifica-tion, fingerprints, and physical evidence. *Modus Operandi* (method of

---

2. Augustine E. Costello, *Our Police Protectors,* (Montclair, NJ: Patterson Smith), 402–403.

3. Ibid., 287.

4. Jack Kuykendall, "The Municipal Police Detective: An Historical Analy-sis, *Criminology* 24, No.1, (1986), 179–193.

operation or m.o.) files and the use of physical evidence to apprehend suspects was initiated. However, detective work was generally not based on scientific evidence but on victims' identification of suspects. Detectives used the *third degree*, or physical abuse applied by investigators, to obtain confessions from suspects.

The "detective as bureaucrat" spent his time "gathering, organizing, and using information."[5] Paperwork—reading and writing reports—was a big part of the detective's job. During the 1970s case management and case screening was initiated. Investigative work was researched for the first time in the 1970s. The screening of cases included looking for solvability factors that could help to identify factors that could solve the case. The criminal cases with the most solvability factors received the highest priority and had the greatest chance of being solved. Generally, detectives focus on cases that are solvable with the exception of cases involving complex crimes, gang activity, and organized crime.

Investigative Units

Most police departments of any size have a full-time investigative or detective unit. A small police department of ten or twelve police officers may have only one full-time detective while a police department of several thousand police officers may have several hundred detectives. The number of police officers assigned to the investigative unit may depend upon the population of the city, the number of police officers, the crime rate, the politics of the city, and the policing philosophy of the police chief and his top assistants.

The investigative unit should be organized around basic managerial principles and the investigative task should be divided according to the type of crimes committed—i.e., crimes against persons or crimes against property. These units can then be further divided. For instance, crimes against persons could be divided into homicide, robbery, assault, and sex crime categories. Crimes against property can be divided into auto theft, burglary, and larceny.

The major purpose of the investigative function is to identify, arrest, and obtain evidence to convict criminal offenders. The major objectives of the investigative unit are to

---

5. Ibid., 184.

1. Identify and apprehend offenders. The identification of the perpetrator is the investigator's primary goal. If the offender can be identified, then the apprehension process is usually one of rote procedure;
2. Gather evidence to prosecute the identified offender. It is important to note that this objective goes somewhat beyond the objective of the police institution itself. One usually conceives that after the police have made an arrest further processing of the individual is the responsibility of the prosecutor. To make an arrest, it is only necessary that the police have sufficient reason to believe that the individual committed the crime, which can be considerably different having sufficient evidence to successfully prosecute the culprit;
3. Help build a favorable public attitude toward the police. Much of the investigation activities are fruitless in terms of contributing to the first two objectives. The only justification for these activities is that of public relations. Investigation activities may increase the public's confidence in the police; or if not that, then the activities may tend to placate the victim, and show that the police, at least, are concerned about their plight.[6]

The Role of the Patrol Officer

Prior to the time that a criminal offense is turned over to the detective unit, the patrol officer performs the preliminary or initial investigation. Normally the patrol officer arrives at the crime scene first in response to a 911 call, and acceptable police procedure dictates that the patrol officer should perform the initial investigation. In police departments that have no criminal investigators, the patrol officer may handle the entire investigation. The criminal investigation requires that the patrol officer

1. Find out what has happened (be observant even while responding to the scene and departing from the patrol vehicle),
2. Locate witnesses (including juveniles) and sources of evidence that will help determine what has happened,

6. Stanley Vanaguanas and James F. Elliott, *Administration of Police Organizations,* (Boston: Allyn and Bacon, 1980), 202.

3. Figure out what further investigative steps should be taken (by either the officer, a technician, or another officer or investigator),
4. Attempt to understand the motivations of the witnesses and evaluate the accuracy of their testimony (deciding whether to act on the testimony and whether some other officer might be successful with a particular witness), and
5. Record what has been done, what has been learned, and what is left to be done.[7]

The Follow-Up Investigation

Upon the completion of the patrol officer's preliminary investigation, and if the crime has not been solved by the patrol officer, it then becomes the responsibility of the detective to do the follow-up investigation. The detective must obtain sufficient evidence to make an arrest and obtain a conviction for the commission of a crime. The detective is responsible for obtaining additional information, making an arrest, recovering stolen property, and working with the prosecutor to obtain a conviction. The following activities are routinely part of a follow-up investigation:

- The identification and apprehension of suspects,
- The interrogation of suspects and the taking of statements when necessary and legal,
- Determining whether the suspects may have committed crimes in addition to the one being investigated,
- Arranging for the analysis and evaluation of evidence,
- The recovery of stolen property for use as evidence or to be returned to the victim,
- The interviewing (or re-interviewing) of victims and witnesses, and the taking of statements if necessary,
- The complete and careful recording of all information obtained,
- The preparation of the case for prosecution and adjudication or other disposition,
- The filing of a complaint with the prosecutor,
- The serving of subpoenas, when required.[8]

---

7. P. Block and D. Weidman, *Managing Criminal Investigations,* (Washington, DC: U.S. Government Printing Office, 1975), 24–25.

8. John P. Kenney and Harry W. More, *Principles of Investigation,* 2nd ed.,

Investigative Methods

There are a wide variety of investigative methods that are used by criminal investigators to solve crimes. *Interviewing* and *interrogation* are two important techniques used for solving crimes. Interviewing usually involves collecting information about a crime from victims and witnesses in a friendly atmosphere. Interrogation implies an adversarial relationship in which the criminal investigator attempts to obtain information from a suspect in a confrontational manner. Since the police become aware of crimes primarily by means of citizens' reports and since a major portion of crimes are solved through the interviewing and interrogation process, investigators need to become proficient in these skills.

An interviewing tool that assists the criminal investigator in determining whether or not a witness, a victim, or a suspect is telling the truth is the *lie detector* or *polygraph*. The operator of the lie detector receives special training on the instrument and on the interviewing techniques that are used with the polygraph test.

Another important method of collecting evidence is a *search of the crime scene*. Physical evidence can be gathered that can support or supplement eye-witness testimony. Investigators should also *canvass the neighborhood* to determine if any residents, business owners, or individuals in the vicinity observed anything suspicious at or around the time when the crime occurred. Some investigators use *informants* to supplement their information. An informant can be anyone who provides information. The informant does not necessarily have to be reimbursed monetarily for his information. There are a variety of other sources that criminal investigators can use such as the department of motor vehicles, telephone directories, licensing bureaus and probation and parole officers.

Special Investigations

Most large police departments divide investigative work into "crimes against persons" and "crimes against property." Within this division there are various types of criminal cases that an investigator may encounter that may require the investigator to have special

_____
(Minneapolis: West, 1994), 13.

training and knowledge. No book can cover every type of crime that an investigator can encounter during his career. Most criminal investigators are generalists, so they develop knowledge and skills to perform various kinds of criminal investigations efficiently. Special investigations can include domestic violence, vice, white-collar crime, organized crime, and sex offenses.

Domestic Violence

Since the late 1960s, *domestic violence* has been a law enforcement issue. Domestic violence includes any violence between couples, married or unmarried. For the last several decades assaults have been a major cause of injury to women in America. Approximately one third of the murders of females are committed by husbands or boyfriends. Approximately sixteen percent of all murders involve a family relationship. The magnitude of domestic violence, though, is largely unknown, since neither police agencies nor social service agencies maintain accurate records of violence between spouses. Violent acts include behavior such as pushing, shoving, grappling, hitting with fists, beating up, threatening with a knife or gun, and using a gun or knife.

The patrol officer, during the preliminary investigation of a domestic violence call, should obtain information pertaining to the nature and extent of the injuries, the amount of force used, the type of weapons used, the threatening language used, the legal status of the relationship, existing court orders against the assailant, and any information on the drug and alcohol abuse problems of the assailant.[9]

As a general rule, police departments do not conduct follow-up investigations of domestic violence cases. Some police departments, like the Baltimore County Police Department, have established a specialized unit within their criminal investigation division. The duties of the unit are to

- Identify repeat offenders (batterers),
- Maintain accurate files on all repeat offenders, including prior offenses, court proceedings and dispositions, and prior counseling received,

9. Nancy Loving, *Responding to Spouse Abuse and Wife Beating*, (Washington, DC: Police Executive Forum, 1980), 95–96.

- Review the quality of reports for prosecution purposes and for any additional investigation that may be needed,
- Conduct follow-up investigations,
- Arrest offenders when appropriate,
- Assist the patrol division in case preparation as needed,
- Identify households where domestic violence is common or where members are prone to assaults on the police,
- Notify precinct stations of violent households in their area (especially if the family has moved from one area to another),
- Provide or coordinate victim assistance with social services by being in contact with both victims and batterers, as well as civic organizations, and public interest groups, to inform them of the services available to them, and
- Follow all cases through all prosecutory stages.[10]

Vice

Vice crimes include gambling, prostitution, and drugs. Not all police departments have vice units. Prostitution and gambling are often handled by a tactical unit that will investigate crimes that criminal investigators cannot handle. The Savannah Police Department of Georgia has such a unit that investigates both gambling and prostitution. In Wichita, Kansas, police officers assigned to community policing investigated and were able to get prostitution under control in their sector. Because of the seriousness of the drug problem in our society many police departments have established drug units to specifically investigate drugs. In some areas of the country, Task Forces comprising local police officers and Drug Enforcement Agents (DEA) have been established to combat the distribution of drugs.

Gambling[11]

Illegal gambling can consist of a lottery known as *numbers, off-track betting, sports wagering,* and *lotteries.* The numbers game consists of "choking" a three-digit number from 000 through 999. The winning number can be determined in several ways—one of which

---

10. G. Goolkasian, *Confronting Domestic Violence: A Guide for Criminal Justice Agencies,* (Washington, DC: U.S. Government Printing Office, 1989), 149.

11. Joseph R. Lentini, *Vice and Narcotics Control,* (Beverly Hills: Glencoe, 1977), 10–21.

is by simply adding the betting totals for selected races at various designated race tracks. *Off-track betting* refers to the practice of betting on horse races (pari-mutuel betting) through a *bookie*, a person who takes bets. Since most states only allow this type of betting at the race track, the bookie fills a void for those individuals who are addicted to betting on horses. New York State is one state that has legalized horse betting, but the final decision to allow the practice is left to the individual counties.

Sports wagering includes betting on sporting events, such as basketball, baseball, football, and hockey games. During the sports season *pool tickets*—lists of professional football teams with a point spreads for individual games—will be distributed in offices, factories, or schools. *Lotteries* are games of chance in which a prize is awarded to the lucky winner. Currently, most Americans are aware of lotteries operated or approved by their state government. However, there are illegal lotteries operated by individuals.

When examining a gambling operation there are several things that the investigator should be cognizant of. Normally, the *runner*, the individual who collects the numbers, the wager, and the money from a bettor, will be susceptible to arrest. The runner can easily be placed under surveillance. If a gambling parlor or office is to be raided, an undercover officer should be placed on the premises to assist the raiding officers. All paraphernalia found in the gambling parlor should be confiscated for possible use as evidence.

Prostitution

There are two kinds of prostitution—male and female. Both male and female prostitutes perform sexual favors with males for payment, and there are various categories of prostitutes, like call girls, escort services, and street walkers. Periodically, because of public pressure, the police crack down on prostitution. This can be accomplished in several ways. First, a police officer works under cover as a *john*, a male who solicits a prostitute to perform a sexual act. When the prostitute makes the offer of sex to the undercover police officer, she is arrested. Conversely, police women will go under cover dressed as prostitutes with the intention of being propositioned by a john. When the john makes the proposition he is arrested by a backup team of police officers. The police officer who works under cover is "wired" so that his or her conversation with the prostitute or john can be monitored, and in many cases, there will be a police van with electronic and video equipment to record the transaction. The same system can work with either a street walker or an escort service.

Narcotics and Drugs

There are a wide variety of illicit drugs and narcotics illegally sold by drug dealers. These include morphine, cocaine and crack, heroin, marijuana, methamphetamine, lysergic acid diethylamide (LSD), phencyclidine (PCP), and designer drugs. The general public, and especially drug users, are usually familiar with the names of these narcotics and drugs. All drugs, and especially illicitly obtained narcotics drugs, can have a detrimental effect on the individual who takes them. Physicians inform their patients that all narcotics and drugs have side effects, and there is generally no way that the individual taking a narcotic or drug will know how that drug will effect them.

The basic investigative techniques used in other crimes generally apply to drug investigations, but there are also some additional techniques that are unique to the investigation of drug-related crimes. These techniques include the use of informers, drug buys, undercover work, drug stings, and other such techniques. *Case screening* is one tool that can help the drug investigator decide whether or not to continue an investigation based on the number of *solvability factors*. Solvability factors are items of information about a specific crime that indicate its likelihood of being solved.

Drug cases are initiated with the receipt and verification of information. The drug investigator finds out who is involved in illegal drug activity through a variety of sources, including the investigator's own organization, other police departments, informants, and public records—i.e., the records of the motor vehicle department. All information pertaining to illegal drug activity must then be corroborated by various methods, such as surveillance, monitoring a drug suspect's movements, or checking information sources. Once the accuracy of the information has been verified, an investigative plan is devised. The drug investigator works the available resources at his disposal—most of which will vary from organization to organization.

White-Collar Crime

White-collar crime can be defined as "illegal acts characterized by guile, deceit, and concealment—and are not dependent upon the application of physical force or violence or threats thereof. They may be committed by individuals acting independently or by those who are part of a well-planned conspiracy. The objective may be to obtain money, property, or services or to secure economic or personal advantage."[12]

Criminal offenses comprising white-collar crimes can include bribes, kickbacks, and payoffs that occur between businesses, between businesses and government, or between both public and private sector management and labor officials. Criminal activities can involve almost anyone in the organization with the authority to purchase supplies, to make personnel decisions, or to make recommendations to the overall operation of the organization.

The investigation of white-collar crime demands patience, imagination, and an awareness of the many approaches utilized in the investigative process. In investigating white-collar crimes it is at times difficult to focus on a specific incident. While white-collar crimes usually have a precise beginning and ending, they generally occur over a period of time, so while evidence may not appear to be useful to an investigator at first, it can become valuable later in the investigation.

Organized Crime

Organized crime consists of two or more persons who engage in such activities as the supplying of illegal goods and services (i.e., gambling, drugs) or predatory crime (i.e., theft, murder)—a definition that includes many more organizations than just the *Mafia*.

Many organized crime activities are not reported by the victim(s), since the crimes usually involve conspiracies. Additionally, the investigation of organized crime activities is tedious and time consuming and requires both surveillance and reviews of financial records. Often an investigation of organized crime requires a financial analysis of the suspects' business. The use of electronic surveillance is another method of collecting information against organized crime figures. Investigators of organized crime figures also use *pen registers* to record the telephone numbers dialed by the suspect. Another effective tool for the organized-crime investigator has been the *confidential informant*. Generally, an informant provides police authorities with information in exchange for immunity from prosecu-

---

12. *A Handbook of White-Collar Crime,* (Washington, DC: U.S. Chamber of Commerce, 1974), 3.

tion or for a reduced charge. Organized-crime investigators also work as *undercover investigators* to collect evidence to arrest and prosecute organize-crime figures.

Sex Offenses

There are numerous sex offenses that the police must investigate. These offenses include rape and other types of sexual deviation such as exhibitionism or indecent exposure. Dealing with sex offenders is often a difficult problem for the police agency. These difficulties can stem from the following problems:

1. The majority of these crimes are committed by abnormal persons whose motivations and behavior frequently elude the understanding of the average police officer;
2. The vicious and revolting nature of some of these crimes creates fear and panic among members of the community, placing additional strain on the police;
3. Lurid sex crimes invariably stimulate a morbid interest on the part of the public, forcing the police to conduct their investigation in the harsh glare of heightened publicity and public interest.[13]

The investigator of a sex offense has to recognize several key points while conducting the investigation. He must keep in mind that a sex offense is different from other types of crimes. Normally, the sex offender is driven by urges and will often be subject to compulsions which may be uncontrollable. Often sexual gratification will be obtained in strange ways that usually have nothing to do with having normal sex.[14]

Like other criminals, sex offenders have a modus operandi. That is, there are certain consistencies in the way they commit their sex offenses. They have established rituals from which they will not deviate. For example, the sex offender may select victims with similar physical features. Although it is important, the motive in these cases may be difficult for the investigator to understand. The actions of some sex offenders may be so grotesque that comprehending the sexual act will be impossible. Furthermore, behavior that is sexually

---

13. Joseph R. Lentini, *Vice and Narcotics Control*, (Beverley Hills: Glencoe, 1977), 77.
14. Ibid., 94.

criminal is often addictive and tends to escalate if the offender is not apprehended.

Criminal Profiling

For several decades criminal profiling has received attention as a tool that aids criminal investigators in solving specific crimes such as rape and homicide. *Criminal profiling* can be defined as "an investigative technique by which to identify the major personality and behavior characteristics of the offender based upon an analysis of the crimes(s) he or she has committed."[15] The criminal profiling process usually involves seven phases:

1. Evaluation of the criminal act itself,
2. Comprehensive evaluation of the specifics of the crime scene(s),
3. Comprehensive analysis of the victim,
4. Evaluation of preliminary police reports,
5. Evaluation of the medical examiner's autopsy protocol,
6. Development of profile with critical offender characteristics, and
7. Investigative suggestions predicated on construction of the profile.[16]

It is important to recognize that there are several assumptions that are fundamental to the criminal profiling process. First, the crime scene reflects the offender's personality. Second, the offender cannot change his personality—the core of an individual's personality will not change, and the same applies to an offender. Third, the method of operation will remain similar for all the crimes committed by the offender.[17]

Criminal offenders are normally profiled for offenses that indicate emotional disturbances or some form of overt sexual activity. Gen-

15. John E. Douglas and Alan E. Burgess, "Criminal Profiling: A Viable Investigative Tool Against Violent Crime," *FBI Law Enforcement Bulletin* 55, No. 12, (1989), 9.

16. Ibid., 9.

17. Ronald M. Holmes, *Profiling Violent Crimes,* (Newbury Park, CA: Sage, 1989), 37–38.

erally, homicides and assaults are the most commonly profiled cases. The profiler in homicide cases must determine if the murderer is either *organized or disorganized*. Using this information, the profiler sketches the behavioral patterns of the offender. In sexual assault cases the profiler obtains information about the offender's verbal, physical, and sexual behavior from the victim in order to make deductions about the offender's motive and personality.[18] Criminal profiling techniques can also be utilized for identifying the behavioral patterns of anonymous-letter writers, rapists, and arsonists.

Criminal profiling cannot provide the identity of the offender, but it can assist in supplying information about the personality type of individual who would be most likely to commit a crime under similar circumstances.

Specialized Units

There are numerous specialized units that exist in a police department that serve to make it operate more efficiently. These specialized units may not be directly connected to the criminal investigative unit but are important to the overall operation of the police department.

Youth Bureaus

Juveniles create an unique problem for the police. For instance, juvenile offenders are usually required by state laws to be segregated from adult offenders. They are status offenders and not criminals like an adult. When the juvenile problem becomes large enough to require a separate unit, that unit is usually called either a juvenile division or a youth division. The Youth Division should have "written policies and procedures that require constant planning, implementation, program evaluation, and refinement based on changing community needs."[19] Juvenile procedures should incorporate legal

---

18. Theodore H. Blau, *Psychological Services for Law Enforcement,* (New York: John Wiley and Sons, 1994), 262–263.

19. *National Advisory Commission on Criminal Justice Standards and Goals,* "Task Force on Police," (Washington, DC. Government Printing Office, 1973), 222.

requirements established by law and by the courts. The Youth Division has the following specific responsibilities:

1. The suppression and prevention of delinquent and criminal behavior by youths. Various codes define juvenile delinquency in terms of acts committed by persons under a certain age limit, usually sixteen to eighteen, but the youth division will find that there is so much overlapping of ages among participants in delinquent acts, particularly in gang activities, car thefts, and burglaries, that they are justified in concerning themselves with persons of all ages up to twenty-one when those over the statutory juvenile age but under twenty-one are involved with younger offenders;

2. The processing of youth arrests. When juveniles, minors with juveniles, and minors engaged in gang activities are taken into custody by any unit of the department, the youth-division personnel should be available to assist in the specialized handling of these cases;

3. The preparation and presentation of court cases. Youth- division personnel should present in court only those cases which have been completely investigated, and each case must be as ready for presentation as it is possible to make it;

4. The diversion of offenders out of the criminal justice system and adjustment of cases. When the best interests of the community and the individual are served by adjusting cases without resorting to court action, youth-division personnel should accomplish this by turning the offender over to his or her parents or other authorized adult and, where feasible, obtaining the assistance of appropriate community agencies;

5. The surveillance of amusement parks, recreational centers, schools, special events, and other places, where youth problems are likely to develop. The youth division must maintain a liaison with the licensing section of the vice division in order that appropriate action must be taken against licensed establishments that contribute to juvenile delinquency.

6. The provision of intelligence relating to youthful offenders, with particular emphasis on gang membership and activities. The youth division should maintain a file on all known offenders and exchange information with the patrol and detective divisions and other crime-prevention agencies in the city as well as with the court;

7. They exercise supervision over police efforts to deal with "status offenders"—youths who have not committed a crime per se but who are by statute given status as potential wards of the juvenile court. In this category are truants, runaways, children who are abandoned or abused by their parents, and so on.[20]

The number of youth officers assigned to the youth division will depend upon the juvenile crime problem and the size of the police department. The *National Advisory Commission on Criminal Justice Standards and Goals* recommends that a police department with seventy-five or fewer police personnel should create a youth division if conditions in the community warrant it. Full-time juvenile investigative officers should be assigned to the youth division unless a juvenile problem does not exist. The youth division conducts investigations of juveniles, assists the field patrol officers with juvenile problems, and coordinates juvenile activities with other criminal justice and social agencies.[21]

Although it does not deal specifically with juvenile crime, an *Exploited and Missing Child Unit* has been established in some cities to investigate criminal cases involving young victims under the age of eighteen. The Wichita/Sedgwick County Exploited and Missing child Unit investigates cases of children under the age of sixteen who have been sexually abused by a non-family member, or a youngster under age eighteen who has been sexually abused by a family member. Investigations originate from police reports, social workers reports, or walk-in reports to the Exploited and Missing Child Unit. The unit is staffed by Wichita Police Department investigators, Sedgwick County Deputy Sheriff's investigators and the Department of Social and Rehabilitation investigators (social workers).

The Crime Laboratory

The crime laboratory serves the important function of analyzing physical evidence. It aids the criminal investigator in answering the questions of who, what, when, why, and how. Usually a crime labo-

---

20. O.W. Wilson and Clinton McLaren, *Police Administration,* 4th ed., (New York: McGraw-Hill, 1977), 413–414.

21. *National Advisory Commission on Criminal Justice Standards and Goals,* "Task Force on Police" (Washington, DC: U.S. Government Printing Office, 1973), 223.

ratory will be manned by *forensic scientists*. Generally, forensic scientists have an education in one of the natural sciences such as biology, chemistry, and physics, and they apply the knowledge and the methods of these disciplines to the investigative process to determine the innocence or guilt of a suspect.

Physical evidence, such as trace evidence and firearms collected by crime scene technicians, is analyzed and evaluated by crime laboratory personnel. The criminal investigator has to recognize that the crime laboratory plays an important part in the investigative process. "It provides this aid by answering, or helping to answer, the vital questions of whether a crime has been committed; how and when it was committed; who committed it and, just as important who could have committed it."[22]

The typical evidence grouping that includes analysis of fingerprints, firearms, and bloodstains/body fluids is usually the most important form of physical evidence in deciding cases. Forensic science is most valuable in the crimes of homicide, rape, and hit-and-run accidents. Good criminal investigators become familiar with the crime lab facility in their jurisdiction. Investigators realize the lab's capabilities of evaluating evidence can save them valuable time in solving a case.

Crime lab technicians, to be effective, have to rely on investigators who understand what physical evidence is, how to collect and preserve it, how to obtain the information it carries, and how to interpret the information. Evidence collection investigators need to collect, preserve, and transmit to lab personnel the clues found during the course of an investigation. The lab technician must be informed about the circumstance and conditions in which the evidence was found. Ultimately, the lab technician complements the criminal investigator's role—the investigator is responsible for collecting and preserving evidence and the lab technician has the responsibility of analyzing its meaning for a criminal case. The criminal investigator and forensic scientist or technician need to develop a cooperative relationship. The investigator is skilled at finding important physical evidence and the forensic scientist or technician has the skills to handle it with care.

---

22. R. H. Fox and C.L. Cunningham, *Crime Scene Search and Physical Evidence Handbook,* (Washington, DC: U.S. Government Printing Office, 1985), 1.

Intelligence Unit

The function of the intelligence unit is to gather information on individuals who are engaging in organized criminal activity. The responsibility of the Intelligence Unit is to keep the police chief abreast of organized criminal activities and "to plan, organize, and efficiently direct enforcement efforts."[23] Intelligence allows the police agency to develop strategies to combat organized types of crimes. Intelligence allows the police chief to "(1) conceptualize organized crime issues; (2) challenge previously held conceptions, assumptions, and stereotypes; (3) re-evaluate and re-order priorities; and (4) establish pragmatic and relevant goals and objectives."[24] Police departments should have written directives that establish procedures of assuring the legality and integrity of the intelligence unit. Those directives should include

- Methods for ensuring informants are secure in their anonymity;
- Procedures for ensuring information collected is limited to criminal conduct and relates to activities that present a threat to the community;
- Procedures for the utilization of intelligence personnel, equipment, and techniques;
- Descriptions of the types or quality of information that may be included in the system; and
- Methods for purging the records of out-of-date information.[25]

Internal Affairs

Internal affairs units were initiated in the late 1950s and early 1960s to investigate charges of corruption in America's largest cities. During the social turmoil of the 1960s citizen complaints against the police grew. Police conduct and behavior were questioned by citizens, especially members of the minority communities.[26]

---

23. Justin J. Dintino and Frederick T. Martens, "An Enduring Enigma: The Concept of Intelligence Analysis," *The Police Chief,* 48, No. 12, (1981), 58.

24. Ibid., 59.

25. Commission on Accreditation for Law Enforcement Agencies. *Standards for law Enforcement Agencies,* 2nd ed., (Fairfax, VA: Commission on Accreditation for Law Enforcement Agencies, 1989), 51–1.

26. Kelvin Krajick, "Police vs. Police," *Police Magazine* 3, No. 3, (1980), 7.

The primary function of the internal affairs unit is to investigate matters of police misconduct, including the excessive use of force, corruption, and any other illegal behavior or violation of departmental policies. The unit investigates the discharge of firearms by police personnel and reviews supervisors' handling of minor complaints. Because of the sensitivity of the internal affairs unit's investigations, police personnel assigned to this unit serve the police executive and the unit reports directly to the police chief.

In order to provide guidelines of appropriate conduct for police officers, the following management system should be put in place (formal guidelines will not only help the police officer but provide the internal affairs unit with a way to assess what should and should not be considered appropriate police behavior):

1. Rules and Regulations: A set of guidelines outlining the unacceptable behavior of personnel. The rules and regulations shall be promulgated by the appropriate authority as designated by municipal ordinance.
2. Policies: Statements of agency principles that provide the basis for the development of procedures and directives.
3. Procedures: Written statements providing specific direction for performing agency activities. Procedures are implemented through policies and directives.
4. Directives: Documents detailing the performance of a specific activity or method of operation. Directives include general orders, personnel orders and special orders.[27]

Planning and Research

Depending upon the size of the police department, the head of the planning and research section either reports directly to the chief of police or to one of his deputies. The Commission on Accreditation for Law Enforcement Agencies had the following to say about police planning and research, "Planning and research activities are essential to effective agency management. Complex demands for services and declining public resources require that law enforcement agencies carefully research operational alternatives and plan future programs."[28]

---

27. *New Jersey Law Enforcement Guidelines,* (Trenton, NJ: Division of Criminal Justice, 1995), 11-6-11-7.

28. *Standards for Law Enforcement Agencies,* 14–1.

The International City Management Association describes planning as "the process of bringing together expectations about the future and data from the past to guide decision making in the present [and research as] the careful, systematic study of a subject."[29]

Research helps illuminate what has been successful in policing. It analyzes community problems, tests new technologies, and examines other practical police concerns.

Planning serves several purposes. Some plans are developed to improve crisis responses. Some plans are developed to improve police performance during specific incidents—such as riots, airplane disasters, and other unplanned events. Operational plans are implemented to make organizations or certain functions of an organization, like the patrol unit, more efficient. Finally, there are strategic plans that generally establish police department goals for five years or longer.[30]

Summary

The idea of police officers performing criminal investigative work has its roots in the London metropolitan police of the nineteenth century. In 1857 the New York City Police Department officially created a detective bureau to investigate crimes. Today, any police department of any size has a detective unit. Investigative sections are usually divided into crimes against persons and crimes against property. The crimes-against-persons unit investigates homicides, robberies, assaults, and sex crimes. The crimes-against-property unit deals with auto theft, burglary, and larceny.

The primary purpose of the investigative unit is to identify, arrest, and obtain evidence to convict criminal offenders. Prior to the time that a criminal offense is turned over to a detective unit, the patrol officer performs the preliminary or initial investigation. Upon the completion of the patrol officer's preliminary investigation—and if the crime has not been solved by the patrol officer—it then becomes the responsibility of the detective to do the follow-up investigation.

---

29. William A. Geller, Ed., *Local Government Police Management,* 3rd ed., (Washington, DC: International City Management Association, 1991), 333.

30. Ibid., 343–345.

Many large police departments divide their detective units into specialized sections. These specialized sections specifically investigate either domestic violence offenses, vice, sex offenses, white-collar crime, or organized crime. Police departments that can justify the need when resources are available will create youth bureaus, crime laboratories, intelligence units, internal affairs units, and planning and research units. The purpose of these specialized units is to assist the police agency to function more effectively and more efficiently.

Key Terms

bookie
confidential informant
forensic science
interviewing
interrogation
informants

lotteries
numbers
off-track betting
pen registers
polygraph
sports betting

Review Questions

1. Discuss the three detective roles as described by Jack Kuykendall.
2. What role does the patrol officer play in a criminal investigation?
3. Describe the functions of two special investigative units.
4. Discuss criminal profiling.
5. Why are specialized police units important to a police agency?

References

Blau, Theodore H. *Psychological Services for Law Enforcement*. New York: John Wiley and Sons, 1994.

Block, P. and D. Weidman. *Managing Criminal Investigations*. Washington: U.S. Government Printing Office, 1975.

Commission on Accreditation for Law Enforcement. *Standards for Law Enforcement Agencies*. 2d ed. Fairfax, VA: Commission on Criminal Justice Standards and Goals, 1989.

Costello, Augustine E. *Our Police Protectors*. Montclair, NJ: Patterson Smith, 1972.

Dintino, Justin and Martens T. Frederick. "An Enduring Enigma: The Concept of Intelligence Analysis." *The Police Chief* 48, no. 12 (1981).

Douglas, John E. and Alan E. Burgess. "Criminal Profiling: A Viable Investigative Tool Against Violent Crime." *FBI Law Enforcement Bulletin* 55, no. 12 (1986).

Ford, Joan Martin. *Evaluation of the Greece Police Youth Division Reorganization Program*. Rochester, NY: Center for Governmental Research, 1976.

Fox, R.H. and C.L. Cunningham. *Crime Scene Search and Physical Evidence Handbook*. Washington: U.S. Government Printing Office, 1984.

Geller, William, Ed. *Local Government Police Management*. 3d ed. Washington: International City Management Association, 1991.

Goolkasian, G. *Confronting Domestic Violence: A Guide for Criminal Justice Agencies*. Washington: U.S. Government Printing Office, 1986.

Handbook of White-Collar Crime. Washington: U.S. Chamber of Commerce, 1974.

Holmes, Ronald. *Profiling Violent Offenders*. Newbury Hills, CA: Sage, 1989.

Kenney, John P. and Harry W. More. *Principles of Investigation*. 2d ed. Minneapolis: West Publishing Company, 1994

Klein, Malcolm W. "Issues and Realities in Police Diversion Program." *Crime and Delinquency* 22 (October 1976).

Klockars, Carl. *The Idea of Police*. Newbury, CA: Sage, 1985.

Krajick, Kelvin. "Police vs Police." *Police Magazine* 3, no 3 (1980).

Kuykendall, Jack. "The Municipal Police Detective: An Historical Analysis." *Criminology* 24, no. 1 (1986).

Lentini, Joseph R. *Vice and Narcotics Control*. Beverley Hills: Glencoe Press, 1977.

Loving, Nancy. *Responding to Spouse Abuse and Wife Beating*. Washington: Police Executive Forum, 1980.

National Advisory Commission on Criminal Justice Standards and Goals. "Task Force on Police." Washington: Government Printing Office, 1973.

New Jersey Law Enforcement Guidelines Trenton, NJ: Division of Criminal Justice, 1995.

Vanagunas, Stanley and James F. Elliott. Boston: Allyn and Bacon, 1980.

Wilson, O.W. and Clinton McLaren. *Police Administration*. 4th ed. New York: McGraw-Hill, 1977.

CHAPTER **8**

Police Use of
Technology

Major Issues

1. Police technology will make policing more effective.
2. Police technology will lead to a loss of our freedoms.
3. Police technology will lead to the police solving more crimes.
4. Police technology will lead to the need for fewer police personnel.

Introduction

As America approaches the next millennium it is fast becoming a society dependent upon sophisticated technology, and this trend in technological advances will continue into the future. Technological advances are occurring in all professions and fields, and policing has not been an exception. Because of these technological advances, the face of policing has been changing for several decades and there is no doubt that it will not be the same in the future as it appears in the present or as it was in the past.

The concept of modern police technology owes a debt to the Sherlock Holmes stories of the 1890s in which the main character used scientific techniques to solve crimes. In 1919, the first modern crime laboratory was opened in San Francisco, California. The first polygraph was constructed in 1921. Because of World War II's explosion of technology, policing was able to make use of equipment developed for military purposes. Radio equipment and surveillance aircraft both found their way into police departments after World War II.

The initiation of the United States Government into police technology can be traced to 1966 when President Lyndon Johnson chartered the President's Commission on Law Enforcement and Administration, often referred to as the Crime Commission Report. The President's Report was divided into nine areas one of which was a *Task Force Report on Science and Technology*. The Task Force found that the police were not using modern technology, and consequently, it recommended and encouraged the development of law-enforcement technology. In 1968 the National Institute of Law Enforcement was created to focus on research and development aimed at improving policing.[1]

---

1. Jeremy Travis, "Criminal Justice Science and Technology Program," *Na-*

The Institute of Law Enforcement initiated communication with other federal agencies such as the Defense Department, the Department of Transportation, the Department of Housing and Urban Development, the Department of Commerce, and the National Aeronautics and Space Administration. The Institute of Law Enforcement worked in cooperation with other agencies on the development of riot control agents, night vision equipment, nonlethal bullets, and personal communicators.[2] In 1971 the Institute established the Law Enforcement Standards Laboratory under the auspices of the National Bureau of Standards, part of the Department of Commerce. The purpose of the laboratory has been to establish scientifically-based, voluntary commercial manufacturing standards so that police agencies could select both high-quality and low-cost equipment. In addition, it requires that laboratories be certified in cases where equipment items can be evaluated according to those standards.[3]

By the mid-1970s, the Institute of Law Enforcement's laboratory had completed standards for the following:

- Portable, mobile, and base station transmitters; mobile receivers; and batteries for portable radios;
- Walk-though and hand-held metal weapon detectors;
- Portable x-ray devices for bomb disarmament;
- Communication equipment such as voice scramblers, car location systems, and radio transmitters, receivers, and repeaters;
- Active and passive night vision devices;
- Magnetic, mechanical, and mercury switches for burglar alarms; and
- Handcuffs, riot helmets, crash helmets, police body armor, ballistic shields, and hearing protectors.[4]

The Justice System Improvement Act of 1979 restructured the National Institute of Justice (NIJ). As a result, the Office of Development, Testing, and Dissemination was created to assess the needs of criminal justice agencies and to develop standards for equipment.

---

tional Institute of Justice: Research in Action, (Washington, DC: National Institute of Justice, 1995), 1-2.

2. Ibid., 2-3.

3. Ibid., 3.

4. Ibid., 4.

In the mid-1980s the Technology Assessment Program Information Center (TAPIC) was created by the National Institute of Justice. TAPIC is responsible for selecting laboratories to test products, for overseeing the testing, and for publishing performance reports and document test results. The National Institute of Justice also established the Technological Assessment Program Advisory Council (TAPAC) which consists of more than eighty federal, state, and local law enforcement officials to confirm that the technology advocated responds to the practical needs of police work.[5]

In 1994 the National Institute of Justice created the National Law Enforcement Technology Center (NLETC) to function as a technology and information center for law enforcement. NLETC disseminates information through Regional Law Enforcement Technology Centers collectively known as the Technology Information Network (TIN), through a news letter known as *Technology Beat*, through national/regional conferences, and by providing access to bulletin boards. The Technology Information Centers assist policing agencies in locating equipment that they use relatively infrequently on an emergency or temporary basis. TIN can ultimately save police departments time and money by tracking down information about technology; by collecting, utilizing, and sharing relevant technological information; by accurately determining police agencies' requirements for technology; and by helping to simplify the technology industry's access to the police market.[6]

During the summer of 1994 the Attorney General of the United States and the Deputy Secretary of Defense signed a Memorandum of Understanding for the purpose of providing for the joint development and sharing of technology systems, allowing for rapid deployment and transition of technologies with applicability for law enforcement and military operations other than war. The 1995 Defense Appropriations Bill allocated funds to support the dual-use technology program. The bill defines the essential technological assistance that will be contributed by the Department of Justice and the Department of Defense to police agencies. These technologies include but may not be limited to:

- Concealed weapons detection,

---

5. Ibid., 9.

6. *Technology Beat,* (Rockville, MD: National Law Enforcement Technology Center, April 1995), 1.

- Authorized-user-only handgun or "safe gun" activities,
- Gunfire localization information,
- Less-than-lethal technologies to halt fleeing vehicles and restrain subjects armed with weapons other than firearms,
- Development of personal status monitors,
- Interactive simulation trainers
- Explosive ordinance detection and disposal,
- Mobile sensor platforms,
- Urban mapping and three dimensional scene generation,
- Advanced sensor integration,
- Sniper identification,
- Response technologies, and
- Support for NIJ national law enforcement technology centers[7]

Technology has made great strides in the past several decades. New technologies are being developed and old technologies are being improved so rapidly that it appears impossible for any police force to keep abreast of all the advances. The modern police department will have difficulties keeping up with technological advances, and even if it could keep up with the advances, it could not afford all the high technology being developed. But with these rapid technological advances has come a better way to keep abreast of all the recent developments.

Computer Use in Policing

The use of computers in policing is a relatively new phenomenon. Since the computer's entry into policing in the 1960s more and more uses for the computer have been found. The closer we come to the twenty-first century the more difficult it becomes to function *without* a computer. The uses of computers in police work seems to know no boundary. In this section we will discuss some of the uses of computers in policing.

Computer Aided Dispatching (CAD)

Computer Aided Dispatching (CAD) has been recognized as being much more efficient than the old method of dispatching po-

---

7. Institute for Law and Justice, *Law Enforcement Options* 1, No. 1, (1995), 3.

lice and other emergency vehicles. The old telephone system required that a seven digit number be used to reach the police. The dispatcher wrote down the information and forwarded it to another dispatcher who would then dispatch the vehicles. Since AT&T's development of the 911 number as an emergency telephone number in the late 1960s, we find it in use across most of America by the late 1990s.

CAD technology spreads dispatching workloads across multiple computers. The dispatcher is assigned to a computer work station designed to perform multiple tasks as efficiently and quickly as the dispatcher can do them. The CAD work station's memory can be divided into several full-screen pages. Each page can access different applications: *Call For Service, CAD Activity Log, Electronic Activity Log, Electronic Messaging, State/NCIC Interface,* and *Host Computer Interface.* With a single key stroke, the dispatcher can switch between applications.[8]

The dispatcher's work station is equipped to display the status of in-service police units and to list calls awaiting dispatch. The dispatcher will dispatch a call according to a priority/time-received sequence. The "CAD Activity Log" records every activity transaction entered into the system—the date, the time, and the user's identification number are all entered along with the work station number. The contents of the "CAD Activity Log" can be displayed either in chronological order, by call number, or by work station identification number. "Electronic messaging" sends and receives messages from other CAD users or from mobile data terminals/computers (MDT/MDC). The "Host Computer Interface" allows one computer system to access records in another system. CAD allows an interface to the "State/NCIC" NLETS to many states. Some states have implemented a computer-to-computer protocol to take advantage of CAD's state/NCIC interface. This process allows CAD to automatically format and transmit vehicle and persons checks. The capabilities of the CAD "State/NCIC" interface can vary according to the protocol adopted by a particular state.[9]

Many communities, such as Sedgwick County, Kansas, have established communication centers. These communication centers

8. Applied Micro Technology Inc., *Public Safety Products Overview* (Cedars Falls, IA).
9. Ibid.

take care of dispatching for all of the police agencies in the county and for other emergency vehicles—fire, rescue, and ambulance services. CAD employs a geographical database (*Geofile*) that validates the location of calls for service and translates the locations to specific police and other emergency service grids. This system divides the responsibility for servicing calls and for collecting statistics between the various agencies.

CAD uses a grid system in three ways. First, grids are used to define jurisdictions when a joint communication center dispatches multiple agencies. Second, when a 911 call has been received, grids are used to determine the geographical area of a police beat. Third, grids are used to compile statistics for various police agencies and to isolate call statistics for specific geographical areas, such as schools, industrial parks, and malls.[10]

Mobile Data Terminal/Computers

Mobile data terminal/computers are units linked to CAD systems providing for prioritized car-to-car and car-to-dispatcher messaging services. CAD forwards call data to the police units when dispatched allowing officers to log remarks to calls. The CAD system allows dispatchers to keep track of where officers are and to efficiently assign patrol units to calls. The mobile data terminal allows patrol officers to query driver's-license files and the National Criminal Information Center (NCIC).

Automatic Vehicle Location (AVL)

The CAD system which has this option can track all police units in service. The AVL allows the CAD dispatcher to dispatch the closest patrol unit to a specific call location.

Laptop Computers

A significant development in computer hardware has been the laptop or notebook computer. When the screen folds it resembles a notebook and is easy to carry. Because of the portability of laptop computers, patrol officers can take them anywhere—from the squad

---

10. Ibid., 10–11.

room to the patrol vehicle to the crime scene. Laptop computers can be mounted in patrol vehicles and with cellular technology the patrol vehicle can be electronically linked to the police department's dispatcher and registration system. The laptop will allow the officer to check license plate numbers and to query the motor vehicle database before leaving the police cruiser. Ultimately, the patrol officer making a traffic stop will be more informed and will know when to call for assistance. The laptop computer will allow the patrol officer to function more effectively and efficiently.[11]

Personal Locator Transmitter (PLT)

With funding from the National Institute of Justice (NIJ), the Department of Energy's Idaho National Engineering Laboratory designed the PLT. The PLT allows police departments to maintain a surveillance on police officers. Designed to be worn around a police officer's shirt collar, the PLT provides a way to constantly monitor the location of and to communicate with the police officer. The PLT provides the officer with a means of communication during each incident he encounters, and if the officer has been injured, his exact location would be known.[12]

Remote Control Information System (RCIS)

The Remote Control Information System provides full-color video and two-way audio communication. It not only monitors an officer's location but it also monitors his vital signs. RCIS monitors incidents and fixes the officer's location. In the future, the RCIS may even replace the hand-held radio.[13]

Timeline Analysis System (TAS)

The Timeline Analysis System can be used to analyze crime trends or to pinpoint cause-and-effect relationships. TAS can assist

---

11. Keith J. Cutri, "Laptop Computers: New Technology for Law Enforcement," *FBI Law Enforcement Bulletin* 65, No. 2/3, (1996), 1-5.

12. Lois Pilant, "High-Technology Solutions," *The Police Chief* 71, No.5, (1996), 38.

13. Ibid., 38.

in intelligence analysis by visually analyzing large amounts of data for patterns and trends.[14]

Crime Analysis

Crime analysis is primarily concerned with the identification of "short term patterns of criminal behavior or events and associated characteristics."[15] Many police departments have established formal crime pattern analysis units to collect, analyze, and disseminate crime information. Crime analysis can be described as a process which provides descriptive and statistical information to facilitate strategic and tactical planning, resource allocation, and the investigative process. A crime analysis system requires that specific records and data be maintained. Records necessary for crime analysis include crime- description files, known-offender files, criminal-history files, suspect-vehicle files, and property files.

The crime analysis unit should direct its efforts toward criminal offenses that the police have the best chance of suppressing or those—like auto theft, burglary, robbery, and rape—that have a high probability of recurrence. In the late 1990s computers play a major role in crime analysis.

Currently, crime analysis units are using *computerized mapping* to solve crimes and to aid in the investigation of crime. The National Institute of Justice had the following to say about the use of computerized mapping in crime control and prevention programs:

> Mapping software has many crime control and prevention applications. In addition to the location of crime, geographic data that can be helpful in crime control and in efforts to apprehend a perpetrator include the perpetrator's last known address, the location of the person who reported the crime, the location of the recovered stolen property, and the locations of persons known or contacted by the perpetrator. Geographical information valuable in planning, conducting, and evaluating crime prevention programs includes the locations of crimes committed during the past month; the locations of abandoned houses, stripped cars, and

---

14. Ibid., 38.

15. *Issues in Crime Analysis in Support of Patrol: A Review and Assessment of the Literature*, (Bloomington, Indiana: Recent Developments in Law Enforcement and Criminal Justice, 1975), 1-1.

other "broken windows" conditions in a neighborhood; and the locations where persons who could benefit from crime prevention and other social programs actually live[16].

The potential uses for computerized mapping software are numerous. Computer-aided dispatch (CAD) and records-management systems that store and maintain service calls, incidents, arrests, and other mappable data are commonly used in large police departments. Geocoding, a CAD feature and a records-management system can verify addresses and can associate other geographic information including police reporting areas, beats, and districts. The crime analysis unit can use mapping software to prepare crime bulletins and for planning operations such as intensive patrol operations or to reconfigure patrol beats. Large police departments—e.g., San Diego, Los Angeles, and Dallas—utilize mapping software in their crime analysis units.[17]

Computerized Data Matching

The computerized comparison of two or more groups of electronic records is known as *computerized data matching*. Many governmental agencies use computers in this way to detect fraud, waste, and abuse.[18]

Computers are currently being used in a large number of criminal investigations. In Washington State investigators have initiated a *Homicide Investigation and Tracking System* (HITS).[19] This system is an electrotonic investigation system that stores, collates, and analyzes the characteristics of all homicides and sexual offenses in the state of Washington. Law enforcement agencies submit data on murders, on attempted murders, on missing persons, on unidentified dead persons believed to be murder victims, and on predatory sex offenders.

16. Thomas F. Rich, "The Use of Computerized Mapping in Crime Control and Prevention Programs," *National Institute of Justice: Research in Action,* (Washington, DC: U.S. Department of Justice, Office of Justice Programs, July 1995), 2.

17. ibid., 3.

18. *Criminal Justice: New Technologies and The Constitution,* (Washington, DC: U.S. Government Printing Office, 1988), 15.

19. Robert D. Keppel and Joseph G. Weiss, "HITS Catching Criminal in the Northwest," *FBI Law Enforcement Bulletin* 62, No. 4, (1993), 14-19.

The HITS homicide file contains information on victims, offenders, and M.O.'s for murder investigations. The sexual assault HIT file contains rape-investigation information on victims, offenders, and M.O.'s. The information contained in the system comes from sexual assault forms that investigators routinely submit. The forms supply information submitted by law enforcement agencies from all over Washington State on predatory sex offenders, non-acquaintance rapists, and serial rapists.

Criminal Justice Information Services

In a 1993 article that appeared in the *FBI Law Enforcement Bulletin*[20] William Sessions, the former Director of the FBI, announced the formation of a new FBI Division, the Criminal Justice Information Services (CJIS), to consolidate criminal justice services and information systems. Sessions professed that the FBI would be building on past successes. Additionally, the *National Crime Information Center* (NCIC) was instituted to provide law enforcement agencies with criminal justice information. NCIC currently maintains records on stolen property; criminal histories; and wanted, missing, and unidentified persons. With the advanced *NCIC-2000* system, law enforcement officers will be able to quickly identify fugitives and missing persons by placing the person's finger on a fingerprint reader located in the patrol vehicle. The fingerprint reader will forward the image to the NCIC computer and the computer will forward the response to the police officer. NCIC-2000 will allow police officers to obtain copies of a suspect's fingerprint, his photograph, his image, his signature, and information about his tattoos from a computer in the patrol vehicle. The patrol officer will also be able to print out images of stolen goods.

The Uniform Crime Report's (UCR) *National Incident-Based Reporting System* (NIBRS) will be adding a crime-fighting instrument. NIBRS will provide information on hate crimes and cover current criminal justice issues that will aid decision makers with comprehensive and reliable data for controlling crime.

---

20. William S. Sessions, "Criminal Justice Information Services," *FBI Law Enforcement Bulletin* 62, No. 12, (1993), 1-3.

The *Integrated, Automated Fingerprint Identification System* (IAFIS) will greatly advance fingerprint identification. IAFIS is "the electronic (paperless) transmittal of fingerprint images to the FBI's Identification Division. This will eventually eliminate fingerprint cards in every step of the process."[21] All fingerprints will be done by live-scan fingerprinting. Fingerprints will be processed by a local police-automated fingerprint identification system and then be forwarded to the state fingerprint identification division. If no match is made with fingerprints already on file, the fingerprints will then be transmitted electronically to the FBI. At that point the fingerprints will be processed by the FBI and the results will be returned electronically to the local police or booking agency.

Electronic Bulletin Boards

As we approach the twenty-first century and with computers becoming more numerous in police departments and with police officers having computers in their police vehicles the use of *electronic bulletin boards* (BBS) will increase. An electronic bulletin board system allows police practitioners to exchange information, send and receive mail, post notices, query online databases, and share software. Bulletins boards function as centers for information exchange and the sharing of resources. Federal, state, and local police agencies, public and private organizations operate bulletin boards that can provide valuable information. Publications are also provided through bulletin boards. Court opinions, criminal justice periodicals, and administrative orders can be placed on bulletin boards. Reports can be disseminated through bulletin boards. The twenty-four-hour-a-day availability of bulletin boards provides a forum for police personnel to communicate, provide technical assistance, query law enforcement databases, and obtain police articles.[22]

Virtual Reality

The best teacher for the police officer may be experience and virtual reality offers the police officer the closest thing to actual experi-

---

21. Ibid., 2.
22. Seth F. Jacobs and David J. Roberts, "Electronic Bulletin Boards," *FBI Law Enforcement Bulletin* 60, No. 3, (1991), 20-24.

ence. *Virtual reality* can provide valuable training that the street patrol officer and the investigator need. Virtual reality "is high-tech illusion. It is a computer-generated, three dimensional environment that engulfs the senses of sight, sound, and touch. Once entered, it becomes reality to the user."[23] Virtual reality may be used in the following areas of law-enforcement training.

Pursuit Driving. The simulator provides users with realistic steering wheel feedback, road feel, and other vehicle motions. The screen possesses a 225-degree field of view standard with 360-degree coverage optional. Simulations can involve one or more drivers, and environments can alternate between city streets, rural roads, and oval tracks. The vehicle itself can be either a police car or a truck or an ambulance or a number of others. Virtual reality driving simulators provide police departments with invaluable training at a fraction of the long-term cost of using actual vehicles. In fact, the simulator is being used by a number of police departments around the country....

Firearms Training. Virtual reality could greatly enhance shoot/don't shoot training simulators currently in use, such as the Firearms Training System.... A virtual reality system would allow officers to enter any three-dimensional environment alone or as a member of a team and confront computer-generated aggressors or other virtual reality users.

High-Risk Incident Management. In addition to weapons training, virtual reality could prove invaluable for SWAT team members before high-risk tactical results. Floor plans and other known facts about a structure or area could be entered into a computer to create a virtual environment for commanders and team members to analyze prior to action.

Incident Re-Creation. Law enforcement agencies could collect data from victims, witnesses, suspects, and crime scenes to re-create traffic accidents, shootings, and other crimes. The virtual environment created from the data could be used to refresh the memories of victims and

23. Jeffrey S. Hormann, "Virtual Reality: The Future of Law Enforcement Training," *FBI Law Enforcement Bulletin* 64, No. 7, (1995), 8.

witnesses, to solve crimes, and ultimately, to prosecute offenders.

Crime Scene Processing. Virtual reality crime scenes
could be used to train both detectives and patrol officers.
Students could search the site and retrieve and analyze
evidence without ever leaving the station. Actual crime
scenes could be re-created to add realism to training or to
evaluate prior police actions.[24]

Virtual realty holds great potential for police training and police
work for the future. For example, it can create strategies prior to implementing a plan of action or evaluate a strategy after the fact to determine its success. Hopefully, virtual reality will assist police officers
in curtailing the mistakes that they would make in real life situations.

Forensic Imaging

For decades, forensic artists have produced drawings and air-
brushed photographs based on witness information to assist criminal
investigators in solving crimes. Today computers are used for age
enhancement. Software exists that helps the computer operator to
alter a photograph to predict the current likeness of an individual.
Typically a forensic artist uses a video camera to digitize photographs for use in the system. The computer operator the "plac[es]
a photograph on a copy stand under an activated video camera to
produce an image on the display monitor. When the photograph has
been properly framed, the camera focused, and the lights adjusted,
the image is 'graphed.' "[25] After this process has been completed, the
computer converts the image into a digital mold and stores it as
memory. This process is repeated each time the forensic artist adds a
new reference image that will be used for the imaging process. It is
expected that in the near future three-dimensional digital skull
imaging will provide forensic artists with the ability to rotate facial
images on the screen and that forensic artists will also have superim-
position capabilities. As we approach the twenty-first century, the
use of forensic imaging will intensify and its facial identification capabilities will improve dramatically.[26]

---

24. Ibid., 8–11.

25. Gene O'Donnell, "Forensic Imaging Comes of Age," *FBI Law Enforcement Bulletin* 63, No. 1, (1994), 6–7.

26. Ibid., 5–10.

Surveillance Equipment

In the last several decades there has been a vast improvement in surveillance technology. These improvements include refinements in imaging technology, remote sensing, telecommunication, computers, and related technologies. Electronic technologies entail the use of "sensing techniques and techniques for aggregating [and] comparing computerized records to reveal additional information about an individual."[27] Electronic surveillance technologies used by law enforcement agencies include the following:

- Closed–circuit television;
- Light vision systems and image intensifiers;
- Parabolic microphones;
- Miniature transmitters;
- Electronic beepers;
- Telephone taps and recorders;
- Pen registers;
- Computer usage monitors;
- Electronic mail monitors;
- Cellular radio interception;
- Satellite beam interception;
- Pattern recognition systems; and
- Intruder detector systems working on vibrations, ultrasound, infrared radiation, etc.[28]

Pen registers are gadgets attached to a telephone line to record the dialed pulses by sensing changes in magnetic energy allowing the interceptor to identify telephone numbers being called. Lasers are used to amplify window vibrations and covert them to audible sound. The parabolic microphones are also used to amplify sound. Night vision observation devices intensify ambient light to allow individuals to be observed.[29]

Night vision devices benefit policing either through *Image Intensification* (II) or through *Thermal Imaging* (TI). Image Intensification is

---

27. *Criminal Justice: New Technologies And The Constitution,* (Washington, DC: U.S. Government Printing Office, 1988), 12.

28. Ibid., 13.

29. Ibid., 13.

used to detect criminal activities or suspects in darkness. One drawback to image intensifiers is that they need minimal light to work effectively, but thermal imaging needs no light at all. Originally developed by the military, thermal imaging uses the heat generated by an object. Thermal imaging converts the heat from vegetation, machinery, and people into a visual image. Essentially, the thermal imaging system measures the thermal energy of an object against it background. It can distinguish minute variations in thermal radiation. The system can electronically display a thermal picture that can be digitized and colorized and viewed by the operation. Ultimately, the thermal imaging system allows officers to search a geographical area without being observed, and the search can be done either from a patrol vehicle or helicopter or airplane.[30]

Videotaping

Videotaping a police interview or the interrogation of a suspect can assist in the criminal investigation by revealing to the judge and jury that the interview was conducted in a fair and impartial manner. If a confession is obtained from the suspect, the video will show that the suspect was not coerced.

Also, expert witnesses who are unable to be present at a hearing or trial can submit to a videotaped deposition. Both the prosecutor and defense attorney can be involved in the deposition to meet any objections that the defense might make. Furthermore, if a victim is unable to appear in court because of medical reasons, his testimony can be videotaped.

The most effective use of the video, however, may be to directly record crimes as they occur. Also, crime scenes can be videotaped to provide the judge and jury with a magnified picture of the crime scene. The use of videotaping provides the police and prosecutor with an effective method of helping the judge and jury to understand the crime.[31]

---

30. "Nightsight," *Police: The Law Officer's Magazine* 19, No. 5, (1995), 59.

31. Michael Giacoppo, "The Expanding Role of Videotape in Court," *The Expanding Role of Videotape in Court* 60, No. 11, (1991), 1-5.

Weapons

Smart Gun

Serious injury and death to police officers are usually caused by firearms. Often, police officers are murdered with their own weapons. Of course, every police officer has faced the potential threat of confronting violent and unpredictable subjects.

Since 1979, an average of nineteen deaths have occurred as a result of an assailant using a police officer's weapon.[32] The *smart gun* or safe gun, however, is a handgun that can "recognize" its user. The goal of smart-gun technology is to prevent an unauthorized user from firing a police officer's weapon by implementing *user recognizing-and-authorizing* safety technology.[33] Although the smart gun is not currently available to police officers, the National Institute of Justice's sponsorship of smart-gun research leaves hope that a smart gun will be available to police officers in the near future.

The Taser

The Taser is a low-powered (5 watt) gadget that operates on a 7.2 volt battery and shoots tiny barbs attached to 15 feet of wire. Electrons flow from the battery to the subject's clothing and skin. The central nervous system closes the electron circuit, which means that the electrical current flows along the subject's central nervous system. The Taser pulses then cause "charlie horse" spasms that cause the subject to lose control of his bodily movements. The Taser will not, however, electrocute someone standing in water nor will it damage the heart, but it should not be used where fires may erupt.[34]

Stun Gun

The basic stun gun is a small, rectangular, plastic box that has two metal posts protruding from the top and is powered by a recharge-

---

32. D.R. Weiss, D.J. Brandt, and K.D. Tweet, "Smart Gun Technology Requirements Preliminary Report," (Albuquerque: Sandi National Laboratories, 1996), 1.

33. Julie Clausen, "Smart Gun Technology Project," (Albuquerque: Sandia National Laboratories, Fax dated March 3, 1996).

34. Lois Pilant, "Selecting Nonlethal Weapons," *The Police Chief* 68, No. 5, (1993), 53.

able nine-volt battery. The stun gun generates an electrical current that delivers a 50,000-volt charge when it is placed against a suspect's body for several seconds. The high voltage provides for disorientation and a temporary loss of muscle control in the subject which thereby allows the police officer to subdue the subject with a minimum amount of force. The amount of time the stun gun is held against the body affects both the size of the charge and its effect on an individual. A charge of less than a second will startle the subject, a charge of one to two seconds will cause the subject to lose the ability to stand up, a three to four second charge will incapacitate a subject leaving him dazed and weak[35].

Pepper Spray

Chemical agents are not effective on all people, including those under the influence of drugs or alcohol, or those who are mentally ill. Chemical irritants act on the central nervous system and induce pain by activating receptor cells within the brain. Oleoresin capsicum, also known as pepper spray, is a natural inflammatory agent that a police officer sprays into the eyes of an uncooperative individual, incapacitating him. Generally, the individual is not injured and can be decontaminated with proper air ventilation and washing of the eyes with water—along with the removal of contact lenses.[36]

The use of *pepper spray* immediately causes a swelling of the eyes and breathing passage. An intense burning occurs in the eyes, throat, and the skin areas sprayed. When pepper spray has been inhaled, breathing will be restricted and the respiratory tract becomes inflamed. The physical effects can include: coughing, choking, involuntary closing of the eyes, nausea, lack of coordination, and loss of upper body strength. Disorientation and fear can also occur.[37]

Pepper spray or oleoresin capsicum (OC) offers a non-lethal approach to handling hostages and in barricade and tactical assault situations. In lieu of using force many police departments have approved the use of pepper spray for getting volatile situations under control.

---

35. Grafton H. Hull, Jr., and Joseph C. Frisbie, "The Stun Gun Debate: More Help Than Hazard?" *The Police Chief* 54, No. 2, (1987), 46.

36. Jami Onnen, "Oleoresin Capsicum," (Alexandria, VA: International Association of Chiefs of Police, 1993), 1-2.

37. Ibid., 2.

Forensic Science

DNA

DNA (deoxyribonucleic acid) is the "material found in the nucleus of human cells that contain our chromosomes. It provides the genetic code that determines the finite building blocks that make up our individual characteristics."[38] DNA profiling assists the criminal investigator by helping to eliminate suspects: it can exonerate a wrongly accused individual and it can make the identity of a suspect more certain.

The profiling methods of DNA have proven that dried human biological material can go through the DNA fingerprinting process and positively establish an identification. The information obtained from DNA can be cataloged, and at a later date it can be compared to information obtained from additional tests to determine the identity of a suspect. It is anticipated that with a large database of DNA profiles, suspects would be more easily identified. Currently, the FBI Laboratories and some private companies will perform DNA testing.

Ultraviolet Forensic Imaging

The same ultraviolet light or rays that cause people to sunburn can be used to provide a detailed analysis of bite marks on human skin. Ultraviolet light provides explicit detail and contrast to an injured locality than standard lighting techniques.

To locate hidden wounds on a victim several technologies have been linked together. A video-intensifier tube sensitive to light waves from the ultraviolet spectrum is modified to catch ultraviolet light rays. The image exposed by the ultraviolet rays is magnified and displayed on a video screen. A victim's entire body can be scrutinized to locate any injuries that would normally not be discovered. In addition to finding difficult-to-detect bodily injuries, the ultraviolet intensifier has great value at crime scenes and can pinpoint evidence such as footprints, fingerprints, and even trace metal fragments. Ultraviolet technology is still being developed and its potential is still largely unknown.[39]

---

38. "DNA Profiling: For Positive Identification," (Washington, DC: National Institute of Justice, 1990), 1.

39. Michael H. West and Robert E. Barsley, "Ultraviolet Forensic Imag-

Crime Control Technology

Police technology is constantly evolving making the police officer's job safer and making it easier to control crime. Technology used by law enforcement agencies is becoming more sophisticated and will play a larger role in the twenty-first century. There are also a variety of important technologies being developed to aid the police in pursuing vehicles.

Auto Arrestor System

The *auto arrestor system* was developed to assist police officers in the pursuit of drivers trying to avoid arrest. High speed police chases are dangerous to police officers, suspects being pursued, pedestrians, and other motorists. Ideally, the police officer would be able to stop a moving vehicle without endangering anyone and have the ability to use non-lethal force. The auto arrestor—using a system initially developed for the defense department—employs an electromagnetic technology that shuts down the ignition system of a speeding automobile. The system consists of a portable, high-energy, pulsed-power source and a conductor strip that a police officer can deploy against a fleeing vehicle. The auto arrestor uses an electromagnetic current to damage the sensitive electronic components of an automobile making the automobile coast to a stop as if it had run out of gas. The auto arrestor is currently being tested by law enforcement and in the near future it will provide police personnel with a safe and effective method of stopping a moving vehicle.[40]

Check-Point Barrier Strip

This technology is a light-weight tire deflator that when activated remotely will deflate the tires of a vehicle. This technology is helpful in situations where a driver attempts to avoid a check point or a traffic stop. The strip consists of an array of ½-inch hardened, hollow steel spikes and support blocks retained magnetically in a 6-foot deflator bar.[41]

---

ing," *FBI Law Enforcement Bulletin* 61, No. 5, (1992), 14-16.

40. Blair Stewart, "Overview of the Jaycor Auto Arrestor Concept," (Colorado Springs: Jaycor Co., 1996), 2.

41. Eagle Research Group, Arlington, VA.

Fleeing Vehicle Tagging System

The *fleeing vehicle tagging system* consists of a launcher and a projectile with an embedded radio-frequency-transmitter tag. An adhesive within the projectile secures the tag to the fleeing automobile.

Retractable Spiked Barrier Strip

A *retractable spiked barrier strip* can be placed across the roadway in advance of a vehicle being pursued. When the vehicle approaches the spiked barrier strip the vehicle's tires are punctured and the spikes are embedded in the tires. Air escapes from the tires rapidly but the vehicle is allowed to come to a controlled stop.[42]

Technologies are also being developed to aid police officers in confrontation situations. The purpose of such technologies is to curtail injuries, to minimize the use of force by police officers, and to reduce the risk of death.

Airbag Restraint for Patrol Vehicles

The *airbag restraint for patrol officers* allows the patrol officer to deploy a rear seat airbag restraint to prevent violent and disruptive behavior from an individual while he is being transported to police headquarters or to jail. The air bag will not explode, but it provides sufficient pressure to restrict the movement of the suspect in the rear seat. The patrol officer will have the opportunity to inflate and deflate the airbag as needed.[43]

Disabling Net and Launcher System

A *disabling net* is yet another means of allowing the police to apprehend a fleeing felon or violent person by use of a non-lethal means. The net is launched as a projectile that immobilizes the suspect.[44]

---

42. The Idaho National Engineering Laboratory, Lockheed Martin Idaho Technologies, Idaho Falls, Id.

43. The Idaho National Engineering Laboratory, Lockheed Martin Idaho Technologies, Idaho Falls, Idaho.

44. Foster Miller, Inc., Waltham, MA.

Disorienting Pulsed Light

The *disorienting pulsed light* induces a temporary impairment of vision and a disorientation. The gadget uses a pulsing white light and the officer operating it wears goggles to prevent impairment.[45]

Projectile Launcher with Impact Velocity Control

A *projectile launcher* has been designed that uses a laser range finder to determine the distance between the launcher and its target and can adjust the velocity of the launch so that the impact of the projectile is constant. The concept allows the launcher to deliver ordnance in a controlled manner.[46] The system uses virtual reality to create an environment of three-dimensional images. The images are viewed thought a mounted head device and goggles which narrow the focus to two video monitors. The monitors can also give the viewer a sense of depth based on the views provided. Users remain stationary and use either a joy stick or track ball to move through the virtual environment. A device contained in a glove may be used to manipulate objects within the virtual environment. The user many also utilize weapons to confront virtual aggressors.

Summary

As America approaches the next millennium it is fast becoming a society dependent upon sophisticated technologies, and the trend in technological advances will certainly continue into the future. Technological advances are occurring in all professions and fields and policing has not been excluded. The concept of modern police technology owes a debt to the Sherlock Holmes stories of the 1890s in which the main character used scientific techniques to solve crimes. In 1919, the first modern crime laboratory was opened in San Francisco, California. The first polygraph was constructed in 1921.

During World War II a technology explosion occurred, and after the war, the police were able to use equipment developed for military purposes. The same thing is happening in the late 1990s. De-

45. Livermore National Laboratory, Livermore, CA.
46. Lawrence Livermore National Laboratory, Livermore, CA.

fense contractors who developed technology for the Cold War are now looking toward law enforcement to peddle their wares. Equipment that would normally be sold to the military is now—with minor adaptations—being sold to police forces.

Most importantly, police departments have adopted the computer as an essential tool. Computer Aided Dispatching (CAD) has been recognized as being much more efficient than the old method of dispatching police and other emergency vehicles. Computers have also been placed in patrol vehicles to make it easier for patrol officers to access information or even to complete reports. All police units use computers either for record keeping, crime scene investigation, or for crime analysis.

The "Criminal Justice Information System" is improving information systems and making information readily accessible to police personnel. Criminal histories, fingerprint identification, and even matching modus operandi have been or will be at an officer's finger tips in the very near future. Police surveillance equipment is also becoming more sophisticated. The use of non-lethal weapons used by the police is becoming a standard part of the police officer's arsenal. Forensic science is vastly improving. Crime control technology will play a bigger role in crime control than it has in the past. Ultimately, the police officer of today has more technology available than the officer of the past, and certainly, the police officer of the future will have more technology available than current police officers.

Key Terms

CAD
cellular-radio interception
closed-circuit television
electronic beepers
electronic mail
geocoding
HITS
intruder-detector system
light-vision systems

NCIC
NCIC-2000
NIJ
NLETC
pen register
parabolic microphones
pattern-recognition systems
satellite-beam interception

Review Questions

1. Why is technology important to policing?
2. Why is the computer important to policing?
3. Why are "Criminal Justice Information Services" important to policing?
4. Why is surveillance equipment important to policing?
5. Why are non-lethal weapons important to policing?

References

Cutri, Keith J. "Laptop Computer: New Technology for Law Enforcement. *FBI Law Enforcement Bulletin* 65, No. 2/3 (1996).

Criminal Justice: New Technologies and the Constitution. Washington, DC: U.S. Government Printing Office, 1988.

Hormann, Jeffrey S. "Virtual Reality: The Future of Law Enforcement Training." *FBI Law Enforcement Bulletin* 64, No. 7 (1995).

Hull, Grafton H., Jr, and Joseph C. Frisbie. "The Stun Gun Debate: More Help Than Hazard?" *The Police Chief* 57, No. 2 (1987).

Institute for Law and Justice. *Law Enforcement Options.* Vol. 1, No. 1. Alexandria, VA: Institute for Law and Justice, 1995.

Jacobs, Seth F. and David J. Roberts. "Electronic Bulletin Boards." *FBI Law Enforcement Bulletin* 60, No. 3 (1991).

Keppel, Robert and Joseph Weis. "HITS Catching Criminals in the Northwest." *FBI Law Enforcement Bulletin* 62, No.4 (1994).

"Nightsight." *Police: The Law Officer's Magazine* 19, No. 5 (1995).

O'Donnell, Gene. "Forensic Imaging Comes of Age." *FBI Law Enforcement Bulletin* 63, No. 1 (1994).

Onnen, Jami. "Oleoresin Capsicum," Alexander, VA: International Association of Chiefs of Police, 1993.

Pilant, Lois. "Selecting Nonlethal Weapons." *The Police Chief* 68, No. 5 (1993).

—-. "High-Technology Solutions," *The Police Chief* 71, No. 5 (1996).

Rich, Thomas F. "The Use of Computerized Mapping in Crime Control and Prevention Programs." *National Institute of Justice.* Washington, DC: U.S. Department of Justice, July, 1995.

Sessions, William S. "Criminal Justice Information Services." *FBI Law Enforcement Bulletin* 62, No. 2 (1993).

Stewart, Blair. "Overview of the Jaycor Auto Arrestor Concept." Colorado Springs, CO: Jaycor, 1996.

Travis, Jeremy. "Criminal Justice Science and Technology Program." *National Institute of Justice*. Washington, DC: NIJ, 1995.

West, Michael H. and Robert E. Barsley. "Ultraviolet Forensic Imaging." *FBI Law Enforcement Bulletin* 61, No. 5 (1992).

CHAPTER 9

The Changing Face of Policing

Major Issues

1. In the future, white males will play a less prominent role in policing.
2. Police departments should mirror the ethnic, racial, and cultural makeup of the community.
3. Affirmative Action should still play an important part in police organizations.

Introduction

With the increase in multicultural awareness in American society it has becomes more commonplace in the last several decades to see groups other than white males providing police service. The roots of the involvement of women and minorities in policing can be traced to the nineteenth century; however, their roles were often limited and allowed for few opportunities for advancement. Throughout the course of the evolution of policing in America various minority groups that had been all but excluded from policework were able to obtain footholds in policing and eventually make their mark. Ultimately, the opening of the door of opportunity for minorities in policing is a result of fundamental changes occurring in American society.

It was not uncommon for ethnic groups such as the Irish, Italians, and Jews to be discriminated against in the competition for specific forms of employment. For example, Mario Cuomo, the former Governor of New York, could not obtain a position on Wall Street upon graduation from St. Johns Law School because he was an Italian, and most Americans are familiar with the exclusion of Afro-Americans from many employment opportunities until recent years. More recently we as Americans have been made aware of discrimination involving Hispanic peoples, Asians, and women.

In the last several decades America has made a concentrated effort to open the doors of opportunity for all Americans. The American government has put clout behind this effort by enacting federal laws and establishing enforcement agencies to carry out the government's mandates. Because of the new opportunities provided to women and minorities, the face of policing is changing.

Women in Policing

The movement to get women involved in police service can be traced to the 1880s. Women's organizations such as the Federation of Women's Clubs, the National League of Women Voters, the National Women's Temperance Union, along with various social agencies and social health groups pushed for women to be involved in police work.[1]

Initially, women worked in police departments as matrons who were put in charge of the women prisoners in the custody of the police agency. In 1877, Portland, Maine, employed the first police matron. In 1888, Massachusetts passed a law requiring the appointment of police matrons for all cities with a population of 20,000 or more. The New York state legislature passed a similar law in the same year. However, the City of Chicago has the distinction of appointing the first police woman, Mrs. Marie Owens, who held the title "patrolman" for her entire thirty-year career. Marie Owens was responsible for assisting detectives in cases involving women and children.[2]

In 1915 the police department of Portland, Oregon, gave Mrs. Lola Baldwin police powers to deal with problems involving females. Mrs. Baldwin was later given a permanent position with the Portland police department and was responsible for dealing with problems pertaining to young girls and women. However, Mrs. Baldwin and the women who were employed to work with her were not called "police women"; instead, they were referred to as "workers" or "operatives."[3]

It was not until 1910 when the Los Angeles Police Department introduced the title "police woman" that the first police woman was recognized. Alice Stebbins Wells, a social worker, was appointed and given the responsibility of supervising dance halls, skating rinks, penny arcades, movie theaters, and places of recreation. Mrs. Wells was also given the responsibility of searching for missing persons.[4] During this early era when women were first entering the police

---

1. Lois Higgins, "Historical Background of Policewomen's Service," *Journal of Criminal Law, Criminology and Police Science* 41 (March/April, 1951), 822.

2. Ibid., 822–823.

3. Ibid., 823.

4. Ibid., 824.

field, those women who came from social-work backgrounds recognized that the police provided the first line of social defense. In other words, the police had an opportunity to intervene before the social services agencies or the courts could.[5]

Women's role in policing was considered a "preventive role." Although women police officers had the same authority to make arrests and to enforce criminal laws and city ordinances, neither female nor male officers thought of their tasks as being similar. The belief was that the female police officer could provide counseling and guidance while the male police officer would make arrests.

In the 1910s the *crime prevention model* was constructed emphasizing crime prevention as the most important function of policing. The "crime prevention model" preceded the *crime control model* which was developed in the 1930s and which emphasized the arrest process. The crime control model has been considered a male-gendered model while the crime prevention model has been considered a female-gendered model. It was thought that females would be more successful at performing crime prevention activities than their male counterparts would be.[6] The crime prevention model has three major tenets:

1. The highest form of policing is social work;
2. Crime prevention is the most important function of the police;
3. Women are inherently better than men at preventing crime.[7]

The movement to increase women police officers spanned the years 1910 to 1940. It was a movement by middle-class women to expand their roles in the public arena. Many of the women entering police service during the 1910s, 1920s, and 1930s were social workers who often had several years of experience.

The evolution of women in policing had its roots in the protection movement, initiated by private organizations to look after the welfare and rights of women and children.[8] Another reason for adding women to police forces was a result of the *white slave scare* of

---

5. Ibid., 227.

6. Janis Appier, "Preventive Justice: The Campaign for Women Police, 1910–1940," *Women and Criminal Justice* 4, No. 1, (1992), 3.

7. Ibid., 5.

8. Ibid., 6–7.

the 1910s and 1920s. In the years preceding 1910 and for several years into that decade there was some concern that women were being abducted and sold into prostitution. The news and entertainment media played an important part in this "white slavery scare." Novels, magazine articles, newspaper reports, and films all had stories about innocent young girls being kidnapped and sold into prostitution. The push to add women to police departments can be attributed to the failure of the enforcement of vice laws and to the sentiments of some women reformers who considered prostitution to be men's fault.[9]

The administration of women police within departments during the early decades of this century had several forms of organization. In larger police departments, a Woman's Division was established with a women director, responsible to the chief of the department. In small-city departments with two or more women, one woman was placed in command to direct the work of the unit. Some police departments placed women in already existing units, such as the detective or special services units and their work was supervised by a male officer. Another administrative method involved assigning women police to precincts and to bureaus where their work would be supervised by the commanding officer. In some cases women worked for private organizations and were given limited police powers while others worked for private organizations that worked in conjunction with the police.[10]

In 1915 the National Association of Policewomen was formed with Alice Stebbins Wells as its first president. The women's organization gained support of the International Association of Chiefs of Police which gave support in drafting a constitution for the Association. The National Association of Policewomen had as its objectives:

> To act as a clearing house for compilation and dissemination of information on the work of women police, to aim for high standards of work and to promote the preventive and protective service by police departments. The suggestions made at the time of the first meeting were that:

9. Ibid., 11–12.
10. Higgins, 828.

1. The work of women police officers should be largely preventive and protective;
2. The need for trained women is urgent;
3. Course instruction in institutes of social sciences or in schools of special work with field work in the police departments is needed;
4. Proper legislation should be secured for the appointment of women police;
5. Women's divisions should be established with the police department and staffed by a woman with a rank not lower than a captain;
6. Careful records should be kept and monthly reports of work should be made to the department;
7. Simple civilian clothes of dark color, preferably navy blue, should be worn on ordinary duty; certain special duties might require special uniforms; and
8. Exchange of women officers by municipalities would provide for enlarged experience and would make for standardization of work and methods.[11]

From the 1910s through the 1940s the police women's work involved exclusively interpersonal, rational work. The work of police women habitually involved tasks that required a high level of affectivity, empathy, attention to detail, and cooperation with others. Police women specialized in services that involved comforting lost children, responding to letters about missing persons, and interviewing female and juvenile offenders and victims of crime. Referrals were made to social service agencies by police women. They also gave advice to parents about mischievous children and to married couples on how to handle domestic relations cases.[12]

In Detroit women police were involved in girl delinquency prevention and many other cities had similar prevention programs. There were five preliminary steps for establishing delinquency-prevention programs for girls:

1. Create in the police department a crime-prevention bureau. Within it, set up a women's division staffed with experts scientifically trained to discover girls in moral peril; interview

11. Higgins, 331.
12. Applier, 17.

them; transport them to the homes or to clean, proper detention places; thoroughly investigate them and refer the cases for solutions to the right public and private agencies.

2. Provide the clean, proper detention places mentioned above.
3. Provide a Children's Court or the equivalent, with competent probation officers. Insist that judge and probation officers be Civil Service, and not political appointees.
4. Finance public and private agencies so that they can give delinquents and potential delinquents the careful long term aid many of the cases require (some cities are not only rehabilitating delinquent girls and boys but are cleaning up the areas that produced them).
5. Punish parents of willful neglect.[13]

In the 1930s the "crime prevention" model began to loose ground to the "crime control" model. The "crime control" model of the 1930s began to emphasize managerial efficiency, technological sophistication, and crime fighting. The crime prevention/social work aspect of policing began to fall into disfavor by police administrators. With the emphasis on the "crime control" model and a deemphasis on "crime prevention" the police women's movement began to stagnate and lose support.[14]

A survey in 1946 found that only 141 police departments out of 417 employed police women. This figure reveals almost no growth in the number of police agencies employing police women since the 1920s. Unlike other occupations during World War II women made no significant gains in the field of law enforcement. Neither were any significant gains made during the 1950s and 1960s. O.W. Wilson, a respected police administrator during this period, advocated in the 1963 edition of his text *Police Administration* that women could serve in juvenile units and some specialized units under the supervision of a male. Wilson, also considered male officers to be better administrators and he considered them to be more rational than female officers.[15]

It was not until the late 1960s that the police women's movement was revived. The 1967 *Task Force Report: The Police* of the President's

---

13. Vera Connolly, "Job For A Lady," *Collier's* (June 10, 1944), 19.

14. Samuel Walker, *A Critical History of Police Reform,* (Lexington, MA: Lexington Books, 1977), 93–94.

15. Ibid., 94.

Commission on Law Enforcement and the Administration of Justice seems to be the first major document advocating a national policy for expanding the role of women police officers. The *Task Force Report: The Police* made the following comments:

> Policewomen can be an invaluable asset to modern law enforcement, and their present role should be broadened. Qualified women should be utilized in such important staff service units as planning and research, training, intelligence, inspection, public information, community relations and legal advisors. Women could also serve in such units as computer programming and laboratory analyses and communications. Their value should not be considered as limited to staff functions or police work with juveniles; women should also serve regularly in patrol, vice, and investigative divisions. Finally, as more and more well-qualified women enter the service, they could assume administrative responsibilities.[16]

Because of the Task Force recommendations on expanding the role of women in policing, a number of police departments began to evaluate the role of women in policing. In 1968, the Police Chief of Indianapolis, Indiana, provided the opportunity for the first police women to assume patrol duties. In 1969, the newly appointed Washington, D.C., Police Chief Jerry Wilson initiated a program utilizing police women throughout the department, including patrol operations. For several years a total of 100 women were recruited and in 1972 they were assigned patrol duties. This was the first time that a large number of women were involved in unisex policing in an American city.[17]

Shortly after Chief Wilson announced that the District of Columbia police department was utilizing women in patrol duties, the Police Foundation agreed to sponsor an evaluation of newly hired female officers to be conducted by The Urban Institute located in Washington. The study was designed to compare an equal number of newly hired female officers with newly hired male officers who

---

16. The President's Commission on Law Enforcement and Administration of Justice, *Task Force Report: The Police*, (Washington, DC: U.S. Government Printing Office, 1967), 125.

17. Kerry Segrave, *Policewomen: A History,* (Jefferson, NC: McFarland & Company, 1995), 116–117.

were placed on patrol duties. The study compared the eighty-six female officers to the same number of male officers. It was discovered that both groups were similar in education (almost thirteen years of schooling), in civil service test scores (81 average for both groups), in the number of jobs previously held (approximately 3.5), and in the ratings they received in their pre-employment interviews. Both groups also had similar scores at the police academy. There were, however, more black women than black men (68 percent for females compared to 42 percent for males) and more females had children than did males (54 percent compared to 31 percent).[18] The height requirement was not changed to recruit more female officers. The minimum height requirement of 5'7" was met by the female officers. The average height of the female officers was slightly shorter than that of the males (about 5'8" compared to about 5'10") and the average weight of the females was about thirty pounds less than that of the males.[19]

The Police Foundation asked three fundamental questions:

> First, is it appropriate, from a performance viewpoint, to hire women for patrol assignments on the same basis as men?
>
> Second, what advantages or disadvantages arise from hiring women on an equal basis for patrol work?
>
> Third, what effect would the use of a substantial number of policewomen have on the nature of police operations?[20]

In answering the three preceding questions, the study found that gender was not a bona fide qualification for performing patrol duties. The work performance of men and women were similar, and both obtained similar results in handling violent and angry citizens. Both male and female officers showed similar respect toward citizens, and citizens reciprocated to both equally. In answering the third question on the impact that women may have on police operations, the study reported that women officers were less aggressive than their male counterparts. The report also indicated that the

---

18. Peter Bloch and Deborah Anderson, *"Police Women on Patrol: Final Report,"* (Washington, DC: Police Foundation, 1974), 1.

19. Ibid., 1.

20. Ibid., 1–3.

presence of women officers could decrease violence and cool down
a potentially violent situation.[21]

In addition to The Police Foundation study there were other
studies done during 1970s that reported that women police officers
could perform police patrol functions successfully. Nevertheless, the
increased number of women in police departments and their expanding role in police service is largely the result of legislation.

The United Stated has developed a body of law that makes it illegal to discriminate on the basis of gender; consequently, hiring
policies and promotion policies in today's police departments are
under the direct influence of the *Equal Employment Opportunity Act
of 1972.*

The core of gender discrimination litigation is based on *Title VII*
of the *Civil Rights Act of 1964.* This federal law made it illegal to
discriminate in employment on the basis of race, color, religion, sex,
or national origin. Initially, the 1964 Civil Rights Act pertained to
the private sector, but in 1972, Congress passed the Equal Employment Opportunity Act by amending Title VII of the 1964 Civil
Rights Act to include public employers, including police departments.

In the last several decades the status of women in policing has
changed. The opportunities for police women to serve in police operations and in administration on a equal footing with their male
counterparts are greater than ever. Police women now serve in all
police divisions including, patrol, traffic, investigations, and training.
Today's police women serve in all the ranks of a police department
as Sergeants, Lieutenants, Captains, Inspectors, and Police Chiefs.

Minority Police Officers

The term minority not only includes women but also Afro-
Americans, Hispanics, Asians, and more recently, gays and lesbians,
and for the last several decades, it has been common for police agencies to actively recruit women, blacks, Hispanics, and Asians. Some
police departments, namely San Francisco's and Philadelphia's, are
actively recruiting gays and lesbians. In addition to the legal requirements that police agencies must meet, a police department should

---

21. Ibid., 3–4.

reflect the cultural, racial, and ethnic makeup of the community. Police officers are recruited from the community they police and service, so it seems only logical and fair-minded that police personnel reflect the cultural makeup of that community.

Of all the minorities it appears that black Americans have the longest history in the field of policing. In 1839 black men were deputized as special police officers when the Mayor of Pittsburgh took this action to allow the black community to defend itself against a white mob.[22] The situation in Pittsburgh, however, was unique due to the fact that prior to the Civil War most blacks were slaves and could not be considered for police service, even as special police for a temporary period of time.

The New Orleans city council in 1805 passed an ordinance allowing "free men of color" to serve as police officers as long as they were commanded by white officers. The "free men of color" performed tasks that white police officers did not want to perform, they were used as *slave catchers*, and they enforced the laws in the black communities. By 1830, the "free men of color" lost their positions on the New Orleans police department. New immigrants, especially the Irish took their positions.[23]

After the Civil War, riots occurred in several Southern cities in which whites attacked blacks. The police of these cities were often incapable or unwilling to protect blacks from white violence, and it became apparent that in order to obtain fair and equitable policing black communities would need to be served by police officers of their own race. In response to this, the city of New Orleans initiated the appointment of black officers in 1867. In 1868, the first black Captain was appointed by the New Orleans Police Department. By 1870, twenty-eight percent of the New Orleans police force was black. Similarly, other cities in the South began to appoint blacks to their police forces.[24]

The black police officers in many of the Southern cites were restricted to policing black areas and to arresting blacks. But when white Southerners' were able to regain political control after the reconstruction period they worked to eliminate black police officers.

---

22. W. Marvin Dulaney, *Black Police in America,* (Bloomington, IN: Indiana University Press, 1996), 4.

23. Ibid., 8–10.

24. Ibid., 11–13.

By the 1890s, most Southern cities had lily-white police departments.[25]

In 1872, the city of Chicago appointed the first black police officer in what may be the first appointment of a black officer outside of the South. This was followed by the appointment of blacks in Philadelphia and Cleveland in 1881, in Columbus, Ohio, in 1885, in Detroit in 1890, and in St. Louis in 1893.[26] During the twentieth century blacks were appointed to many large and small American cities as police officers. Often, their numbers did not reflect the black population of their city. Usually their numbers on the police force represented one or two percent of the total number of sworn police personnel. Typically, black officers were denied access to choice assignments, they found promotions difficult to obtain, and they were generally not given command positions. Although black officers' opportunities increased after World War II, it was not until the 1960s that they began to make big strides in policing.

The 1960s was a period of turmoil. There was a great deal of unrest that was reflected in the riots in America's urban ghettos. These riots were quite severe causing death and billions of dollars of property damage. Riots occurred in many of America's major cities, mid-sized cities, and small cities alike. As a result, a number of studies and national commissions were initiated to examine the causes of urban unrest and to find possible solutions to prevent further violence in America's urban ghettos. President Johnson's Commission on Law Enforcement and Administration of Justice in its *Task Force Report: The Police*, published in 1967, recommended that police forces with a considerable minority population need to vigorously recruit black police officers. The Commission explained that a police department dominated by whites policing a black neighborhood caused annoyance and resentment among black residents. The *Task Force* also stated that the police department should reflect the whole composition of the city and that black police officers policing black neighborhoods would have an understanding of the language and subculture of those communities. In their findings *The Task Force: The Police* found that

> In short, in every city, county, and State where statistics are available, Negroes are under represented, usually substantially,

---

25. Ibid., 15.
26. Ibid., 18–19.

on police forces. Although the number of Negroes in police departments has been increasing, in some places rapidly, there is indication that the percentage of Negroes on police forces may level off well below their percentage of the population unless police departments are much more effective in recruiting in the future.[27]

One year after the publication of the President's Commission on Law Enforcement and the Administration of Justice, the National Advisory Commission on Civil Disorders (Kerner Report) issued its report. To a large extent the Kerner Report reiterated many of the findings pertaining to policing that were advocated by the President's Commission. The Kerner Report suggested that police agencies take a close look at their internal operations, including the recruiting and training of black police officers. The Report also recommended that police departments develop better rapport with black communities and impartially enforce the law when dealing with blacks.

In 1973, the National Advisory Commission on Criminal Justice Standards and Goals, *The Police*, reemphasized that qualified blacks should be recruited as police officers in communities with black residents. Because there is often a distrust between the black community and the police, it is extremely important that blacks and other minorities be recruited to overcome that distrust of the police. The Commission's report, *The Police*, recommended that

1. Every police agency should engage in positive efforts to employ ethnic minority group members. When a substantial ethnic minority population resides within the jurisdiction, the police agency should take affirmative action to achieve a ratio of minority group employees in approximate proportion to the makeup of the population.
2. Every police agency seeking to employ members of an ethnic minority group should direct recruitment efforts toward attracting large numbers of minority applicants. In establishing selection standards for recruitment, special abilities such as the ability to speak a foreign language, strength and agility, or any

---

27. The President's Commission on Law Enforcement and Administration of Justice, *Task Force Report: The Police,* (Washington, DC: U.S. Government Printing Office, 1967), 168.

other compensating factor should be taken into consideration
in addition to height and weight requirements.
3. Every police agency seeking to employ qualified ethnic minority members should research, develop, and implement specialized minority recruitment methods. These methods should
include:

  a. Assignment of minority police officers to the specialized
     recruitment effort,
  b. Liaison with local minority community leaders to em-
     phasize police sincerity and encourage referral of minor-
     ity applicants to the police agency,
  c. Recruitment advertising and other material that depict
     minority group police personnel performing the police
     function,
  d. Active cooperation of the minority medial as well as the
     general medial in minority recruitment efforts,
  e. Emphasis on the community service aspect of police
     work, and
  f. Regular personal contact with the minority applicant
     from initial application to final determination of employ-
     ability.

4. Every police chief executive should insure that hiring, assignment, and promotion policies and practices do not discriminate against minority group members.
5. Every police agency should evaluate continually the effectiveness of specialized minority recruitment methods so that
successful methods are emphasized and unsuccessful ones discarded.[28]

Ultimately, the various government commissions have influenced
the recruitment of blacks and other minorities by police departments. Many cities have established recruitment programs to attract
minority candidates. These programs include using billboards along
highways and using television, radio, and newspapers advertisements. Some police departments have offered cash incentives for
police officers who have recruited minority officers. Great strides
have taken place in recruiting, promoting, and increasing the number of blacks on American's police forces. There are now more

28. National Advisory Commission on Criminal Justice Standards and
Goals, *Police,* (Washington, DC: U.S. Government Printing Office, 1973), 329.

black police administrators running American police departments than ever before in the history of American policing.

But in a study done in the 1980s of the fifty largest cities in the United States it was found that the departments fell below desirable levels in employing blacks and Hispanic police officers. It was revealed that only two of the fifty police departments achieved population representation for both blacks and Hispanics. Two reasons given for not achieving compliance were budgetary constraints and police officer layoffs.[29] In the 1990s, Blacks and Hispanics still seem to be playing catch up in many American cities. For example, while New York City has a black population of approximately twenty-nine percent, its police department has a black representation of only eleven percent. While thirty-nine percent of Chicago's population is black, black police officers total only twenty-five percent of the city's police force. In Philadelphia, which has a black population of forty percent, only twenty-five percent of its police force is black.[30] In a report published by the U.S. Justice Department it was reported that "Black officers accounted for 11.3 percent of the total in 1993, compared to 10.5 percent in 1990 and 9.3 percent in 1987. The percentage of Hispanic offices was 6.2 percent in 1993, 5.2 percent in 1990 and 4.5 percent in 1987."[31]

Another group that has been added to the list of minorities in policing is the homosexual police officer. Currently, gays and lesbians cannot be denied the opportunity to be police officers, and in some cities homosexual police officers are "coming out of the closet," while in others they are remaining quiet. In the early 1990s there were at least ten cities that actively recruited homosexuals: Boston, Minneapolis, Madison, Seattle, Portland, Atlanta, Philadelphia, San Francisco, Los Angeles, and New York City.[32]

---

29. Sam Walker, "Employment of Black and Hispanic Police Officers," *Review of Applied Urban Research* XI, No. 6, (October 1983), 1.

30. Paul Glastries, "The Thin White Line," *U.S. News & World Report* 117, No. 7, (August 15, 1994), 53.

31. Bureau of Justice Statistics, *Local Police Departments, 1993,* (Washington DC: U.S. Department of Justice, 1993), iii.

32. Stephen H. Leinen, *Gay Cops,* (New Brunswick, NJ: Rutgers University Press, 1993). 11.

Affirmative Action

The face of policing has been changing for several decades. There are now more women, blacks, Hispanics, Asians and homosexuals on America's police forces than ever before in the history of policing. One of the primary reasons for this is *affirmative action*. The term affirmative action can be defined as "results-oriented practices to ensure that women, minorities, handicapped persons, and other protected classes of people will be equitably represented in the organization. Put another way, affirmative action is any action that is taken specifically to overcome the results of past discriminatory employment practices."[33]

The concept of affirmative action can be traced to 1935 when the Wagner Act made it illegal for employers to harass union organizers and members. In 1941 President Roosevelt, by Executive Order, prohibited labor discrimination by defense contractors. President Truman, by Executive Order, mandated fair employment for all federal government agencies. In 1961, President Kennedy, by Executive Order, barred discrimination for government contractors based upon race, color, or creed. In 1965 President Johnson, by Executive Order, barred discrimination for federal employees and job applicants based on race, color, religion, or national origin.[34]

In addition to Presidential Executive Orders, several federal laws play an important part in affirmative action. *The Equal Pay Act of 1963* requires that equal pay be given for equal work. Positions that require equal skills, efforts, and responsibility and that are accomplished under similar work conditions should be considered equal work. The *Civil Rights Act of 1964* and its 1972 Amendments, Title VII of the Civil Rights Act of 1964, prohibits discrimination in employment based on race, color, sex, religion, or national origin.[35] Generally, these laws are designed to prevent unlawful discrimination

---

33. Francine S. Hall and Maryann H. Albrecht, *The Management of Affirmative Action,* (Santa Monica, CA: Goodyear, 1979), 26.

34. George T. Felkenes, "Affirmative Action: Concept, Development, and Legality," *Diversity, Affirmative Action and Law Enforcement,* George T. Felkenes and Peter Charles Unsinger, Ed.s, (Springfield, IL: Charles C. Thomas, 1992), 4–6.

35. Francine S. Hall and Maryann H. Albrecht, 16.

1. In employee hiring or firing, wages and salaries, promotions, or in any terms, conditions, or privileges of employment;
2. In union membership, classification, or referrals for employment which cause or attempt to cause an employer to discriminate;
3. In employment agency discrimination in classifying or referring for employment;
4. In employer labor unions, or joint labor-management committee training, retraining, apprenticeship, or employment advertising.[36]

In the latter part of the twentieth century, however, there is still some controversy regarding affirmative action. There are individuals who consider affirmative action programs to be quota systems that lead to preferential treatment for select groups of people. Former St. Louis Police Chief Clarence Harmon sued the St. Louis police department in 1980 forcing them to adopt an affirmative action plan which resulted in the hiring and promotion of black and female police officers. In the mid-1980s Harmon began to change his mind when he noticed that the department was hiring black recruits who scored poorly on entrance examinations. He came to believe that many young black police officers were using affirmative action as a kind of crutch. He explained that "Some of [his] younger colleagues will be loath to admit this but for many of them affirmative action has meant that they didn't have to do some of the things they should have done to compete."[37]

Those who support affirmative action believe that it is still needed to correct the discriminatory practices of the past. They believe that the playing field is still not equal. On the other hand, some organizations believe that the white-male work force is shrinking and that a smaller hiring pool would not be good for their companies. They claim that affirmative action provides corporations and governmental agencies with a larger work pool to draw from.

Regardless of what one believes it should at least be recognized that the face of policing has changed. There are women and minorities performing police functions who owe their jobs primarily to affirmative action, but regardless of whether or not affirmative

---

36. ibid., 16.
37. "Black and Blue," *U.S. News and World Report* 118, No. 6, (February 1995), 43.

action will continue to be a part of America's future, women and minorities will continue to staff our nation's police departments, and their numbers will only increase. They have established their importance in the field of policing.

Summary

With the increase in multicultural awareness in American society it has becomes more commonplace in the last several decades to see groups other than white males providing police service. The roots of the involvement of women and minorities in policing can be traced to the nineteenth century; however, their roles were often limited and allowed for few opportunities for advancement. Throughout the course of the evolution of policing in America various minority groups that had been all but excluded from policework were able to obtain footholds in policing and eventually make their mark. Ultimately, the opening of the door of opportunity for minorities in policing is a result of fundamental changes occurring in American society.

A movement to get women involved in police service can be traced to the 1880s when women began to serve as matrons. It was not until 1910 that the first police woman was officially appointed by the Los Angeles Police Department. Other big city police departments followed the example. However, until the 1970s women's roles in policing were limited to dealing with juveniles, with women, and with prevention programs. In the 1970s federal legislation and affirmation action programs guaranteed opportunities for women to perform tasks identical to those assigned to their male counterparts. Today, women serve in all operational and administrative positions.

Black police officers have been involved in policing since the early nineteenth century. New Orleans had black police officers as early as 1805. Black police officers were primarily used to catch "runaway slaves" and to police free-black communities. It was not until the twentieth century that the role of black police officers increased. Northern cities began to employ blacks in greater numbers. However, it was not until the 1960s when federal legislation and affirmative action programs were implemented that blacks began to make great strides. Today, there are more black police officers, supervisors, and administrators than ever before in American policing.

Key Terms

Alice Stebbins Wells
Civil Rights Act of 1964
Chief Clarence Harmon
Chief Jerry Wilson
Equal Pay Act of 1963

Equal Employment
   Opportunity Act
Indianapolis, Indiana
slave catchers
white-slave scare

Review Questions

1. What role did the early police women play in policing?
2. What role did the early black police officers play in policing?
3. What role do women play in today's police departments?
4. What role do blacks play in today's police departments?
5. What led to the changes in the involvement of minorities in policing?

References

Applier, Janis. "Preventive Justice: The Campaign for Women Police." *Women and Criminal Justice* 3, No. 2 (1992).

"Black and Blue." *U.S. News and World Report* 118, No. 6, (February 1995).

Bloch, Peter B. and Deborah Anderson. *Policewomen on Patrol: Final Report.* Washington, DC: Police Foundation, 1974.

Bureau of Justice Statistics. *Local Police Departments, 1993.* Washington, DC: U.S. Department of Justice, 1993.

Dulaney, W. Marvin. *Black Police in America.* Bloomington, IN: Indiana University Press, 1996.

Felkenes, George T. and Peter Charles Unsinger. *Diversity, Affirmative Action, and Law Enforcement.* Springfield, IL: Charles C. Thomas, 1992.

Glastris, Paul. "The Thin White Line." *U.S. News & World Report* 117, No. 7, 1994.

Hall, Francine S. and Maryann Albrecht. *The Management of Affirmative Action.* Santa Monica, CA: Goodyear, 1979.

Higgins, Lois. "Historical Background of Policewomen's Service." *Journal of Criminal Law, Criminology, and Police Science* 41 (March/April 1951).

Leinen, Stephen H. *Gay Cops*. New Brunswick, NJ: Rutgers University Press, 1993.

National Advisory Commission on Criminal Justice Standards and Goals. *Police*. Washington, DC: U.S. Government Printing Office, 1973.

Segrave, Kerry. *Policewomen: A History*. Jefferson, NC: McFarland 1995.

President's Commission on Law Enforcement and Administration of Justice. *Task Force Report: The Police*. Washington, DC: U.S. Government Printing Office, 1967.

Walker, Samuel. *A Critical History of Police Reform*. Lexington, MA: Lexington Books, 1977,

Walker, Samuel. "Employment of Black and Hispanic Police Officers." *Review of Applied Urban Research* XI, No. 6, 1983.

CHAPTER 10

Police Recruiting, Education, and Training

Major Issues

1. Should the major phases of police recruiting be uniform for all police agencies?
2. All police officers hired should possess a college degree.
3. Police training needs to be updated to prepare police officers for the multi-cultural dynamics of society.

Introduction

The importance of recruiting, education, and training cannot be overstated if our communities expect to have quality police officers. Our society should demand that all police officers enforce our laws impartially and fairly without regard to race, ethnic background, gender, or socio-economic status.

The initial stage of recruiting and hiring and the selection of a person to become a police officer can have unforseen implications for the community. Often it is the new recruit who is most likely to be found guilty of brutality or to be in violation of departmental policies. All police candidates need to be carefully recruited and selected and only the best candidates should be hired.

A team is "only as good as its weakest link." The same philosophy holds true for a police organization. If poorly qualified candidates are hired who can not adapt to the pressures of police work, should we not be surprised when those individuals find themselves in difficulties that embarrass the police agency that hired them?

In a era when a large number of Americans have obtained a college degree, should we not expect the same from our police officers? Furthermore, if policing is as complex, demanding, and difficult as police administrators, police officers, and scholars claim, then we as citizens should demand that all police officers possess at least a bachelors degree. We should require our police officers to have the kind of professionalism that comes with a college education. The police vocation will never be recognized as a professional occupation until all police officers possess a college education.

Another requirement of professionalism is training. Police officers need training before they enter the profession. They must also be expected to continue their training throughout their police careers.

Police officers have to be trained to handle the various situations they will encounter, like handling a domestic dispute or interviewing a witness to a crime. They need continuous training to keep abreast of the changes in policing. Only by lifelong training can police officers function as professionals.

But professionalism begins with the recruiting process. Only by recruiting quality police officers can a police department hope to have a quality police department.

Recruiting

Outstanding police officers are usually the result of outstanding recruitment programs, and the President's Crime Commission *Task Force Report: The Police* concurs. The *Report* states, "Complexities inherent in the policing function dictate that officers possess a high degree of intelligence, education, tact, sound judgement, physical courage, emotional stability, impartiality, and honesty."[1] The *Task Force* on the police considered it gross negligence that professional standards for the police service had never been set. The failure to establish police standards has been costly to both the police and to society.

In the late 1960s the *Task Force* found that—with the exception of the physical requirements for new police officers—the selection requirements and the procedures used by a majority of police departments did not generally screen out unsuitable candidates. Because of the poor selection process, many police officers were hired who were incompetent, corrupt, abusive, and were unable to gain the respect of their fellow police officers. Potentially, an incompetent and abusive officer could trigger a riot, damage the relationship between the community and the police agency, and probably do permanent damage to the reputation of any of the citizens of the community.[2]

The recruitment and selection of police personnel is ultimately a responsibility of police administrators. Police managers are obligated to organize, plan, and budget funds for police officer recruitment.

---

1. The President's Commission on Law Enforcement and Administration of Justice, *Task Force Report: The Police,* (Washington, DC: U.S. Government Printing Office, 1967), 125.

2. Ibid., 125.

The National Advisory Commission on Criminal Justice Standards and Goals advocates that all police agencies should aggressively recruit applicants to fill police officer vacancies. Additionally, the National Advisory Commission had the following recommendations for police recruiting:

1. The agency should administer its own recruitment program.
   a. The agency should assign to specialized recruitment activities employees who are thoroughly familiar with the policies and procedures of the agency and with the ideals and practices of professional law enforcement.
   b. Agencies without the expertise to recruit police applicants successfully should seek expertise from the central personnel agency at the appropriate level of State or local government, or form cooperative personnel systems with other police agencies that are likely to benefit from such an association: every police agency, however, should retain administrative control of its recruitment activities.
2. The police agency should direct recruitment exclusively toward attracting the best qualified candidates. In so doing, it:
   a. Should make college-educated applicants the primary targets of recruitment efforts,
   b. Should concentrate recruitment resources according to the agency's need for personnel from varied ethnic backgrounds.
3. Residency should be eliminated as a pre-employment requirement.
4. The police agency should provide application and testing procedures at decentralized locations in order to facilitate the applicant's access to the selection process.
   a. The initial application form should be a short, simple record of the minimum information necessary to initiate the selection process.
5. The police agency should allow for the completion of minor routine requirements, such as obtaining a valid driver's license, after the initial application but before employment.
6. The police agency, through various incentives, should involve all agency personnel in the recruitment and selection process.
7. The police agency should seek professional assistance—such as that available in advertising, media, and public relations

firms—to research and develop increasingly effective recruitment methods.

8. The police agency should evaluate the effectiveness of all recruitment methods continually so that successful methods may be emphasized and unsuccessful ones discarded.[3]

Many police agencies have adopted many of the National Advisory Commission's recommendations. Progressive police departments are continuously evaluating their recruitment process. However, before the recruiting of police officers can begin there must be *openings* for police officers. Openings for police officers occur because of termination, attrition, retirement, or a general increase in the need for sworn police officers. Vacancy announcements are advertised in newspapers, television, radio, state unemployment offices, city personnel offices, police personnel offices, college criminal justice departments, police department bulletin boards, church bulletin boards, and a variety of other sources.

Vacancy announcements often include a job description that outlines the duties of a sworn police officer. The job description should list the specific tasks and skills required for the position. The announcement should indicate that the right candidate should have a college education, have no record of felony arrests, and be free from drug use. Age minimums and maximums and weight or height requirements should also be included.

Normally all candidates interested in applying for a police position are required to complete a written application. The application, depending upon the requirements of the police agency, can be quite extensive. General information requirements include: name, nickname, date of birth, current residence, past residence(s), social security number, driver's license number, schools and college attended, and current employment and past employment. Questions pertaining to the applicant's use of medication and the applicant's arrest and driving record should also be included. Applicants may be requested to provide documentation—a birth certificate, a driver's license, high school and college transcripts—to verify information requested in the application.

After the applicant has applied for the position of police officer, the first step in the hiring process is the written examination. The written examination's date, time, and location should be described

---

3. National Advisory Commission on Criminal Justice Standards and Goals, *Police,* (Washington, DC: U.S. Government Printing Office, 1973), 321.

in the job announcement. If the applicant does not take the written examination or fails to obtain the minimum passing score, he will be eliminated from the hiring process. The written examination often tests math skills, reading comprehension, and possibly grammar and writing skills. The written examination may vary from agency to agency.

Applicants who successfully pass the written examination are often required to pass an agility test. Candidates are informed of the date, location, and composition of the agility test, and those who fail to take the agility test or to meet the minimum passing requirements are eliminated from the hiring process. The agility test may differ for various police agencies, but the general purpose of the agility test is to determine the physical strength, endurance, and motor skills of the candidate.

The third stage of the hiring process is the background investigation of the candidates who have successfully passed the agility test. Depending upon the police agency conducting the background investigation, the candidate's background check can either be superficial or very thorough. At the very minimum, the background check will require that the applicant be finger-printed and that the candidate's fingerprints be forwarded to the state fingerprint depository and to the FBI. The purpose of this process is to determine whether or not the candidate has a criminal record, which would mean that he could not be a police officer. Progressive police agencies conduct a thorough background investigation that takes several months. The background check can determine if the applicant had any financial difficulties or indebtedness; had any record of substance abuse, including the abuse of drugs or alcohol; or falsified or misrepresented any information on the written application. All employment positions and schools and colleges will be verified by a background check. The background investigation will include interviewing college professors, high school teachers, fellow workers, prior employers, neighbors, friends and acquaintances to evaluate the candidate's character, adaptability, and fitness to perform police work.

If the candidate successfully meets the requirements of the police agency for the background investigation, then he proceeds to the next step. However, if the candidate does not meet the criteria of the background investigation, the candidate will no longer be considered for a position as a police officer.

The next step the candidate must successfully complete for many police agencies is the polygraph test. It should be noted that not all police agencies have this requirement. The use of the polygraph is used to determine an applicant's suitability for police service. The polygraph is used to verify information supplied by the applicant in the written application for police employment or if pertinent information was overlooked. The polygraph test usually focuses on the candidate's morals, use of drugs and alcohol, and any other illegal activities. Depending upon the policy of the police agency, a person may not be disqualified if they are unsuccessful in passing the polygraph test. Some police departments may also give the candidate a second chance to be reexamined.

The medical examination of the applicant usually follows the polygraph examination. Police agencies expect candidates to be healthy if they are to function as police officers. Generally, their weight has to be proportionate to their height—for example, a five-foot-tall person should not weigh 250 pounds (though it is important to note that police departments are no longer legally permitted to have height requirements). Most police agencies also require all candidates to be tested for the use of illegal drugs, and the thoroughness of the medical examination depends upon the police agency. The medical examination can be in depth, requiring that the applicant submit to all kinds of sophisticated medical tests. It is also normal for all applicants to required to submit to eye examinations. The applicant is then either eliminated from the hiring process or continues to the next phase if the results of the medical examination are acceptable.

A psychological examination of all candidates is usually the norm for police agencies, and often such exams are conducted by a clinical psychologist. The purpose of the psychological exam is to determine the "emotional fitness" of the candidate to perform police service and to determine if the candidate suffers from mental illness which would eliminate him from further consideration. There are a wide variety of psychological tests that the psychologist can give the applicant. Psychological testing could include either an intellectual assessment, a personality assessment, or a clinical interview. The psychological test consists of either a questionnaire and/or a face-to-face interview in which the psychologist has the opportunity to observe the applicant's behavior. The psychologist's report can also eliminate the candidate from further consideration.

An oral interview conducted by the police chief, by deputies, or by an oral board is usually part of the screening process. The purpose of the oral interview is to provide the police administration with a way to assess a candidate's suitability for police service. During the interview process the police interviewer should follow a structured interview that asks the same questions of all of the candidates. Specific questions pertaining to sex, religion, race, age, and ethnic origin should not be asked. The police interviewer should be familiar with affirmative action and equal employment-opportunity-commission guidelines. All police interviews conducted by a police administrator should follow all state and federal laws and guidelines established for the pre-employment interview.

If the candidate successfully passes all of the phases of the screening process, then he or she is considered for a position. Most police hiring lists have some kind of sequence for ranking the candidates. Based on his or her ranking, the candidate may or not be hired. For example, if a police department has one opening it can usually offer the police position to any one of the top three candidates on the list, but it is entirely possible that the job may never be offered to the first candidate on the list.

The screening process and its various phases may differ from police agency to police agency. Police departments often develop screening processes that meet their own unique requirements. Although there are similarities in the screening processes used by the police, candidates for police service are best advised to be aware of the differences.

Education

Criminal justice education can be traced to 1916 when the University of California at Berkeley established a law enforcement program for police officers. The initial impetus for the development of crime-related studies came primarily from Police Chief August Vollmer in Berkeley, California. Chief Vollmer, in conjunction with a Berkeley law faculty member, devised a program in criminology.[4]

In the summer of 1918, the University of California at Los Angeles offered a program in the Department of Criminology for police women. The University of California at Berkeley recorded a "first" in 1923 when it awarded an A.B. degree to a police officer in Criminology. In 1925, the Graduate School of Harvard University established the Bureau of Street Traffic Research program. Al-

---

4. University of California at Berkeley, *Bulletin of School of Criminology,* (1966–67), 7.

though this was not a degree program, it was the initial entry of prestigious Eastern universities into criminal justice post-secondary education. Through the 1920s cooperation between institutions of higher education and criminal justice increased.[5]

The period between 1930 and 1945 represents a time of gradual expansion for criminal justice education. The National Commission on Law Observance and Enforcement, in 1931, proposed the application of science to police work in the hope of better coping with the problem of crime[6]—

> Universities and colleges responded to the National Commission's recommendation by establishing new criminal justice programs and expanding existing ones. In 1933, the University of California, Berkeley, authorized a bachelor's degree program in Criminology. A baccalaureate degree program in Police Administration was begun in 1935 by Michigan State University. This program was characterized by four years of academic study followed by eighteen months of field instruction. Such institutions as Ohio State, Texas, A&M, Northwestern, and the Universities of Florida, Hawaii, and Texas all offered criminal justice course work. The programs established during this period were primarily designed for police personnel.[7]

Following World War II, veterans who were interested in the criminal justice field received financial assistance from the G.I. Bill. This prompted institutions of higher education to expand their programs to meet the resulting demands.

In 1949, twenty-six post-secondary institutions offering degree programs in criminal justice were identified; of these, eleven were concentrated in law enforcement, five in corrections, four in other criminal justice fields, and six in related areas.[8] In 1959, there were seventy-seven criminal justice programs among fifty-six different

---

5. William E. Caldwell, "LEEP—Its Development and Potential," *The Police Chief* 37 (August 1970), 24.

6. *National Commission on Law Observance and Enforcement: Report on the Police,* (Washington, DC: Government Printing Office, 1931), 85.

7. Charles W. Tenney, Jr., *Higher Education in Criminal Justice: A Status Report,* (Washington, DC: U.S. Department of Justice, LEAA, 1971), 26.

8. The National Manpower Survey of the Criminal Justice System, *Criminal Justice Education and Training* 5, (Washington, DC: Government Printing Office, 1977), 49.

institutions in nineteen states. These included twenty-six associate, twenty-one baccalaureate, twenty-one master's, and nine doctoral programs.[9]

The first major thrust for improving criminal justice education occurred in 1963 when the Ford Foundation provided a grant to the International Association of Chiefs of Police. As a result of this grant, many community colleges and universities established law enforcement programs. The grant resulted in the establishment of over two hundred programs throughout the United States over a four-year period. Prior to the Ford Foundation Grant, there were fewer than one hundred such programs, most of which were in California.[10]

The impetus for criminal justice education began in 1967. During that year, the President's Commission on Law Enforcement and Administration of Justice made recommendations that appeared in *The Challenge of Crime in a Free Society*. The report recommended that "The ultimate aim of all police departments should be that all personnel with general enforcement powers have baccalaureate degrees."[11] The President's Commission had the following to say about the quality of police personnel and education:

> The police personnel need that the Commission has found to be almost universal is improved quality. Generally, law enforcement have met their difficult responsibilities with commendable zeal, determination, and devotion to duty, however, Commission surveys reflect that there is substantial variance in the quality of police personnel from top to bottom.
>
> The Commission believes that substantially raising the quality of police personnel would inject into police work knowledge, expertise, initiative, and integrity that would contribute importantly to improved crime control.
>
> The word "quality" is used here in a comprehensive sense. One thing it means is a high standard of education

9. Ibid., 26–27.

10. Charles E. Grant, "Police Science Programs in American Universities-Colleges-Junior Colleges," *The Police Chief* 32 (May 1965), 32–34.

11. The President's Commission on Law Enforcement and the Administration of Justice, *The Challenge of Crime in a Free Society,* (Washington, DC: Government Printing Officer), 109.

for policemen.... A policemen today is poorly equipped for his job if he does not understand the legal issues involved in his everyday work, the nature of the social problems he constantly encounters, the psychology of those people whose attitudes towards the law differ from his. Such understanding is not easy to acquire without the kind of broad general knowledge that higher education imparts, and without such understanding a policemen's response to many of the situations he meets is likely to be impulsive or doctrinaire. Police candidates must be sought in colleges.[12]

The 1960s was a decade of social disruption and violence. It was common during that era for police to confront students at universities and to confront anti-Vietnam war protesters. Also, the inability of the police to cope with the ghetto riots and their apparent helplessness in curtailing the spiraling crime rate led both liberal and conservative politicians to believe that higher education for police officers was desirable.

The police were charged not only with being ineffective in controlling disorder but also with aggravating and precipitating violence through harassment of minority ghetto dwellers, student dissidents, and other citizens.

The National Advisory Commission on Civil Disorders discovered that, in the cities, aggressive police patrolling and harassment were a result of society's fear of crime, and that these practices only created hostility and conflict between the police and minorities.

In Newark, in Detroit, in Watts, in Harlem—in practically every city that has experienced racial disruption since the summer of 1964—abrasive relationships between police and Negroes and other minority groups have been a major source of grievance, tension, and ultimately disorder.[13]

Finally, President Johnson's Campus on Campus Unrest also advocated the belief that education for the police might assist in decreasing police/citizen confrontation. The Commission stated that

---

12. Ibid., 107.

13. *Report of the National Advisory Commission on Civil Disorders,* (Washington, DC: U.S. Government Printing Office, 1968), 229.

> Law enforcement agencies desperately need better educated
> and better trained policemen.... There should be special mon-
> etary incentives for all who enter the police service with col-
> lege degrees or who obtain degrees while in police service.[14]

The national Commission's consensus was that, in order to improve law enforcement, the quality of police personnel had to be
upgraded through education. There is little doubt that police personnel had limited education. The median educational level of police personnel in 1966 was 12.4 years. *Fortune* magazine estimated,
in December of 1968, that fewer than ten percent of American police officers had been to college; in October, 1968, *Time* reported
that Detroit police recruits were from the bottom 25 percent of
their high school graduating class.[15]

Education is usually based on a solid foundation of liberal arts. A
criminal justice practitioner or potential practitioner must understand
how criminal justice relates to American society and the democratic
process. Higher education exposes students to ideas, concepts, and
problem-solving techniques. The educational process aims to develop
individuals who know how to live within a group, individuals who
understand conflicts in our society, and who possess an understanding of the motivations, the stress, and the tensions of other people in
society. An individual with this knowledge and understanding has
the ability to apply past information to new situations.[16]

A college education will not transform an intellectually wanting
person into an accomplished one. But all things being equal, the
college educated individual is more qualified than the high school
graduate. The college trained person has more experience with
people and with new situations. His or her responsibility and adaptability to new surroundings have been tested. In addition, he or she
has been exposed to various cultural characteristics and ethical and
racial backgrounds. This exposure should eliminate or reduce prejudice and bias. More importantly, a formal education should teach

14. *U.S. President's Commission on Campus Unrest,* (Washington, DC: Government Printing Office), 154.

15. James B. Jacobs and Samuel B. Magdovitz, "At LEEP's End? A Review
of the Law Enforcement Education Program," *Journal of Police Science and Administration* 5, (March 1977), 2.

16. William H. Hewitt, *The Objectives of Formal Police Education* 9 (Novem-
ber-December 1964), 26.

individuals to check their judgments regarding their own prejudices in favor of applying more tranquil analysis.[17]

One of the primary benefits of higher education—not only for the police but also for the field of criminal justice—is the improvement of policing and the criminal justice process. Academic study of policing and the criminal justice process is needed to identify problems and to identify ways in which those problems can be solved.

The importance of setting educational standards for the selection of police officers has been recognized for several decades. The National Advisory Commission of Criminal Justice Standards and Goals recommended, in the early 1970s, that in order for police officers to perform their police duties properly every police department should establish guidelines for entry level educational requirements. These recommendations are that

1. Every police agency should require immediately, as a condition of immediate employment, the completion of at least 1 year of education (30 semester units) at an accredited college or university. Otherwise qualified police applicants who do not satisfy this condition, but have earned a high school diploma or its equivalent, should be employed under a contract requiring completion of the educational requirement within 3 years of initial employment;

2. Every police agency should, no later than 1975, require as a condition of initial employment the completion of at least 2 years of education (60 semester units) at a accredited college or university;

3. Every police agency should, no later than 1978, require as a condition of initial employment the completion of at least 3 years of education (90 semester units) at an accredited college or university;

4. Every police agency should no later than 1982, require as a condition of initial employment the completion of at least 4 years of education (120 semester units or a baccalaureate degree) at an accredited college or university.[18]

---

17. Ibid., 27.

18. National Advisory Commission on Criminal Justice Standards and Goals, *The Police,* (Washington, DC: U.S. Government Printing Office, 1973), 369.

Although the National Advisory Commission on Criminal Justice Standards and Goals has not been mandated by all police agencies there are more police departments requiring a baccalaureate degree than when the National Advisory Commission made its recommendations. Even though most police departments have not made it a requirement to have a baccalaureate degree to be a police officer, there are more college educated police officers in American police departments than in all of this country's previous history. Many departments require a baccalaureate degree, while others require a two-year Associate Degree and still others require that an officer must have a degree in order to be promoted.

Studies conducted by the Police Executive Forum (PERF) found that approximately 62 percent of the nation's police agencies serving communities with more than 50,000 inhabitants had some kind of educational incentive program. However, only approximately 14 percent of police agencies required some amount of higher education as a prerequisite to obtaining employment.[19] One constant theme was discovered by Carter, Sapp, and Stephens in a study of education for police agencies. They discovered that agencies were apprehensive that if a higher education requirement was challenged, either in court or through labor arbitration, two problems would surface:

1. They did not feel that a higher education requirement could be quantitatively validated to show job-relatedness, and
2. They feared such a requirement would be shown to be discriminatory toward minorities, thus not meeting the provisions of Title VII of the Civil Rights Act of 1964 nor being consistent with the Equal Employment Opportunity Commission (EEOC) guidelines.[20]

Although the two preceding reasons for not making higher education mandatory have been rationalized by some police administrators, there have been sufficient governmental studies, court decisions, and research that substantiate the value of higher education for today's police officer. The world of the late 1990s is much more

19. David L. Carter, Allen D. Sapp, and Darrel W. Stephens, "Higher Education as a Bona Fide Occupational Qualifications (BFOQ) for Police: A Blueprint," *American Journal of Police* 7, No.2, (1988), 1.

20. Ibid., 1.

sophisticated and complex than any preceding period of American history. Today's police officer needs to interact within a multi-cultural environment and have the ability to use highly technical equipment. The police officer of the late 1990s will be held more accountable for his actions and is expected to have a more thorough knowledge of legal rights of both suspects and victims, to be a problem-solver, and to be a negotiator rather than an enforcer. The advantages of a college education for police officers are numerous:

1. It develops a broader base of information for decision making;
2. It allows for additional years and experiences for maturity;
3. Course Requirements and achievements inculcate responsibility in the individual;
4. Both general education courses and course-work in the major (particularly a criminal justice major) permit the individual to learn more about the history of the country and the democratic process and to appreciate constitutional rights, values, and the democratic form of government;
5. A college education engenders the ability to flexibly handle difficult or ambiguous situations with greater creativity or innovation;
6. For criminal justice majors, the academic experience permits a better view of the "big picture" of the criminal justice system and provides both a better understanding of and appreciation for the prosecutorial, courts, and correctional roles;
7. Higher education develops a greater empathy for minorities and their discriminatory experiences through both course-work and interaction within the academic environment;
8. It allows a greater understanding and tolerance for persons with differing lifestyles and ideologies which can translate into more effective communications and community relationships in the practice of policing;
9. The college-educated officer is likely to be less rigid in decision-making in fulfilling the role of the police while balancing that role with the spirit of the democratic process in dealing with variable situations and is likely to have a greater tendency to wisely use discretion to deal with individual cases rather than applying the same rules to all cases;
10. The college experience will help officers communicate and respond to crime and to service the needs of the public in a competent manner with civility and humanity;

11. The educated officer is more innovative and flexible when dealing with complex policing programs and strategies such as problem-oriented policing, community policing, task force responses, etc.;

12. The college-officer is better equipped to perform tasks and make continual policing decisions with minimal, and sometimes no, supervision;

13. College helps develop better overall community relations skills including the ability to engender the respect and confidence of the community;

14. More "professional" demeanor and performance is exhibited by college-educated officers;

15. The educated officer is able to cope better with stress and is more likely to seek assistance with personal or stress-related problems, thereby making the officer a more stable and reliable employee;

16. The officer can better adapt his/her style of communication and behavior to a wider range of social conditions and "classes";

17. The college experience tends to make the officer less authoritarian and less cynical with respect to the milieu of policing; and

18. Organizational change is more readily acceptable by and adapted to by a college-educated officer.[21]

Training

There is evidence that New York City developed a rudimentary training program in 1853. However, it would be an exaggeration to use the word "school" to describe it. Referring to the program as the first to be established as a unit independent of the police department, Raymond Fosdick commented:

> Because of the varied use of the term "school," it is difficult to determine when the New York institution was first inaugurated. If a single instructor, a number of students, and a certain amount of time devoted to instruction constitute a school, then the New York department has been equipped with a school for half a century. In early times, however, the instruc-

---

21. Ibid., 16–18.

tion was of the elementary kind. Police recruits were taught for a period of thirty days by a sergeant specially detailed for that purpose, and in addition the students were sent out on patrol during certain hours of the day and night.[22]

The New York training program represents more than 100 years of development, but that progress has not always been in a forward direction. As Fosdick states,

> The development of these educational activities in New York has been irregular and uncertain, dependent upon the interest and enthusiasm of the changing police commissioners. At times the teaching corps has been enlarged and the instruction broadened only to be reduced by succeeding commissioners. The elementary preparatory instruction in laws, ordinances and rules has for the most part remained fairly constant, and has never been discarded altogether, although considerable fluctuation has occurred in the amount and variety of physical drill.[23]

The New York City training school was known as the "School of Instruction" and included on-the-job training in its thirty- day curriculum. By 1914, the need for refresher training was recognized, and senior members were retrained in laws, procedures, regulations, and ordinances in order to keep them abreast of current changes. In addition, specialized training was conducted for police officers assigned to bicycles, to motorcycles, and to traffic duty. In 1914, New York City police training was divided into four branches: recruit, refresher, specialized, and pre-promotion. At this time, recruit training was increased from thirty days to six weeks and, shortly thereafter, to twelve weeks. The New York program was probably the best offered by any police department in the country.[24]

Fosdick stressed the importance of training and utilized the example of New York City:

> Surely, the experience not only of New York but of other large cities—like London and Paris—amply demonstrate the

22. Raymond Fosdick, *American Police Systems,* (New York: Century Company, 1920), 299.

23. Ibid., 300.

24. The U.S. Department of Justice, *Police Training and Performance Study,* (Washington, DC: U.S. Government Printing Office, 1970), 7.

fact that a properly equipped and administered school is perhaps the most indispensable single feature of the police force of
a modern community. For it must be repeated that the primary problem in police administration is the problem of personnel. The establishment of reporting systems and the building up of organizational schemes cannot be wisely disregarded
or slighted, for they are important and have a definite place in
regulating the daily work of the force. But they are aids and
means, not ends. The heart of police work is the contact of
the individual policemen with the citizen.[25]

Although the City of New York was at the vanguard of police
training, other cities were also becoming involved. For instance,
Berkeley established a training school for police officers in 1911, and
Philadelphia followed suit in 1913. In 1916, the University of California at Berkeley created the first training school for police officers
at a university.[26] During the 1920s, the Los Angeles Police Department underwent broad changes: standards for personnel were ele-
vated and their training program was lengthened and intensified.
The New Orleans Police Department initiated a medical training
program for its officers, and in 1922, it received a national award for
being the only police department fully equipped to provide first aid
to its citizens.[27]

During the 1930s, significant developments occurred in police
training. By the end of the decade, every state, with the exception
of Wisconsin, had created a state police department. These state organizations were leaders in implementing progressive training programs, most of which were three months in duration. New York
established the first state police academy, with Pennsylvania following suit. By 1934, Michigan, New Jersey, Connecticut, Oregon,
Washington, and Texas had established police academies. These early
training schools motivated municipal police departments to implement training programs of their own.[28]

In 1935, the Federal Bureau of Investigation initiated their own
involvement in the training of police personnel of state and local

25. Fosdick., 305–307.
26. William J. Bopp and Donald O. Schultz, *A Short History of American Law Enforcement,* (Springfield, IL: Charles C. Thomas, 1972), 84–85.
27. Ibid., 104.
28. Ibid., 111.

government with the establishment of the Police Training School. Presently, the FBI offers four types of training assistance to local and state governments. The first is the National Academy, the successor to the Police Training School. The National Academy is an eleven-week, college-level training program that enrolls approximately 1,000 police officers yearly at the municipal and state level. The Bureau also offers specialized training that ranges from three days to four weeks and covers such topics as hostage negotiation and training instruction. Their third effort offers the services of FBI agents as lecturers at sites designated by state and local police agencies. Finally, there is the National Executive Institute, a management training program for chiefs and deputy chiefs.[29]

The post World War II period saw more progress in police training. Recruit and in-service training programs burgeoned in local police agencies. In 1948, the Los Angeles Police Department became the first police department to inaugurate roll call training in which officers were given short periods of training prior to going on duty. By the end of the decade, most police departments of any size had established a police academy. Those that did not either sent their officers to training schools nearby or engaged in on-the-job training. The South, which was behind the rest of the country in establishing training schools, began to develop them as New Orleans, Miami, and Augusta inaugurated training programs.[30]

In 1967, the President's Commission on Law Enforcement and Administration of Justice *The Task Force Report: The Police* made the following comments pertaining to recruit training: "No person, regardless of his individual qualifications, is prepared to perform police work on native ability alone."[31] The *Task Force Report* further stated that "Training is one of the most importance means of upgrading the services for a police department."[32]

The National Advisory Commission on Criminal Justice Standards and Goals on the *Police* recommended that all states make basic police training mandatory. The Commission also recommended that a state police training commission be established by the

---

29. The National Manpower Survey of the Criminal Justice System, 246.

30. Bopp and Schultz, 122.

31. The President's Commission on Law Enforcement and Administration of Justice *Task Force Report: The Police,* (Washington, DC: U.S. Government Printing Office, 1967), 137.

32. Ibid., 137.

state government to oversee mandatory police training; that the states should establish a minimum curriculum, certify all police training facilities, inspect and evaluate training facilities, and certify police graduates; and that the state police training commission should be represented by local police agencies to guarantee that police training programs meet the need of local police agencies.[33]

The basic police training curriculum generally covers six categories: law, the criminal justice field, patrol, investigation, human values, police proficiency (i.e., first aid, firearms, and self-defense tactics), and administration. The Commission recommended that all police recruits receive at least a minimum 400 hours of training. They recommended that the formalized classroom training be followed by field training for at least four months.[34] The Commission encouraged all police training facilities to develop effective training programs that covered specific subject matters that are fundamental to meeting the needs of the police agencies and their communities. The Commission recommended that

1. Every police training academy should insure that the duration and content of its training programs cover the subject every employee needs to learn to perform acceptably the tasks he will be assigned;
2. Every police training academy should define specific courses according to the performance objective of the course and should specify what the trainee must do to demonstrate achievement of the performance objective;
3. Every police training academy serving more than one police agency should enable the police chief executives of participating agencies to choose for their personnel elective subjects in addition to minimum training;
4. Every police training academy should insure that its training programs satisfy State standards for police training as well as meet the needs of participating police agencies and that its training is timely and effective. These measures should at least include:

33. National Advisory Commission on Criminal Justice Standards and Goals, *Police,* (Washington, DC: U.S. Government Printing Office, 1973), 381.
34. Ibid., 381–382.

a. Regular review and evaluation of all training programs by an advisory body composed of police practitioners from participating agencies;

b. Periodic field observation of the operations of participating police agencies by the training staff; and

c. Continual critique of training programs through feedback from police employees who have completed the training programs and have subsequently utilized that training in field operations and from their field supervisors.[35]

The first states to establish the Peace Officers' Standards and Training Commissions (POST) were New York and California in 1959. By the early 1980s most states had established POST bodies. Most states like Kansas have enacted legislation creating a Peace Officers' Standards and Training Commission. The Kansas POST consists of twelve members including the Superintendent of the Kansas Highway Patrol, the Director of the Kansas Bureau of Investigation, three sheriffs, three police chiefs, a training officer from a training facility, a commissioned police officer, a district attorney, and a member representing the public at large. The Kansas POST Commission is responsible for overseeing the Kansas Law Enforcement Training Act.

The Kansas Law Enforcement Training Act requires that all full-time police officers who work at least 1,000 hours per year must receive at least 320 hours of police training. Those part-time police officers who work less than 1,000 hours per year are required to receive 80 hours of police training. The training for both full-time and part-time police officers has to be completed within the first year of police service. All full- time police officers beginning in the second year of police service are required on a annual basis to complete 40 hours of police training. Failure of a full-time police officer to complete his annual training—usually referred to as in-service training—will be suspended from work without pay until the police officer has completed his annual training (the Kansas Law Enforcement Training Act makes no mention of annual training for part-time police officers). Under the Kansas Law Enforcement Training Act a recruit must meet the following criteria in order to be admitted to an approved police training facility:

1. The recruit must be a citizen of the United States;

---

35. Ibid., 388.

2. He or she must have been finger-printed and a search of local, state and national fingerprint files must have been made to determine whether or not the applicant has a criminal record;

3. He or she must not have been convicted, must not have an expunged conviction, and on or after July, 1995, he or she must not have been placed on diversion by any state or the federal government for a crime which is a felony or its equivalent under the uniform code of military justice;

4. He or she must be the holder of a high school diploma or furnish evidence of successful completion of an examination indicating an equivalent achievement;

5. He or she must be of good moral character;

6. He or she must be free of any physical or mental condition that might adversely affect the applicant's performance of a police officer's or law enforcement officer's duties; and

7. He or she must be at least 21 years of age.[36]

The POST Commissions established throughout the country enable a state agency to establish standards for policing without taking control over police training programs away from the local agencies.

There is some degree of diversity among the state POST Commissions. Some POST Commissions are deeply involved in program areas while others are not. For instance, some states have set in motion mandatory selection standards while other have not, and the minimum amount of basic police training varies from state to state—some states may require six weeks of training while others may require sixteen weeks.

The POST Commissions throughout the country have also collaborated to create a professional organization—*The International Association of Directors of Law Enforcement Standards and Training* (IADLEST)—comprised of POST commission directors and staff members for the specific purpose of promoting shared programs and goals.[37]

Training for police officers begins with basic recruit training and continues throughout the course of an officer's career. All police officers need to maintain their skills with firearms and first aid. In addition, police officers are often called upon to obtain new and spe-

---

36. Kansas Law Enforcement Training Center.

37. Albert A. Apa, "Police Officer Standards & Training Commissions: Three Decades of Growth, *The Police Chief* 57 (November 1990), 30.

Wichita Police Department
Police Basic Training Curriculum Comparison

The basic law enforcement course curriculum of "Not less than 320 Hours" as mandated by K.S.A. 74-5604(a) in comparison to the basic law enforcement curriculum of the wichita Police Training Academy.

	Mandated	WPD
I. LAW	47 hours	
A. U.S. Constitution and Bill of Rights	2	2
B. Kansas Criminal Justice System	2	2
C. Testifying in Court	2	2
D. Kansas Criminal Code and Procedure	10	11
E. Laws of Arrest, Search and Seizure	8	8
F. Kansas Juvenile Code and Procedures	2	2
G. Kansas Alcohol Beverage Control Laws	2	2
H. Kansas Traffic Code (Title 11)	4	4
I. Laws of Evidence	2	2
J. Civil and Criminal Liabilities of Police	2	3
K. Use of Force - Legal Aspects	3	10
L. Civil Process	4	N/A
M. Legal Guidelines in Interrogation	8	8
II. POLICE PATROL PROCEDURES	40 hours	
A. Introduction to Patrol	3	3
B. Crowd Control/Chemical Agents	2	5
C. Officer Survival	4	8
D. Mechanics of Arrest	3	3
E. Introduction to EVOC	4	4
F. Criminal Justice Information Systems	2	4
G. DUI Recognition and Apprehension	8	20
H. Vehicle Stops	4	4
I. Building Searches	1	2
J. Crimes in Progress Calls	1	1
K. Hazardous Material Awareness Level	4	4
L. Handcuffing and Search Techniques	2	8
M. Occupant Protection Usage and Enforcement	2	2
III. POLICE INVESTIGATION PROCEDURES	72 hours	
A. Collecting, Recording and Protecting Physical Evidence	5	8
B. Narcotics and Dangerous Drugs	6	7
C. Laboratory Services and Polygraphy	4	4
D. Techniques of Interviews, Admissions and Statements	5	6
E. Accident Investigation	33	32
F. Arson Investigation	3	4
G. Developing Informants	1	1
H. Bomb Calls, Threats and Investigations	2	8
I. Crimes Against Persons	11	30.5
a. Assaults		1.5
b. Robbery		4
c. Sex Crimes		4
d. Hostage Situations		4

Wichita Police Department
Police Basic Training Curriculum Comparison *continued*

	Mandated	WPD
e. Death Investigation		7
f. Hate-bias Crimes		1
g. Physical and Sexual Abuse of Children		8
J. Crimes Against Property	5	9
a. Credit Card Frauds		1
b. Checks and Frauds		1
c. Burglary		2.5
d. Theft		2
e. Vehicle		2.5
IV. HUMAN RELATIONS	35 hours	
A. Interpersonal Communications	10	23
a. Communications Process		7
b. Cultural Awareness		8
c. Police Professionalism		8
B. Crisis Situations	15	45.5
a. Domestic Violence		16
b. Crisis Intervention		8
c. Abnormal Behavior		11
d. Stress Management		10.5
C. Police-Community Relations	10	27
a. Crime Prevention		4
b. Community and Public Relations		23
V. DEMONSTRABLE PROFICIENCY AREAS	124 hours	
A. Report Writing	10	25
B. Defensive Tactics	11	54.5
C. Firearms	32	84
D. Fingerprinting	4	4
E. Emergency Vehicle Operation	8	8
F. Practical Problem in Felony Stops	8	8
G. Practical Problem in Criminal Investigation	10	10
H. Moot Court	6	6
I. Practical Problem in Officer Survival	8	8
J. Practical Problem in Crisis Intervention	4	8
K. Physical Training	15	23.5
VI. MEDICAL/EMERGENCY CARE		
A. Basic First Aid	8	8
B. CPR	8	8
C. Infectious Diseases	1	3
VII. COURSE ADMINISTRATION		
A. Orientation Pretest	2	2
B. Notetaking and Notebooks	1	1
C. Examinations	4	27.5
D. Graduation Exercises	1	1

*Information obtained from the Wichita Police Department

cialized training in areas such as supervision, stress management, and traffic accident reconstruction in order to supplement their skills and to increase their value to their departments.

Summary

The importance of recruiting, education, and training cannot be overstated if our communities expect to have quality police officers. Our society should demand that all police officers enforce our laws impartially and fairly without regard to race, ethnic background, gender, or socio-economical status.

The initial stages of recruiting, hiring, and selecting a person to become a police officer can have unforseen implications for the community.

For a community to have outstanding police officers, its police department must have an outstanding recruiting program.

The recruitment and selection of police personnel is the responsibility of police administrators. Police managers are obligated to organize, plan, and budget funds for police officer recruitment. Vacancy announcements are advertised in newspapers, on television and radio, and through state unemployment officers. Usually, vacancy announcements include a job description and a list of qualifications for the police officer position. Normally, candidates must submit a written application for the position, and before an applicant can be offered a position, there are several phases of the application process that must be successfully completed. These can include a written examination, a background investigation, an agility test, a polygraph examination, a medical examination, a psychological examination, and an oral interview.

For the past several decades, experts have recommended that higher education be a requirement for all police officers. Generally, a college education is based on a solid foundation of liberal arts. A criminal justice practitioner, or a prospective criminal justice practitioner, must understand the role of criminal justice in American society and the democratic process. Higher education also exposes students to ideas, concepts, and problem-solving techniques that are fundamental to effective policing. The educational process aims to develop individuals who know how to live within a group, who understand the conflicts inherent in our society, and who possess an understanding of the motivations and anxieties of our society. Most importantly, an individual with this knowledge has the ability to apply past information to new situations.

It is no longer acceptable to give a person a badge and gun and claim he or she is a police officer. The police officer of our decade must be properly trained before the work of policing can begin. The basic police training curriculum generally covers six categories: law, the criminal justice field, patrol, criminal investigation, human values, and police proficiency—such as the appropriate and effective use of firearms. Training for the new police recruit can vary in duration lasting anywhere from six weeks to more than a year, yet sworn police officers are expected to continue their police training throughout their careers. Most states see to this by requiring an additional forty hours of continuous training for officers each year.

Key Terms

agility test   medical examination
background investigation   oral interview
basic training   polygraph examination
continuous training   psychological examination
drug testing   vacancy announcement
higher education   written examination

Review Questions

1. Describe the phases of the police selection process.
2. Why is the recruiting process important to a police agency?
3. Why is higher education important for police service?
4. Do all police agencies have the same educational standards?
5. Discuss the need for police training.

References

Bopp, William J. and Donald O. Schultz. *A Short History American Law Enforcement.* Springfield, IL: Charles C. Thomas, 1972.

Caldwell, William E. "LEEP—Its Development and Potential." *The Police Chief* 37 (August 1970).

Carter, David L., Allen D. Sapp, and Darrel W. Stephens. "Higher Education as a Bona Fide Occupational Qualification (BFOQ) for Police: A Blueprint." *American Journal of Police* 7, No. 2 (1988).

Fosdick, Raymond. *American Police Systems.* New York: The Century Company, 1920.

Grant, Charles E. "Police Science Programs in American Universities-Colleges-Junior Colleges." *The Police Chief* 32 (May 1965).

Jacobs, James B. and Samuel B. Magdovitz. "At LEEP's End? A Review of the Law Enforcement Education Program." *Journal of Police Science and Administration* 5 (March 1977).

National Advisory Commission on Criminal Justice Standards and Goals. *The Police.* Washington, DC: U.S. Government Printing Office, 1973.

National Commission on Law Observance and Enforcement. *Report on the Police.* Washington, DC: U.S. Government Printing Office, 1931.

National Manpower Survey of the Criminal Justice System. *Criminal Justice Education and Training* 5. Washington, DC: U.S. Government Printing Office, 1977.

President's Commission on Law Enforcement and the Administration of Justice, *The Challenge of Crime in a Free Society.* Washington, DC: U.S. Government Printing Office, 1967.

President's Commission on Law Enforcement and Administration of Justice. *Task Force Report: The Police.* Washington, DC: U.S. Government Printing Office, 1967.

Report of the National Advisory Commission on Civil Disorders. Washington, DC: U.S. Government Printing Office, 1968.

U.S. Department of Justice. *Police Training and Performance Productivity.* Washington, DC: U.S. Government Printing Office, 1970.

U.S. President's Commission on Campus Unrest. Washington, DC: U.S. Government Printing Office, 1968.

University of California at Berkeley. *Bulletin of School of Criminology.* 1966–1967.

CHAPTER 11

Crime Prevention

1. Crime prevention is an important aspect of American policing.
2. Environmental design is an important aspect of crime prevention.
3. Crime prevention programs can curtail America's crime rate.
4. The police can prevent crime without citizen cooperation.

Introduction

The concept of crime prevention can be traced to ancient times when barbaric punishments were used to deter potential offenders from committing barbaric crimes. As society became more sophisticated, formal policing was implemented—eliminating the need for citizens who functioned as peacekeepers. It was during the Industrial Revolution of the 19th century that modern policing as we know it today was created to combat the crime wave of that period. In 1829 the Metropolitan Police of London were established to maintain order. One of the principal responsibilities of the New Police was to work toward

> The prevention of crime. To this great end, every effort of the police is to be directed. The security of person and property, the preservation of public tranquility, and all other objects of a police establishment will thus be better effected by detection and punishment of the offender after he has succeeded in committing the crime.[1]

As the responsibilities of the New Police evolved, the prevention of crime became an essential aspect of their duty. Although crime detection was an important part of their objective, it was so because it ultimately supported the principle of crime prevention.

According to the National Crime Prevention Institute the principles of crime prevention are

1. To prevent crime and disorder, as an alterative to their repression by military force and severity of legal punishment;

---

1. Stanley Bailey, "Crime Prevention on a Shoestring," *The Police Chief,* (March 1985), 67.

2. To maintain at all times a relationship with the public that gives reality to the historic tradition that the police and the public are the police. The police being the only members of the public who are paid to give full-time attention to duties which are incumbent on every citizen, in the interests of community welfare and existence and;

3. To recognize always that the test of police efficiency is the absence of crime and disorder and not the visible evidence of police action in dealing with them.[2]

Although the New Police were created primarily for the prevention of crime, it was not until 1963 that the United Kingdom established the National Crime Prevention Centre. In the United States, the National Crime Prevention Institute (NCPI) was established at the University of Louisville in 1971. Since that time crime prevention training has been expanded to state and regional training facilities. In addition there have been numerous scholarly studies and practical applications of various crime prevention programs.

Defining Crime Prevention

Various individuals may assign various meanings to what the term "*crime prevention*" means, so it is important to define the concept for the sake of discussion. Crime prevention is a method of eliminating crime from society by "bring[ing] together for the first time the ingredients of crime prevention practice, thus to provide a roadmap for those who wish to take part in this fascinating and demanding field."[3]

The formal definition of crime prevention, as adopted in several countries, is: "*The anticipation, recognition and appraisal of a crime risk and the initiation of some action to remove or reduce it.*"[4] In other words, crime prevention is the effort to directly reduce criminal opportunity. According to C. Ray Jefferies, "Direct controls of crime include only those which reduce environmental opportunities for crime. Indirect controls include all other measures, such as job

---

2. National Crime Prevention Institute, *Understanding Crime Prevention,* (Stoneham, MA: Butterworth, 1986), 13.

3. National Crime Prevention Institute, *Understanding Crime Prevention,* Vol. 1, (Louisville, KY: Crime Prevention Library, 1978), 1–1.

4. Ibid., 1–2.

training, remedial education, police surveillance, police apprehension, court action, imprisonment, probation and parole."[5] The important operating assumptions taught to crime prevention practitioners by the National Crime Prevention Institute are that

1. Potential crime victims or those responsible for them must be helped to take action which reduces their vulnerability to crimes and which reduces their likelihood of injury or loss should crime occur;
2. At the same time, it must be recognized that potential victims (and those responsible for them) are limited in the action they can take by the limits of their control over their environments;
3. The environment to be controlled is that of the potential victim, not of the potential criminal;
4. Direct control over the victim's environment can nevertheless affect criminal motivation in that reduced criminal opportunity means less temptation to commit offenses and learn criminal behavior and, consequently, fewer offenders. In this sense, crime prevention is a practical rather than a moralistic approach to reducing criminal motivations. The intent is to discourage the offender;
5. The traditional approaches used by the criminal justice system (such as punishment and rehabilitation capabilities of courts and prisons and the investigative and apprehension functions of police) can increase the risk perceived by the criminal, and thus have a significant (but secondary) role in criminal opportunity reduction;
6. Law enforcement agencies have a preliminary role in crime prevention to the extent that they are effective in providing opportunity reduction education, information and guidance to the public and to various organizations, institutions and agencies in the community;
7. Many skills and interest groups need to operate in an active and coordinated fashion if crime prevention is to be effective in a community-wide sense;
8. Crime prevention can be both a cause and an effect of efforts to revitalize urban and rural communities;
9. The knowledge of crime prevention is interdisciplinary and is a continual process of discovery, as well as discarding misinfor-

---

5. Ibid., 1–1.

mation. There must be a continual sifting and integration of discoveries as well as a constant sharing of new knowledge among practitioners;

10. Crime prevention strategies and techniques must remain flexible and specific. What will work for one crime in one place may not work for the same crime in another place. Crime prevention is a "thinking person's" practice, and countermeasures must be taken after a thorough analysis of the problem, not before.[6]

National Commission Reports

In 1967 the President's Commission on Law Enforcement and Administration of Justice *Task Force Report: The Police* recognized that the community had a role in crime prevention. The *Task Force Report* recognized that the police could not- -through their own efforts— solve or prevent crime; consequently, "The police need help from citizens, from private organizations, from other municipal agencies, and from crime prevention legislation."[7] The *Task Force Report* further indicated that business has a responsibility to take action that could decrease thievery, robberies, and burglaries. The Commission also recommended educational programs in crime prevention and crime prevention campaigns. One method discussed was to have professional and social organizations provide crime prevention messages for their members. Such organizations could also play a part in getting the crime prevention message to the community.

The *Task Force* suggested that various aspects of crime prevention strategies could be built into community planning. "A Commission-sponsored survey of 95 high ranking public officials in 4 large cities revealed that the police were not significantly involved in community planning"[8]; however, the Commission did find some examples of collaboration between the police and other governmental agencies in crime prevention. For example, one police department surveyed residents of high-crime areas regarding their perception of the most serious crime problem and what could be done about it.

---

6. *Understanding Crime Prevention*, 1986, 20–21.

7. *Task Force Report: The Police*, 221.

8. Ibid., 225.

The citizens' responses indicated that crime prevention is a multi-departmental task. In other words,

1. The fire department should eliminate fire hazards and burn off lots being used for juvenile behavior,
2. Schools should provide better perimeter lighting for the school yards and structures after lighting,
3. The recreational department should offer more attractive programs designed to use up idle youth energy,
4. Juvenile probation officers should intensify their contact with probationers in the area,
5. Public utilities should provide additional street lighting,
6. The alcoholic beverage commission should crack down on liquid dealers who sell to minors.[9]

The Commission concluded that "To reduce crime in their communities citizens must be prepared to back up their police force with more than slogans. They need to keep in mind, but in perspective, the possibilities of crime in their daily lives and take reasonable steps to limit criminal opportunities."[10] Also, the municipal government has to become more involved in crime prevention by providing "the mechanism for coordination of all the local agencies whose activities and policies can have an effect on crime prevention and on opportunities for the detection and apprehension of criminals after crimes have been committed."[11]

In 1971 the Administrator of the Law Enforcement Assistance Administration (LEAA) appointed the National Advisory Commission on Criminal Justice Standards and Goals. The goal of the Commission was to establish national criminal justice standards and goals for crime reduction and crime prevention at the local and state levels. In 1973 the Commission completed its task. Standards for crime prevention appeared in the *Report on Police*. The standards for crime prevention as it applies to the police are as follows:

> Every police agency should immediately establish programs that encourage members of the public to take an active role in preventing crime, that provide information leading to the arrest and conviction of criminal offenders, that facilitate the

---

9. Ibid., 225.
10. Ibid., 228.
11. Ibid., 228.

identification and recovery of stolen property, and that increase
liaison with private industry in security efforts.[12]

1. Every police agency should assist actively in the establishment
   of volunteer neighborhood security programs that involve the
   public in neighborhood crime prevention and reduction;
   a. The police agency should provide the community with
      information and assistance regarding means to avoid
      being victimized by crime and should make every effort
      to inform neighborhoods of developing crime trends that
      may effect their area;
   b. The police agency should instruct neighborhood volun-
      teers to telephone the police concerning suspicious situa-
      tions and to identify themselves as volunteers and provide
      necessary information;
   c. Participating volunteers should not take enforcement ac-
      tion themselves;
   d. Police units should respond directly to the incident rather
      than to the reporting volunteer;
   e. If further information is required from the volunteer, the
      police agency should contact him by telephone;
   f. If an arrest results from the volunteers' information, the
      police agency should immediately notify him by telephone;
   g. The police agency should acknowledge through personal
      contact, telephone call, or letter, every person who pro-
      vides information;
2. Every police agency should establish or assist programs that
   involve trade, business, industry, and community participation in preventing and reducing commercial crimes;
3. Every police agency should seek the enactment of local ordinances that establish minimum security standards for all new
   construction and for existing commercial structures. Once
   regulated buildings are constructed, ordinances should be enforced through inspection by operational police personnel;
4. Every police agency should conduct, upon request, security,
   inspections of businesses and resistances and recommend
   measures to avoid being victimized by crime.[13]

---

12. National Advisory Commission on Criminal Justice Standards and
Goals, *Police,* (Washington, DC: U.S. Government Printing Office), 66.

13. National Advisory Commission on Criminal Justice Standards and Goals,

Environmental Design and Defensible Space

The relationship between crime and environment was ignored until the 1970s. During that time, researchers—often supported by government grants—began to study how physical environment affected crime.

It is now widely recognized that alternative means of preventing crime—like those resulting from the study of physical environment—must be recognized and put into place. The assumption that all the responsibility for crime prevention belongs to the local police—who have not been entirely successful—must be changed. Non-criminal-justice solutions to preventing crime have been receiving more and more recognition. The International Society of Crime Prevention Practitioners recognizes three new crime prevention categories:

1. Punitive Action
   a. This type of prevention involves taking steps taken by various authorities to publicize the fact that punishment will be severe if crime is committed.
2. Corrective Action
   a. This category of prevention is based on the premise that criminal behavior is caused by a variety of related and unrelated factors.
   b. Emphasis is placed on working with individuals or the social conditions within a community that channel individuals into crime.
3. Mechanical Action
   a. Deals with the placement of obstacles in the path of criminals to make the commission of a crime riskier or more difficult.
   b. This is the most recent approach to crime prevention.
   c. Includes better alarm system, locks, security guards, closed circuit television, etc.[14]

Various studies found that convenient stores, service stations, and liquor stores are vulnerable to armed robberies simply because they are open late at night, they keep cash on hand, and they are often

---

The Police, (Washington, DC: U.S. Government Printing Office, 1973), 66.

14. Thomas J. Chuda, Basic Crime Prevention Curriculum, (Columbus, OH: International Society of Crime Prevention Practitioners, 1990), 4–5.

located in isolated areas. Studies of burglaries indicate that burglars usually take the easiest route—they don't want to take a long time to enter the dwelling they are going to burglarize. Consequently, a dwelling that is easy to enter has a greater chance of being burglarized than a dwelling with obstructions to access. This basic concept holds true for most crimes; therefore, one of the goals of crime prevention is to eliminate or to decrease, as much as possible, the potential for crime to be committed.

The concept of *defensible space* has been offered as one strategy to eliminate or decrease the possibility of crime. The term defensible space was born at Washington University in 1964 in St. Louis, Missouri, with a study of a high-crime public housing development. An inquiry was made into the effects of architectural settings on crime and vandalism on the public housing area.[15]

Oscar Newman explains the term *defensible space* as

> A residential environment whose physical characteristics—building layout and site plan—function to allow inhabitants themselves to become the key agents in ensuring their own security. However, a housing development is "defensible" only when residents choose to adopt this intentional role—a choice that is facilitated by the development's design. Defensible space therefore is a sociophysical phenomenon.[16]

Physical elements are important in creating defensible space, but ultimately, the goal of creating defensible space is to create a sense of community and territoriality among residents.

The term *defensible space* describes physical design characteristics in which residents can control behavior—including criminal actions—within a residential community. Defensible space provides for a residential environment that provides clear definition of areas as being either public, private, or semiprivate. The concept of *defensible space* includes architectural design and physical planning[17] and the following strategies for creating defensible environments:

---

15. Oscar Newman, *Architectural Design for Crime Prevention,* (Washington, DC: U.S. Government Printing Office, 1971), 1.

16. Oscar Newman, *Design Guidelines for Creating Defensible Space,* (Washington, DC: U.S. Government Printing Office, 1975), 5.

17. U.S. Department of Housing and Urban Development, *A Design for Improving Residential Security,* (Washington, DC: U.S. Government Printing Office, 1973), 5.

1. The assignment to different resident groups the specific environments they are best able to utilize and control, as determined by their ages, life styles, socialization proclivities, background, incomes, and family structures;
2. The territorial definition of space in residential developments to reflect the zones of influence of specific inhabitants. Residential environments should be subdivided into zones toward which adjacent residents can easily adopt proprietary attitudes;
3. The juxtaposition of dwelling interiors with exterior spaces and the placement of windows to allow residents to naturally survey the exterior and interior public areas of their living environments and the areas assigned for their use;
4. The juxtaposition of dwellings—their entries and amenities—with city streets so as to incorporate the streets within the sphere of influence of the residential environment;
5. The adoption of building forms and idioms that avoid the stigma of peculiarity that allows others to perceive the vulnerability and isolation of a particular group of inhabitants.[18]

There are a number of concepts that architects should take into consideration when designing space to prevent crime. The first concept to consider is *intrusion time*. The architectural design of a building should make it more difficult for the intruder to escape. The length of time that it takes for a criminal to commit a crime is crucial. Locking devices should be more functional than decorative and burglar alarms should be considered before crime has an opportunity to occur. The second concept to consider is the *time of detection*—the time it takes to establish communication with the police once a crime occurs. The third concept, *crime prevention deterrence* combines the entrance factor with the deterrence factor. Deterrence involves making it more difficult for the potential criminal to commit a criminal offense by reducing the number of opportunities to do so. The fourth concept, *economic consideration*, plays a key role in an individual's decision to obtain additional security to protect his property. This can include adding solid core doors, protective gratings, and so forth, but the crime prevention practitioner—the police officer- -has to properly advise citizens on the cost effectiveness of additional securities. The fifth, concept, *configuration of business*, refers to the practice of designing commercial establish-

---

18. *Design Guidelines for Creating Defensible Space,* 6.

ments to make it difficult for criminals to have easy access and to escape easily. The sixth concept, *multi-purpose protection systems* involves including a system for monitoring not only for crime but also for smoke, fire, gas leaks, and so forth. The seventh concept, *false alarms* has as its main goal the elimination of false alarms. The eighth concept, *design in the community* includes integrating physical designs that decrease criminal opportunity into the aesthetic design of the community.[19]

Theories of Environmental Design

Crime prevention through environmental design, or CPTED, describes the attempt to apply physical design, citizen participation, and law enforcement strategies to neighborhoods, communities, schools, and public transportation. "CPTED is the proper design and effective use of the built environment that can lead to a reduction in the fear and incident of crime, and an improvement in the quality of life."[20]

Oscar Newman developed three concepts describing the physical design of buildings intended to reduce crime. Such design creates *territoriality* (the sense of protectiveness within a specific space area), *natural surveillance* (an environment that makes it easy for people to look out for the physical welfare of others), and *defensible space* (an environment that extends the sense of territoriality and provides opportunities for natural surveillance and protection of property).[21]

During the 1970s global objectives for environmental design were developed and carried out through four types of strategies: *territorial defense*, *personal defense*, *law enforcement*, and *confidential restoration*. A territorial defense strategy involves preventing property-related crimes like burglary, larceny, and auto theft. This strategy involved five different approaches:

> *Land use planning strategies* involving planning activities aimed at avoiding land use mixtures that have a negative im-

---

19. Thomas J. Chuda, 5–6.
20. Thomas J. Chuda, 6.
21. Ibid., 7.

pact on neighborhood security, through zoning ordinances and development plan reviews;

Building perimeter ground security strategies providing the first line of defense against unauthorized entry sites and offering social control mechanisms to prevent dangerous and destructive behavior of visitors. The emphasis is on the access control and surveillance aspects of architectural design. The target environment might be a residential street, the side of a housing complex, or alleyways behind or between business establishments;

Building interior security strategies providing the third line of defense for protecting site occupants and property by preventing unauthorized access to interior spaces and valuables through physical barriers, surveillance and intrusion detection systems, and social mechanisms; and

Construction standards strategies involving building security codes which require construction techniques and materials that tend to reduce crime and safety hazards. These strategies deal both with code adoption and code enforcement.[22]

Personal defense strategies that focus on violent crime such as rape and assault have four approaches:

Safe-streets-for-people strategies involving planning principles derived primarily from CPTED concepts of surveillance and activity support. Surveillance operates to discourage potential offenders because of the apparent risk of being seen and can be improved through various design modifications of physical elements of the street environment (e.g. lighting, fencing, landscaping). Pedestrian traffic areas can be channeled to increase their use and, hence, the number of observers through such measures as creating malls, eliminating on-street parking, and providing centralized parking areas;

Transportation strategies aiming at reducing exposure to crime by improving public transportation. For example, transit waiting stations (bus, trolley) can be located near areas of safe activity and good surveillance, or the distance between stations can be reduced, thus improving accessibility to specific residences, business establishments, and other traffic generating points;

---

22. *Understanding Crime Prevention 1978*, 6- 14-6-15.

Cash-off-the-streets strategies reducing incentives for crime by urging people not to carry unnecessary cash and providing commercial services that minimize the need to carry cash; and

Citizen intervention which, unlike the three previous activities, consists of implementing strategies aimed at organizing and mobilizing residents to adopt propriety interest and to assume responsibility for the maintenance of security.[23]

Law enforcement is the third strategy which involves community support to prevent crime. The law enforcement strategies are of two types:

Police patrol strategies focusing on ways in which police deployment procedures can improve their efficiency and effectiveness in responding to calls and apprehending offenders and

Citizen/police support strategies consisting of police operational support activities that improve citizen/police relations and encourages citizens to cooperate with the police in preventing and reporting incidents.[24]

The confidential restoration strategies focus on residential and commercial environments and on obtaining community and neighborhood support and interest for CPTED. This strategy has two specific approaches:

Investor confidence strategies promoting economic investment and, therefore, social and economic vitality and

Neighborhood identity strategies building community pride and fostering social cohesion.[25]

Crime Analysis

Crime prevention practitioners are frequently asked to analyze specific crimes. After providing an analysis of a crime, they are usually expected to provide strategies for preventing similar crimes from occurring.

---

23. Ibid., 6-15-6-16.
24. Ibid., 6–16.
25. Ibid., 6–16.

The primary source of information for crime analysis comes from police reports. Generally, police reports include the type of incident, the location of the incident, the victim's and the suspect's descriptions, and any unique characteristics of the incident—the type of weapon, verbal expressions, and so forth.

The purpose of crime analysis is to provide practical information about crime patterns, crime trends, and possible suspects, but for crime analysis to be useful, it must be forwarded to the patrol officer who has the primary responsibility in crime prevention.

Crime analysis consists of a process of collecting, analyzing, and disseminating information so that it can be put to use by the patrol officer and the criminal investigator. In a study by the International Association of Chiefs of Police, seven crime analysis functions were identified as being universal for effective law enforcement operation:

1. *Crime pattern detection*: monitoring and discovering crime occurrences that share common attributes or characteristics such as 1.) geographical location or occurrence, 2.) time of occurrence, 3.) modus operandi (M.O.) information;

2. *Crime suspect correlation*: providing information to operation personnel on possible suspects;

3. *Target profiling*: analyzing victimized persons and/or premises by specific geographical areas to specify the nature of the objects that might be attached;

4. *Forecasting crime potential*: predicting the exact time and location of future crime events for short-range purposes;

5. *Monitoring exceptional crime trends*: periodically monitoring at fixed intervals (i. e. daily, weekly, or monthly) the occurrence of crime incidents city-wide or by geographical area to identify "out-of-control" points based on crime thresholds;

6. *Forecasting crime trends*: analyzing crime incidents by type, area and or time to identify trends in support of long-term police action. Forecasting crime trends involves the prediction of crime volume in time domain, i.e. forecasting by time of day, day of week, based on the historical crime data by using statistical methods and techniques; and

7. *Resource allocation*: allocating available manpower for 1.) patrol operation and 2.) criminal investigation for the sake of achieving some department operational goals and objectives.[26]

---

26. Samuel Chang, William H. Simms, Carl M. Makres, et al., *Crime*

The use of crime analysis in crime prevention assists in developing victim profiles that can be used in crime prevention programs. Crime analysis can provide specific modus operandi information that can be used to prevent crime.

Crime Prevention Programs

Crime prevention programs involve a cooperation between citizens and municipal police agencies for the sake of reducing the number of opportunities available for crimes to be committed. In crime prevention programs the crime prevention practitioner works with citizens to develop and implement productive crime prevention programs. Knowledgeable police scholars and practitioners recognize that only through citizen support and cooperation can crime prevention programs work. The model approach involves

1. *Developing and organizing community background data* such as crime and loss patterns, police patrol districts, census tracts, natural geographic boundaries, and other socio-economic and demographic patterns. The purpose of the background data is to provide a reasonably complete picture of crime patterns and related socio-economic conditions, and to help determine how variety and cohesiveness of the neighborhood population;
2. *Using collected data to select target areas-* -high priority areas are identified along with control areas so that the true impact of the project may be assessed. A control area is a comparable neighborhood that does not participate;
3. *Establishing criteria for levels, kinds, and distribution of participation.* The practitioner should make determinations prior to attempting to organize a neighborhood as to what a workable participatory model for that neighborhood should look like. For example, what percentage of residents should be involved? How should their residents be distributed? Should residents remain anonymous for surveillance and reporting purposes? What residents should take organizing lead? Should police present a low profile at first? What kind of project ac-

---

Analysis Support System, (Gaithersburg, Maryland: IACP, 1979), xvi-xviii.

tivities are likely to be best received at first? What level of acceptance is likely? And so on;

4. *Approaching neighborhood leaders*—people who have been identified as having significant influence in the area should be approached first. After they have been informed as to the possible nature of a project and its potential value to the area, they may be asked to invite friends and other potential group members to participate in preliminary, exploratory meetings. It is important to remember that local leaders serve many important group functions such as information dissemination, recruitment, and stimulation of group interest. They can also provide the practitioner with valuable feedback on the progress and interest in their areas;

5. *Providing education and training*—group members and related police personnel should become acquainted with their respective roles in the crime prevention efforts. The goal is to build the basic mechanism necessary for citizens and police working together. Initial citizen education and training would probably include crime reporting procedures, guidance on what to report, the basic security and personal safety tips. As interest is generated and people begin to increase interaction with police, the police must encourage the actions of the group members and provide guidance for further contacts. It is imperative that not only the beat officer, but other police personnel, such as the patrol commander and radio dispatcher, be aware of the group and lend their cooperation;

6. *Providing feedback to police and citizens*—if a citizen's call results in a good arrest, he should be notified and recognized....If the call resulted in an officer being dispatched in a situation where police responses were inappropriate, he should also be notified and courteously advised on what should and should not be notified to the police. Citizens should also provide feedback to the police department on police response. Was it timely, courteous, accurate?

7. *Formulating crime-specific tactics*—when project performance reaches a level that reflects a capacity for the project to function as an efficient, unified, and directed entity, it is time to look back to the crime data files to determine the most serious crime problems facing project areas and devise crime specific tactics to address the problems. Times, places, and methods of criminal attack must be considered to identify what specific

things a citizen can do to reduce the chances of criminal victimization...;

8. *Implementing crime-specific tactics* throughout the organization as they are developed. This may be accomplished by having the practitioner or local police patrol attending the periodic group meetings to provide specific training, or training sessions for group leaders, who, in turn, train the groups and supervise the process of implementation. Crime-specific tactics should be implemented comprehensively throughout the project to achieve maximum effectiveness and to avoid displacement;

9. *Assessing the performance of the organization.* Performance assessment should come in the form of formal and informal feedback throughout the organizational period. At some point, however, the determination must be made that the project is sufficiently organized, educated, and trained to become essentially self-sustaining and regenerative with only logistical support from the police.

10. *Evaluating the impact on crime in the project area.* The project goal of reducing crime can only be reliably and validly assessed relative to crime specific tactics. Also, it is important that the tactics be quickly assessed so that they can be revised as necessary. When refined tactics have been implemented, the practitioner can legitimately establish that specific actions by citizens are affecting the rate of crime in the neighborhood.

11. *Encouraging the group to take on other needed changes*—once the mechanism for community action has been established and has been proven effective, it can take on various community improvement projects. Widening the scope of the activities of the organization can help sustain the crime prevention effort by offering participants a diversity of activities to meet their interests. Many of these projects will probably overlap, reinforcing each other, and increasing the total chance of success.[27]

The crime prevention practitioner needs to be involved in planning crime prevention programs. He or she has to be involved in applying environmental designs and selecting security devices and procedures. In addition, the crime prevention practitioner must develop citizen participation and be deeply involved in crime prevention program planning. This includes designing the organization,

---

27. *Understanding Crime Prevention*, 1986, 146–147.

defining the crime problems and priorities, and developing program objectives.[28]

But while the crime prevention practitioner is responsible for guiding the community in developing and planning crime prevention programs, it seems that when the community and its citizens are committed to crime prevention crime prevention programs have a greater chance of being successful. Generally, those neighborhoods where neighbors keep an eye out for each other have been found to be the safest.

Operation Identification

There is a natural tendency to want to mark one's belongings for identification. As a modern crime prevention technique the practice was used in 1963 in Monterey Park, California, to deter a rash of hub-cap thefts. The Police Chief recommended that residents engrave their license numbers on their hub caps and eventually their household items for identification purposes.

When implementing an operation-identification program, the crime prevention practitioner has to require that the number selected is permanently engraved onto the property marked. The numbering system used should be a standardized system that is acceptable to the National Crime Information Center (NCIC). The crime prevention practitioner must create a recording system that will provide for an inventory and a description of the property that also includes serial numbers if they are available. Also, the crime practitioner should make citizens aware that property that cannot be engraved should be photographed. It is also recommended that entire rooms be photographed to show the items that are in them.[29]

Neighborhood Watch

The neighborhood watch, or block watch, works toward making the community become more aware of and more knowledgeable about the crime that occurs there. The aim of the program is to reduce the fear of crime and also to reduce the opportunities available for crimes to occur. The Neighborhood Watch Program is meant to contribute to building a sense of community in a neighborhood

28. Ibid., 150.
29. Thomas J. Chauda, 4–8.

which results in a greater sense of safety among its residents. Neighborhood residents provide a constant surveillance, looking for any unusual occurrences in their neighborhood. A strong neighborhood organization, working in cooperation with a crime prevention practitioner, can do much to reduce crime in a neighborhood and provide a sense of security. The program also provides the crime prevention practitioner with an opportunity to teach neighborhood residences the techniques of crime prevention.

Another crime prevention strategy that residents can become involved in is *citizen patrols*. Neighborhood residents provide surveillance of their community by actively engaging in patrolling. But citizen patrols provide only surveillance and they are instructed to notify the police when they observe a criminal offense. Patrol by neighborhood residents can be either by foot patrol or by some other form of mobile patrol. Almost any age group or sex can be involved in citizen patrol, since duties are limited to observation and do not involve enforcement, and it is normally up to the community to decide what kind and how many neighborhood patrols they want to man.

Other types of citizen patrols that have been implemented have included using taxi drivers, truck drivers, and individuals with cellular telephones in their automobiles to notify the police when suspicious activities are observed.

Crime Stoppers

Crime Stoppers, also known as Silent Witness, Crime Line, etc., is also a valuable crime prevention program. The program involves the local news media, the local police, and the community to get citizens involved in the campaign against crime. The premise of Crime Stoppers is that for various reasons some individuals do not want to cooperate with the police—whether in some kind of retaliation, because of a sense of apathy, or simply because they have reason to dislike their local police department. Crime Stoppers offers both rewards and anonymity to individuals who are willing to provide specific details leading to the arrest or indictment of criminal offenders.

Silent Witness—Savannah, Georgia's, version of Crime Stoppers—is operated by an Executive Director whose responsibilities include interacting with a board of directors to determine the monetary amount of all rewards, maintaining and operating an around-the-clock telephone hotline, preparing crime synopses for distribution as news releases, selecting and videotaping "Crime of the

Week" simulations for local television, and interacting with an established Finance Committee for fund-raising efforts.

Monetary rewards for information relating to specific crimes range from $100 to $2,000—the maximum amount normally going only for information pertaining to capital offenses. As calls are received on the hotline in response to Silent Witness publicity, information is immediately forwarded to the appropriate police agency. Written follow-up reports are then distributed to officers once each week. Callers are asked to provide a 4-digit/1-letter alphanumeric code to assist in their future identification for reward entitlement. To collect a reward, tipsters must re-contact Silent Witness administrators and submit a claim, citing their private alphanumeric code.

Crime Stoppers programs are generally dependent upon the business community for financial support, and to a great extent, they depend upon the news media for publicity. As a mechanism for preventing and controlling crime, Crime Stoppers seems to be worthwhile.

Innovative programs such as Crime Stoppers can effectively stimulate community participation in crime prevention and crime control and have a tremendous impact on the effort to reduce crime rates and to apprehend offenders.

Crimes Against the Elderly

In some communities crime prevention practitioners may have to develop and to administrate crime prevention programs geared specifically to the elderly. National studies have found that the elderly have a smaller chance of becoming victims of crime than any other age group. But when they *are* victimized they are more likely to be victims of property crime than of crimes against their person.

Senior citizens may be victims of crimes because of their poor physical health or their isolation from family and friends. Often the elderly live in high crime areas where they are statistically more likely to become victims of crime. Despite some of these problems, senior citizens can still be involved in crime prevention strategies. The crime prevention practitioner can work with the elderly to teach them how to deter street crimes—such as mugging and purse snatching. It should also be the responsibility of the crime prevention practitioner to advise senior citizens on the precautions they can observe when they take public transportation or when they walk in public, on personal safety at home, on safety on the telephone, and on how to protect money and valuables. The crime prevention practitioner can also offer valuable advice on confidence games and consumer fraud, since older citizens are often the victims of unscrupulous individuals and their scams.

Police agencies that serve a substantial elderly population should establish crime prevention programs for the elderly. When they become aware of crime prevention techniques and strategies, the elderly can make an excellent contribution to the deterrence and prevention of crime.

Marketing Crime Prevention

The crime prevention practitioner needs to know and understand the community and should be familiar with the socio-economic make up of its citizens. Do crimes such as robbery, burglary, and other serious crimes occur there? Does the community have a domestic violence problem, a child abuse problem, or a drug problem? In order for the crime prevention practitioner to take any action or to develop plans to prevent and control crime, the practitioner needs to know what the community's crime problems are. Once the crime prevention practitioner knows his or her objective, crime prevention programs can be developed that meet the community's needs.

As any police officer knows, the police cannot succeed in solving or preventing crime without the community's assistance. Crime prevention programs have to involve the community and have to deal with community problems to be effective. When crime prevention programs are successful they usually have the full support and participation of the community. The crime prevention practitioner must sell programs to the police department and to the citizens of the community, must function as a catalyst and initiate programs to fill the community's needs, and must work to overcome any resistance to crime prevention programs by educating the community on how the programs work. The crime prevention practitioner is the most important link between the community and the police.

Summary

The concept of crime prevention can be traced to ancient times when barbaric punishments were used to deter potential offenders from committing barbaric crimes. As society became more sophisticated, more formal policing methods were implemented. When the Metropolitan Police of London were established, one of their main responsibilities was to be involved in crime prevention. The formal definition of crime prevention is "The anticipation, recognition, and appraisal of a crime risk and the initiation of some action to remove or reduce it." The purpose of crime prevention is to reduce criminal opportunity. In 1967 the President's Commission on Law Enforcement and Administration of Justice recognized that the community has a role to play in crime prevention. The President's Commission suggested that business had a responsibility to take actions that could decrease thievery, robberies, and burglaries. The Commission also recommended the initiation of educational programs in crime prevention.

In 1971 the Administration of the Law Enforcement Assistance Administration (LEAA) appointed the national Advisory Commission on Criminal Justice Standards and Goals. The goal of the Commission was to establish national criminal justice standards and goals for the crime reduction and crime prevention at the local and state levels. The Commission recommended that the police establish crime-prevention programs and encourage members of the public to take an active role in preventing crime.

During the 1970s researchers—often supported by government grants—began to study the relationship between environment and crime. As a result, it is now understood that alternative means of preventing crime must be recognized and put into place. Placing all of the responsibility for crime prevention on the police is not entirely effective.

The concept of defensible space suggests that communities or buildings can be designed to eliminate or decrease the potential for crime to occur by creating a sense of community and territoriality among residents.

Crime Prevention through Environment Design or CPTED is the attempt to apply physical design, citizen participation, and law enforcement strategies to neighborhoods, communities, schools, and public transportation. CPTED "is the proper design and effective use of the built environment that can lead to a reduction in the fear and incidence of crime and an improvement in the quality of life."

Crime-prevention practitioners are frequently asked to analyze specific crimes and to develop strategies to prevent similar crimes from occurring. Crime analysis consists of a process of collecting, analyzing, and disseminating information so that it can be put to use by the patrol officer and the criminal investigator. The use of crime analysis in crime prevention assists in developing victim profiles that can be used in crime-prevention programs. Crime analysis can provide specific modus-operandi information that can be used to prevent crime.

Crime-prevention programs should encourage citizen participation with the municipal police agencies for the sake of reducing the number of opportunities that crime has to occur. In crime- prevention programs, the crime-prevention practitioner works with citizens to develop and implement productive crime- prevention programs, to apply environmental designs, and to select security devices and procedures. For such programs to be successful, the crime-prevention practitioner must recognize that community support is essential.

Key Terms

building-ground
   security strategies
building-interior
   security strategies
building-perimeter
   security strategies
building-perimeter
   security strategies
cash-off-the-streets strategies
cash-off-the-streets strategies
citizen intervention
citizen/police-support strategies
confidential restoration
configuration of business
crime prevention
construction-standard strategies
CPTED
crime deterrence
crime stoppers

defensible space
design in the community
economic consideration
false alarms
intrusion space
investor-confidence strategies
land-use planning strategies
LEAA
National Advisory Commission
   on Criminal Justice Standards
   and Goals
natural surveillance
NCPI
neighborhood-identity strategies
President's Crime Commission
safe-streets-for-people strategies
territoriality
time of detection
transportation strategies

Review Questions

1. Describe the concept of crime prevention.
2. Define the concept of crime prevention.
3. Describe and compare some of the major findings of the national crime commissions as they relate to crime prevention.
4. Explain the concept of environmental design and defensible space as it relates to crime prevention.
5. Explain the theories of environmental design or CPTED.
6. Discuss the concept of crime analysis and explain its importance to crime prevention.
7. Review several crime prevention programs with which you are familiar.
8. What should a crime prevention practitioner do in order to establish a successful neighborhood crime prevention program?

References

Bailey, Stanley. "Crime Prevention on a Shoestring." *The Police Chief* (March 1985).

Chang, Samuel, et al. *Crime Analysis Systems Support*, Gaithersburg, MD: IACP, 1979.

Chuda, Thomas J. *Basic Crime Prevention Curriculum*, Columbus, OH: International Society of Crime Prevention Practitioners, 1990.

National Advisory Commission on Criminal Justice Standards and Goals. *A National Strategy to Reduce Crime*. Washington: U.S. Government Printing Office, 1973.

National Advisory Commission on Criminal Justice Standards and Goals. *Police*. Washington: U.S. Government Printing Office, 1973.

National Crime Prevention Institute. *Understanding Crime Prevention*. Louisville, KY: The Crime Prevention Library, 1978.

National Crime Prevention Institute. *Understanding Crime Prevention*. Stoneham, MA: Butterworth, 1986.

Newman, Oscar. *Architectural Design for Crime Prevention*. Washington: U.S. Government Printing Office, 1975.

Newman, Oscar. *Design Guidelines for Creating Defensible Space* Washington: U.S. Government Printing Office, 1975.

President's Commission on Law Enforcement and Administration of Justice. *Task Force Report: The Police*. Washington: Government Printing Office, 1967.

Rosenbaum, Dennis P., Arthur J. Lurigio, and Paul J. Lavrakas. "Crime Stoppers—A National Evaluation." Washington: National Institute of Justice, September 1986.

U.S. Department of Housing and Urban Development. *A Design for Improving Residential Security.* Washington: U.S. Government Printing Office, 1973.

CHAPTER 12

Current Issues
in Policing

Major Issues

1. Is police discretion necessary for police work?
2. How does multiculturalism affect police work?
3. How does the Americans with Disabilities Act affect the police?
4. How does the homeless problem affect the police?
5. How does the AIDS epidemic affect the police?
6. How does stress affect police officers?

Introduction

There are numerous current issues relating to policing that are of concern to citizens of the community, politicians, police administrators, and to police officers themselves. These issues include the matter of police discretion, the accreditation of police agencies, multiculturalism, the Americans with Disabilities Act, homelessness, AIDS, and stress.

Discretion

In the 1950s it was common practice for police administrators to claim that police officers investigated all crimes and enforced all laws. They claimed that all crimes were investigated with equal effort and that all laws were enforced with the same priority. But students of policing realize that it is impossible for the police to investigate every crime reported or to enforce every law. Often the police do not have sufficient information to conduct an investigation, or on the practical side, they may not always have the manpower available to devote to the thorough investigation of a crime. Consequently, the police have established a set of priorities in criminal investigations; that is, the more serious the crime the higher the priority. For example, a murder investigation will require more time, effort, and resources than, say, the theft of a car stereo. Furthermore, we can not expect the police to enforce all of the state and federal laws. No police department has sufficient police officers to enforce all laws. So since the police cannot be expected to inves-

tigate all crime or to enforce all laws, then we should presume that
the police are able to exercise a certain amount of discretion in
choosing which laws to enforce and which crimes to investigate.
Without the "use of discretion" the police would have a difficult
time functioning.

Roscoe Pound defines discretion as "an authority conferred by
law to act in certain conditions or situations in accordance with an
official's or an official agency's own considered judgement and con-
science. It is an idea of morals, belonging to the twilight zone between laws and morals."[1] It has been argued, however, that since
discretion means that a police officer must make decisions that are
not regulated by legal guidelines but by personal values and judgments, the exercise of discretion by police officers is improper. Discretionary acts by police officers often result directly in a citizen's
loss of freedom, or at the very least, they result in someone's being
inconvenienced.

But if the police are denied the opportunity to use discretion,
then a "full enforcement" policy of enforcing all laws would be in
effect. The police would not have the authority to ignore or to
overlook certain violations or even provide an offender with a
warning to avoid illegal actions. Police functions would become
rather mechanical and would not take into account the actions behind a specific act being committed.

On the other hand, the exercise of discretion implies that the police must consider a variety of factors before taking legal action. Police officers may choose not to make an arrest—even if probable
cause exists—if they consider not making an arrest to be an appropriate action. For example, there are situations where police officers
did not arrest college students who had marijuana in their automobile, since they knew the students wanted to become attorneys and
an arrest for possession of drugs may have affected their chances of
becoming attorneys.

Herman Goldstein believes that, if police officers are to be
granted discretion, then the need for criteria in the use of discretion
becomes essential.

1. There is a general reluctance to spell out criteria as to those
   conditions under which an arrest is to take place lest this writ-

---

1. Roscoe Pound, "Discretion, Dispensation and Mitigation: The Problem
of the Individual Special Case," 35 N.Y.U.L. Rev. 925, 926 (1960).

ten modification of existing laws be attacked as presumptuous on the part of an administrative agency and contemptuous of the legislative body;

2. In the absence of written instructions, it is extremely difficult to communicate to large number of policemen the bounds of the discretion to be exercised;

3. An officer cannot be forced to exercise discretion, since the broad oath which he takes places him under obligation to enforce all laws and he can maintain that he is adhering to this higher authority; and

4. If a written document is desired, the preparation of criteria for the exercise of discretion requires an expert draftsman—one more skilled than the legislative draftsman who may have tried and failed.[2]

Developing the criteria recommended by Herman Goldstein places the police administrator in a difficult position. How can the police chief develop discretionary guidelines that will be clearly understood and followed by all police officers? Often in the past it was much easier for the police chief to avoid the issue by taking no action at all.

In the 1970s the *National Advisory Commission of Criminal Justice Standards and Goals on the Police* recommended that every police agency recognize that discretion exists both at the administrative and the operational levels. The Commission recommended that police agencies establish policy statements limiting discretion and that they provide guidelines for the exercise of discretion within departmental policies. With the establishment of the *Commission on Accreditation for Law Enforcement Agencies* in 1980, written directives became a requirement in order for police agencies to obtain accreditation.

The Commission standard specifies that "A written directive governs the use of discretion by sworn officers."[3] This standard requires that discretion be defined by written enforcement policies and reinforced by training and supervision. The Commission suggests that

2. Herman Goldstein, "Police Discretion: The Ideal versus the Real," *Police Administration Review* 23, (September 1963), 144.

3. Standards For Law Enforcement Agencies, *The Standards Manual of the Law Enforcement Agency Accreditation Program,* (Fairfax, VA: Commission on Accreditation for Law Enforcement Agencies, 1989), 1-2.

written directives limit individual discretion and provide guidelines for the exercise of discretion.

Another standard that the Commission recommends states that, "A written directive defines the authority, guidelines, and circumstances when sworn personnel should exercise alternatives to arrest and/or alternatives to prearranged confinement."[4] The implication of the directive is that police officers should be authorized to use alternatives to arrest like citations, summonses, referrals, informal resolution, and warnings.

In addition to police department policies, procedures, and guidelines, some other branches of government are also involved in maintaining a check on police discretion. The courts, for example, have checked police discretion by such court decisions as *Miranda, Mapp,* and *Escobeda.* The police are also required to follow guidelines established by federal and state courts of appeal. Additionally, police officers who overstep the boundaries of discretion may be in violation criminal laws and can either be arrested and/or become defendants in a civil suit. State and Federal legislative bodies will from time to time pass laws that limit police discretion. But one of the most important means of controlling police discretion is peer pressure. The rookie police officer usually learns quickly what is the acceptable norm for discretion, and as a result, he or she usually falls into line.

The police have long worked for a professional status for their field. Generally, one of the symbols of professionalism is the recognition of the need for discretion founded on professional competence and efficiency. Public recognition of the discretionary role of the police would provide greater respect for the police and at the same time reinforce the idea that the police are working toward professionalism.

Accreditation

The police in America for decades have worked toward obtaining recognition as professionals, and although over the last several decades, the police have upgraded police training and research on policing has become more acceptable, they still have not obtained a

4. Ibid., 1-2.

professional status. If the Police in America are to become professionals, they must be recognized by the society as professionals.

Although there have been concentrated attempts by numerous police agencies to achieve professionalism, these attempts have fallen short of the mark, especially when the images that the public sees on national television are of a police officer clubbing what appears to be a defenseless African-American (i.e., Rodney King), or dragging an African-American woman from her vehicle for not responding quickly enough to a state police officer's request (a South Carolina State Police Officer did this in the spring of 1996), or a police detective of one of the largest police agencies in the country being accused of racism (i.e., Detective Mark Furman of the Los Angeles Police Department.)

Careers that have long been recognized as being professional careers are the medical, the legal, and the ministerial fields. These fields have a legacy of education and research, they have accumulated a body of knowledge, they involve life-long training, and for the most part, they involve self-employment. The police scholar Peter Manning claims that the professional mandate cannot be easily obtained. He writes, "Professions claim a body of theory and practice to justify their right to discover, define, and deal with problems."[5] James Q. Wilson, a nationally recognized researcher on policing adds

> Occupations whose members exercise, as do the police, wide discretion alone and with respect to matters of the greatest importance are typically "professions"—the medical profession, for example. The right to handle emergency situations, to be privy to "guilty information," and to make decisions involving questions of life and death or honor and dishonor is usually, as with a doctor or a priest, conferred by the organized profession. The profession certifies that the member has acquired by education, certain information, and by apprenticeship certain arts and skills, that render him competent to perform these functions and that he is willing to subject himself to the code of ethics and sense of duty of his colleagues (or, in the case of the priest, to the laws and punishment of God). Failure to per-

---

5. Peter K. Manning, "The Police: Mandate, Strategies, and Appearances," *The Police and Society: Touchstone Reading,* Victor E. Kappeler, Ed., (Prospect Heights, IL: Waveland Press, 1995), 98.

form his duties properly will, if detected, be dealt with by professional sanctions—primarily, loss of respect. Members of professions tend to govern themselves through collegial bodies, to restrict the authority of their nominal superiors, to take seriously the reputation among fellow professionals, and to encourage some of their kind to devote themselves to adding systematically to the knowledge of the profession through writing and research. The police are not in any senses professionals. They acquire most of their knowledge and skill on the job, not in separate academies; they are emphatically subject to the authority of their superiors; they have no serious professional society, only a union-like bargaining agent; and they do not produce, in systematic written form, new knowledge about their craft.[6]

Wilson's comments were written in the late 1960s, but for many students they still hold true as we approach the year 2000. Police administrators, police organizations, and individual police officers continue to work for the recognition of policing as a profession. In 1979 four police organizations banded together to strive toward achieving the recognition of police professionalism. These organizations, the International Association of Chiefs of Police (IACP), the National Organization of Black Law Enforcement Executives (NOBLE), the National Sheriff's Association (NSA), and the Police Executive Research Forum (PERF), formally established the *Commission on Accreditation for Law Enforcement Agencies (CALEA)*. They appointed a Board of Directors from their members including representatives of police agencies, public officials, college professors, and business executives. The Commission established a body of standards designed to

1. Increase an agency's capabilities to prevent and control crime,
2. Increase effectiveness and efficiency in the delivery of services,
3. Increase cooperation and coordination with other agencies, and
4. Increase citizen and employee confidence in the goals, objectives, policies, and practices of agencies.[7]

---

6. James Q. Wilson, *Varieties of Police Behavior*, (Cambridge, MA: Harvard University Press), 29-30.

7. Standards For Law Enforcement Agencies, *The Standards Manual of the*

The Commission on Accreditation for Law Enforcement Agencies specified forty-eight topics as standards that would be addressed by police agencies being evaluated for accreditation. There are 944 standards which are divided into mandatory and non-mandatory standards. Mandatory standards apply to all police agencies if they are applicable. For example, if police agencies have a lockup, then the same standard applies to all police departments that have lockups. If the police agency has no lockup, then this standard does not apply to the police agency.

The Commission expects a police department that applies for accreditation to initially meet eighty percent of the non-mandatory standards. The police agency determines which of the non-mandatory standards that they will meet. However, police agencies are encouraged to exceed meeting eighty percent of the standards. The standards defined by the Commission involve such matters as organizational management and administration, crime analysis, training, operations, traffic, and auxiliary and technical services.

For those police departments that desire to obtain accreditation there is a five step process:

1. Application: The accreditation process begins when an agency applies to the Commission for applicant status;
2. Agency questionnaire: The agency completes and files an Agency Profile Questionnaire (APQ), thereby providing information that the Commission needs to determine the standards with which the agency must comply;
3. Self-assessment: The agency then initiates the self- assessment process, which involves examination by the agency to determine whether it complies with all applicable standards. The agency then prepares "proofs of compliance" and assembles documentation to facilitate the on-site assessment;
4. On-site assessment: After the agency is satisfied that it has reached compliance with all applicable standards, it notifies the Commission. The Commission then identifies a team of assessors, allows the candidate agency to review the team make-up to avoid conflict of interest, and dispatches the team to the agency. The assessors examine proofs of compliance to determine if the agency complies with all applicable standards; and

---

Law Enforcement Agency Accreditation Program, (Fairfax, VA: Commission on Accreditation for Law Enforcement Agencies, 1989), xi.

5. Commission review: The on-site assessment team submits a report to the Commission, whereupon the Commission grants
full accreditation or defers accreditation status. In the case of
the latter, the Commission advises the agency of the steps to
gain accreditation.[8]

Police agencies that are successful receive accreditation for five
years. Departments are expected to continue to comply with the accreditation standards, and if they want to be reaccredited, they have
to reapply for accreditation and an on-site assessment is required.
Accreditation usually also requires a monetary commitment on the
part of the police department. Not only must the police department
cover the Commission fee for accreditation but the police department may have added expenses such as purchasing new equipment
or providing all sworn officers with departmental policies and procedures.

Agencies that make the investment of money and man-hours to
obtain accreditation expect to receive a number of benefits. They
hope that their image in the community they serve will be improved, or if that image is already excellent, that it will be reinforced. Police departments also seek accreditation hoping that it will
give them recognition as professionals.

Multiculturalism

As we approach the twenty-first century, multiculturalism is
quickly becoming an issue of primary importance. It is being recognized that America is a multicultural society made up of not one
but many different cultures. In the last U.S. Census (1990) approximately seventy-six percent of the population of the United States
were white, twelve percent were black, nine percent were Hispanics, and three percent were Asians/Pacific Islanders and various
other groups. Females constituted over fifty percent of the population while males accounted for less than fifty percent of the United
States population. What is even more interesting is that in the
twenty-first century it has been projected that the white population
will no longer constitute a clear majority of the population, the

---

8. Ibid., xiii.

white population will have a larger number of Americans 65 and older, white males will be a minority in the work force while females and the traditional minorities will comprise the majority of workers in the workplace.

The term multiculturalism "refers to a society that is made up of many different ethnic and racial groups and does not refer to a 'movement' or political force."[9] America is a country of diversity. Since the discovery of America by Christopher Columbus and the settling of America by Europeans it has been a country of immigrants. The immigration of people from other countries of the world have brought together peoples with different cultures. But while the immigration from other parts of the world still continues, the number of Europeans immigrating to the United States has decreased. For several decades immigrants have come from Asia, Mexico, Central America, South America, and the countries of the Caribbean. Of course, peoples immigrating to the United States bring their cultures with them, and sometimes these cultures are not understood by many Americans and as a result this can lead to conflicts with the police. When we consider the various cultures already in America, along with recent arrivals to our shores, we as Americans should recognize that we are a multicultural society and that we should work toward understanding the complexity of implications inherent in that fact.

Progressive police agencies are responding to multicultural changes in their community. California police departments are concentrating on including diverse members of their community. These programs involve new employment strategies, citizen participation, multicultural training programs for police employees and members of the community, and community outreach programs. The San Jose Police Department concentrated on recruiting and hiring culturally diverse applicants. As an incentive to San Jose police officers, the department rewards officers with forty hours of paid vacation if the individuals they recruit become police officers. The Long Beach Police Department, in collaboration with the National Conference of Christian and Jews, developed a forty hour course on cultural awareness for all department employees. Substa-

---

9. Robert M. Shusta, Deena R. Levine, Philip R. Harris, et al., *Multicultural Law Enforcement: Strategies for Peacekeeping in a Diverse Society,* (Englewood Cliffs NJ: Prentice-Hall, 1995), 3.

tions were placed in distinct neighborhoods by the San Jose and Garden Grove police departments, and police employees and citizen volunteers who were capable of speaking the residents' language manned the substations.[10]

The Lakewood, Colorado, Police Department recognized that police officers could not relate to an increasing number of Hispanics in their community because of the language barrier and a variety of cultural differences. To address the problem, the Lakewood Police Department employed an educational consultant to educate police officers on Hispanic culture and to establish a language training program for its officers.[11]

Multicultural issues are also a concern of federal agencies. The U.S. Border Patrol established a community resource development program for Border Patrol agents to gain the cooperation of the community. The program consisted of forty hours of discussion for ten weeks. Participants came from the Chicano Federation, the Federation for American Immigration Reform, the Legal Aid Society, the District Attorney, and the electronic and print media. The purpose of the program was to open lines of communication among diverse groups within the community. Border Patrol officers regularly have contact with people often under difficult situations from different cultures. Border Patrol agents, like all police officers in America, need to be made aware of cultural differences in their communities.

Multicultural awareness is becoming an important part of police training regardless of where in America the police officer works. It has been suggested that police officers perform the following activities in order to improve their relationship with multicultural communities:

- Make positive contact with minority-group members. Don't let them see you only when something negative has happened;
- Allow the public to see you as much as possible in a nonenforcement role;

---

10. Brad R. Bennett, "Incorporating Diversity: Police Response to Multicultural Changes in Their Community," *FBI Law Enforcement Bulletin* 64, No. 12, (December 1995), 1–3.

11. Alan A. Younger and Ana Novas, "Accelerated Learning: A New Approach to Cross-Cultural Training," *FBI Law Enforcement Bulletin* 64, No. 3, (March 1995), 14–15.

- Make a conscious effort in your mind, en route to every situation, to treat all segments of society objectively and fairly;
- Remember that all groups have some bad, some average, and some good people within them;
- Go out of your way to be personable and friendly with minority-group members. Remember, many don't expect it;
- Don't appear uncomfortable or avoid discussing racial/minority issues with other officers and citizens;
- Take responsibility for patiently educating citizens and the public, in general, about the role of the officer and about standard operating procedures in law enforcement. Remember, the citizens do not understand police "culture";
- Don't be afraid to be a change agent in your organization when it comes to improving cross-cultural relations within your department and between police and community. It may not be a popular thing to do, but it is the right thing to do.[12]

The Americans with Disabilities Act

The Americans for Disabilities Act (ADA) was signed by President Bush in 1990. The law was enacted on the premise that people with disabilities have been discriminated against in the workplace and in society and that individuals with disabilities were isolated and segregated because of their disabilities. The ADA created guidelines for access to government facilities, for the delivery of services, and for governmental programs of agencies, and although the ADA does not specifically address police agencies, it also does not exempt police agencies. Police agencies, too, have to follow the ADA guidelines where they are appropriate.

On July 26, 1992, Title I of ADA took effect. Title I prohibits private companies, state and local government agencies, and labor unions from discriminating against disabled individuals through job application procedures, hiring practices, firing practices, advancement, compensation, job training, or any of the privileges of em-

---

12. Robert M. Shusta, Deena R. Levine, Phillip R. Harris, et al., *Multicultural Law Enforcement: Strategies for Peacekeeping in a Diverse Society,* (Englewood Cliffs, NJ: Prentice-Hall, 1995), 30–31.

ployment they are entitled to, if they are qualified to hold an announced position. A person with a disability is defined as one who:

> Has a physical or mental impairment that substantially limits one or more major life actions,
> Has a record of such an impairment, or
> Is regarded as having an impairment.[13]

The ADA explicitly states that specific conditions are not included under this law. This includes homosexuality, bisexuality, transsexualism, transvestism, voyeurism, exhibitionism, pedophilia, sexual disorders, kleptomania, pyromania, and compulsive gambling. To qualify under the ADA an individual must have a mental or physical impairment that substantially limits such activities such as talking, walking, breathing, sitting, standing, or learning.

Employers cannot ask applicants any questions about their disability or even about the nature or severity of their disability. Applicants can only be asked questions about their ability to perform specific job functions. Job offers, however, can be conditional based upon the results of a medical examination—provided that the medical examination is required for all employees for similar positions.

Employees and applicants currently using illegal drug substances, however, are not protected by the ADA. Testing for illegal drug abusers does not violate the ADA guidelines. Illegal drug users and alcoholics can be held to the same standards as other employees.

It needs to be noted, however, that the ADA does not guarantee jobs, nor should it be considered an Affirmative Action law. To determine whether or not a person qualifies for a job, two questions should be asked:

1. Does this person meet the initial job requirements, such as work experience, education, skills, certificates, or licenses?
2. If so, can the person perform the essential functions of the job, with or without reasonable accommodation?[14]

---

13. Paula N. Rubin, "The Americans with Disability Act and Criminal Justice: An Overview," *National Institute of Justice Research in Action,* (Washington, DC: U.S. Department of Justice, September, 1993), 2.

14. Ibid., 4.

The ADA has an enormous impact on police agencies, especially in the hiring process. To follow ADA requirements a "department cannot even remotely investigate an applicants's disability or potential disability until the applicant's other qualifications have been evaluated and a contingent offer of employment has been made to the candidate."[15] Police agencies can use screening devices provided they follow the ADA guidelines. Currently, police departments use a variety of screening devices to determine who should be hired. Most police departments use the following screening devices: agility tests, drug tests, polygraph tests, background checks, medical examinations, and psychological examinations. Police departments can still utilize screening devices provided they follow established ADA guidelines and provided the intent is not to discriminate against a person with a disability either intentionally or unintentionally.

To address ADA standards police administrators should evaluate the jobs and tasks performed in their organization, and they should identify essential functions for specific positions in their department. The next step is to determine the standards and criteria that accurately indicate and measure the basic components of the position. When this has been done the police administrator can make a fair and impartial decision regarding a disabled person's ability to perform a precise function or to hold a certain position. Decisions on hiring or promoting should be made on a case-by-case basis.

Like other governmental agencies police agencies cannot discriminate against individuals with disabilities. They are not required to employ or to promote a disabled person, but they must be able to justify their decisions not to do so. For example, police officers are occasionally called upon—as a part of their job—to use physical, and possibly, deadly force. Some disabilities may prevent an individual from performing this function.

Additionally, police agencies, like other governmental employers, are not obliged to make changes—including reconstruction—if changing causes an undue hardship to the organization, and the ADA provides several factors that assist agencies in deciding whether a modification or a particular act creates a hardship. The following factors have to be considered:

15. T. Schneid and L. Gaines, "The American with Disability Act: Implications for Police Administrators," *Police Liability Review,* (Winter, 1994), 4.

1. The nature and cost of the accommodation;
2. The overall financial resources of the employer and the particular facility where the accommodation is needed;
3. The number of persons employed at such facilities and by the employer in general; and
4. The impact of the accommodation upon the operation of the facility.[16]

Homelessness

There are individuals in America who have no jobs or who have jobs that do not pay them enough to be able to afford a place to live. To be homeless means "not having customary and regular access to a conventional dwelling; it mainly applies to those who do not rent or own a residence. Thus people we find sleeping in abandoned buildings or on steam grates who do not have an apartment or house they could go to are clearly among the literally homeless."[17]

The current pattern of homelessness can be traced to the late 1970s. Homelessness began to grow during this period, and America still has a substantial homeless population. As we approach the twenty-first century, we find that there are over three million people who are homeless for at least one night during the year. The majority of individuals who are homeless are single males. Children comprise approximately twenty-five percent of the homeless. Many of the children are runaways or "throwaways" whose parents don't want them at home any longer. The homeless are not only found in our cities but also in our affluent suburbs, rural areas, and small towns.

The homeless often cause a problem to the police. Frequently, the police are called to remove homeless people from parks and streets. The homeless have a stifling effect on businesses and often they attract crime because they create an appearance of community neglect. Weather conditions such as subfreezing days can put the

---

16. Jeffrey Higginbotham, "The Americans with Disability Act," *FBI Law Enforcement Bulletin* 60, No. 8, (March 1992), 30.

17. Peter H. Rossi, *Down and Out In America,* (Chicago, IL: University of Chicago Press, 1989), 10.

homeless in physical danger, and this too is a situation to which the police must sometimes respond.

Essentially, the homeless situation raises three distinct issues for the police:

1. The conflict over the use of public facilities,
2. Public demand for enforcement action against activities that are often marginally criminal, and
3. The need to provide police service to an economically disenfranchised class of people.[18]

Traditionally, policing would advise the homeless to leave an area where residents consider them to be an "eyesore." Since making the homeless move from a specific area has not become an acceptable practice from a legal and moral standpoint, the police in many situations can no longer take any action.

Panhandling is another problem that part of the homeless community creates for the police. Panhandling is often considered a form of harassment, that for some, borders on being a form of robbery. Since panhandling is not a normal or acceptable practice for the average citizen, the police should take action against it including arresting panhandlers when necessary.

Another problem the homeless can create is an increase in the need for police service—because of crimes committed by the homeless such as assaults, rapes, and robberies and because of the public's apprehension of the homeless.[19]

Society has no clear answer to the question of homelessness, but in the meantime, the matter of dealing with the situation is the responsibility of the police. The situation requires that police officers cooperate with social service agencies and, at times, refer the homeless to these agencies. Police officers need to be aware of the location of soup kitchens and shelters where the homeless can spend an evening.

But the homeless are citizens, and as such, they have rights and they enjoy the protection of the U.S. Constitution and of the laws of the states—even if it makes a police officer's job more difficult.

------

18. Barney Melekian, "Police and the Homeless," *FBI Law Enforcement Bulletin* 59, No. 11, (1990), 2.

19. Ibid., 2–6.

The police officer is best advised to remember that the majority of people who are homeless don't want to be homeless.

AIDS and the Police Officer

Since Acquired Immunodeficiency Syndrome (AIDS) was first recognized as a deadly disease in 1981, it has become one of our nation's most important health issues. Even as we approach the twenty-first century, scientists have not discovered a cure for the disease and it is almost always fatal. AIDS belongs to a group of viruses known as retroviruses which attack critical cells within the immune system. The immune system's functions are curtailed, thereby leaving the person totally vulnerable to a multitude of diseases that can lead to death.[20]

The disease of AIDS is caused by the Human Immunodeficiency Virus (HIV) which infects and destroys white blood cells which damages the body's immune system. When the body becomes infected, the immune system cannot fight the infection. Individuals can be infected with HIV indefinitely without developing any symptoms, and in spite of not having symptoms, a person with HIV can transmit the infection to others.[21]

AIDS has been determined to be contagious but not in the same way that illnesses like the common cold, influenza, measles, and chicken pox which are contagious. It cannot be caught by casual contact through hugging, handshaking, touching, using the same toilet, or through any other nonsexual activity or contact. The AIDS disease can be easily destroyed outside the human body with soap, liquid bleach, alcohol, or other disinfectants. The human body contracts the AIDS virus most frequently through sexual contact or through needles or syringes contaminated with the virus after being shared by intravenous drug users. It can also be contacted through blood transfusions with blood containing the virus and, possibly, by

---

20. Daniel B. Kennedy, Robert J. Homant, and George L. Emery, "AIDS Concerns Among Crime Scene Investigators," *Journal of Police Science and Administration* 17, No. 1, (1990), 12.

21. Theodore M. Hammett, *AIDS and the Law Enforcement Officer: Concerns and Policy Responses,* (Washington, DC: National Institute of Justice, 1987), 1.

virus-infected mothers passing the disease on their new born babies.[22]

Initially, AIDS was considered to be a homosexual disease but in recent years it has become a concern of the general population. AIDS causes anxiety not only among individuals but also among professionals who have contact with AIDS victims. This includes health workers, social-service workers, and police officers. The AIDS epidemic does have an impact on police personnel. Four potential routes of impact for the police have been identified:

1. The nature of police work will often place the officer in contact with high risk populations, most specifically intravenous drug users;
2. Many officers perceive themselves at risk for contamination because of the nature of their work. Officers are regularly called upon to render first-aid to accident victims; aid which may expose them to body fluids which carry the virus;
3. The police could serve as an important conduit of information to those populations that most need information about this problem;
4. Officers could potentially be infected through contact with other personnel in their departments who have contacted the disease.[23]

Crime scene investigators who are involved in death investigation—whether the cause of death can be attributed to an accident or to a disease—can often encounter substantial quantities of blood or body fluids at the crime scene. Unlike the health worker who usually works in a controlled environment, the crime scene investigator has to confront less manageable conditions. One study of crime scene investigators indicated that they needed more information about methods of dealing effectively with the AIDS problem. Many of the crime scene investigators felt that department guidelines dealing with AIDS were insufficient, and many crime scene investigators were still concerned about their own safety even though the quality of their work was maintained. Ultimately, police

22. *AIDS Concern Among Crime Scene Investigators*, 12–13.

23. Patrick T. Kinkade and Matthew C. Leone, "To Protect and Serve? Public Perception of Policing Responsibility and the AIDS Virus.", *American Journal of Police* XIII, No. 4, (1994), 137–138.

departments must support not only crime scene investigators but all police officers with strong departmental measures. At a minimum, clear guidelines should be incorporated into the most recent information on AIDS prevention and this information should be developed, published, and disseminated to all police personnel. The police department should also consider issuing appropriate clothing when officers are called upon to deal with AIDS victims or with evidence contaminated with the AIDS virus.[24] Most questions among police officers come from the concern that they might become infected with HIV by handling potentially contaminated objects. The following recommendations address these concerns:

- Provide education and training on AIDS for law enforcement officers and other departmental staff;
- Issue specific AIDS policies and procedures, or revise existing communicable disease policies to address AIDS issues. Such policies may help to avoid incidents caused by overreaction and fear. On the other hand, promulgating specific AIDS policies may heighten concern by calling attention to the issue. The alternative is simply to apply existing disease policies, based on experience with Hepatitis-B and other infections— i.e., emphasizing basic hygiene and cleanup of body fluid spills;
- Educate officers on the low risk of HIV infections associated with assault, human bites, and other disruptive behavior by subjects but recommend responsible precautions. To establish low risks, emphasize saliva and needle stick studies. Reasonable precautions include polishing "defensive skills" to minimize physical contact and practicing good hygiene if contact occurs;
- Ensure careful supervision of lockup areas to prevent incidents in which HIV infection may be transmitted among prisoners;
- Counsel caution and use of gloves in searches and evidence handling, but educate on low risk. Needlestick studies establish the extremely low risk of infection, but officers should wear gloves and use mirrors when possible to examine places hidden from view. Punctured-proof containers should be provided for evidence and potentially infectious material should be labeled;
- Use masks or airways for CPR, but educate on low risk of infection. Saliva studies establish the low risk of infections, but

---

24. "AIDS Concerns Among Crime Scene Investigators," 18.

protective devices make sense from the point of view of general hygiene;

- Follow infection control procedures for first aid. When there is likely to be contact with blood, all cuts or open wounds should be covered with clean bandages and gloves should be worn. There should be careful hand washing after contact and spills should be cleaned up promptly with a household bleach solution;
- Ensure that no staff touch bodies of deceased individuals unless transmitted by any form of casual contact. Departments should keep continuously abreast of research developments in this area and pass all new information on to staff;
- Provide clear education on the fact that HIV infection is not transmitted by any form of casual contact. Departments should keep continuously abreast of research development in this area and pass all new information on to staff.
- Coordinate educational efforts with public health departments, hospitals, emergency medical services, fire Departments, Community-Based AIDS Action Groups, and Gay/Lesbian Organizations. Cooperative ties with the last two organizational categories are currently rare in law enforcement agencies and probably should be expanded.[25]

Stress Related to Police Work

For the last several decades the public and private sectors have recognized that stress in the workplace can affect a worker's job performance and health, and since the 1970s police work has been recognized as being stressful. Police officers are exposed to acts that are aggressive, cruel, and violent.

Stress can be defined as "a physical, chemical or emotional factor that causes bodily or mental tension, resulting from factors that tend to alter an existent equilibrium."[26] Data indicates the following about stress:

25. *Aids and the Law Enforcement Officer,* 35–36.

26. Joseph A. De Santo and Lawrence J. Fennelly, " Stress and the Police," *Law and Order,* (February 1979), 54.

Stress in daily life is common, pervasive, unavoidable, and thus to be expected;

Depending on how one copes with stressful events, the experience of stress can be positive (healthy & happy) or negative (sick & unhappy);

Since people differ in a variety of ways, each person's means and success in coping with stressful situations will vary;

There is a mental-physiological mechanism, known as the general adaptation syndrome, that assists one in adjusting to demands for change;

By definition, stress is the non-specific response of the body to any demand for change. (The demand can be from within, or from one's surrounding environment);

Police managers are subjected to unusually high demands for change. As a result, they typically experience high levels of stress.[27]

Hans Seyle, the noted authority on stress, describes three stages in adapting to stress—1. the *alarm reaction stage* (a situation in which the human organism is totally aroused and all resources are focused on the stress agent), 2. the *resistance stage* (in which reactions become specialized in an attempt to bring the effects of the stress agent to within tolerable levels), and 3. the *exhaustion stage* (in which defenses against stress give way and the effects of stress become dominant).[28]

Stress is a highly complex condition that may elicit a variety of individual responses to the same stressful situation. The stress over a particular situation does not occur because of the situation but because of the perceived difficulty or the ability of the individual to handle the situation. In other words, when situations become severely stressful, the individual may not feel capable of coping with the environment or with the situation. These stressful events are referred to as *stressors*. These stressors can include such minor incidents as traveling on vacation, getting engaged, and even receiving a promotion. It is important to understand, however, that what might be a stressor to one person may, in fact, motivate another person.

27. Paul M. Whisenard, *The Effective Police Manager*, (Englewood Cliffs, NJ: Prentice-Hall, 1981), 262.

28. Hans Seyle, *The Stress of Life*, (New York: McGraw-Hill, 1956), 31.

Police officers, like other employees, are exposed to stressors. These stressors can be categorized in four ways:

1. *External stressors* to the law enforcement organization:
   A. Frustration with the criminal justice system;
      1. Courts' leniency with offenders,
      2. Decisions restricting criminal suppression,
      3. Endless waiting,
      4. Inconsiderate scheduling of judicial proceedings,
   B. Negative or distorted media presentation;
   C. Unfavorable attitudes of some minority communities;
   D. Attitudes of administrative bodies that restrict funding.
2. *Internal stressors* within the agencies. This can include poor training, poor supervision, poor pay, inadequate opportunities, poor reward for work well done, policies that are viewed as offensive, excessive paperwork, failure of administrators and citizenry to appreciate officer's work, political influence and implications.
3. *Stressors* in police work itself. This can include shift work, rotating shifts, court time, overtime, the interplay between fear and danger, fragmented nature of the job which does not allow a person to follow through a case, boredom alternated with the need to become totally alert, and responsibility for other people's safety.
4. *Stressors* confronting the individual officer. These can include worries about one's competency, being fear ridden, the necessity to conform, being a member of a minority, being a female, martial and family difficulties, necessity of taking a second job, continuing education to aid in advancement.[29]

Medically it has become recognized that stress can impair the social, psychological, and physical functioning of an individual. Individuals suffering from stress are also often experiencing job dissatisfaction, decreased productivity, poor judgment, increased accidents, and slower reaction time. Psychological reactions to stress can be exhibited by irritability, anxiety, tension, feeling "uptight," or "flying off the handle." Additionally, the immune system of the stressed individual is more susceptible to disease, and consequently, they are

---

29. John G. Stratton, "Police Stress: An Overview," *The Police Chief* XLV, No. 4, (April 1978), 59–60.

more likely to be absent from work. Those individuals suffering from continuous stress are also prone to behavior that could include substance abuse, marital difficulties, and suicide. Long term stress can lead to chronic diseases that can include high blood pressure, heart disease, asthma attacks, and diabetes.[30]

Police officers suffering from stress have a wide range of strategies they may use to deal with stress. These include

- Handling specific stressful situations that officers frequently encounter on the job (e.g., family crises, racial conflict, deaths);
- Understanding human behavior and psychological processes relevant to police work;
- Maintaining physical health and well-being though diet and exercise;
- Increasing body awareness and relaxation through biofeedback, meditation, yoga, etc.;
- Communicating effectively with others (family members, peers, supervisors, citizens); and
- Restructuring attitudes or thoughts that contribute to stress.[31]

Summary

There are currently numerous issues relevant to policing that are of concern to citizens of the community, politicians, police administrators, and police officers themselves. These issues include police discretion, the accreditation of police agencies, multiculturalism, the Americans with Disabilities Act, homelessness, AIDS, and stress.

In the 1950s it was common practice for police administrators to claim that police officers investigated all crimes and that they enforced all laws. Police administrators claimed that all crimes were investigated with equal effort and that all laws were enforced with the same priority. Of course, this was not accurate. When the police lack sufficient information to conduct an investigation they usually

---

30. Jennifer M. Brown and Elizabeth A. Campbell, *Stress and Policing,* (New York: John Wiley and Sons, 1994), 17–18.

31. Gail A. Goolkasian, Ronald W. Geddes, and William De Jong, *Coping With Stress,* (Washington, DC: U.S. Government Printing Office, 1985), 93–94.

do not continue the investigative process. The police cannot be expected to investigate all crimes or to enforce all laws. Consequently, we assume that the police are able to exercise a certain amount of discretion.

For decades the police have worked toward obtaining recognition as professionals. If the police in America are to be recognized as professionals, then they must be recognized by society as such. The traditional professions long recognized as being professional are the medical, legal, and ministerial fields. These fields have a legacy of education and research, a body of knowledge, a life-long commitment to training, and a history of self-employment. In the late 1970s four police organizations banded together to strive toward achieving the recognition of police professionalism. These organizations created the *Commission on Accreditation for Law Enforcement Agencies (CALEA)*. The Commission established professional standards that police agencies must adhere to in order to obtain accreditation.

Multiculturalism has become a major issue as we approach the twenty-first century. America has been recognized as a multicultural society with not one dominant culture but many distinct cultures within its borders. Progressive police agencies are responding to multicultural changes in their communities by providing multicultural training for their officers, establishing community outreach programs, and recruiting officers from multicultural backgrounds.

The Americans with Disabilities Act (ADA) became a law in 1990. The law was enacted on the assumption that people with disabilities have been discriminated against in the workplace and in society. Although the ADA does not specifically address police agencies it also does not exempt police agencies. Police agencies have to follow the ADA law where it is appropriate. The ADA has an enormous impact on police agencies, especially in the hiring process. Police agencies can use screening devices for hiring provided they follow the ADA guidelines, but the use of screening devices by police agencies cannot have the intent of discriminating against a person with a disability, either intentionally or unintentionally.

The homeless are those who—through unemployment or underemployment—cannot afford a place to live. The majority of the homeless population are single males. The homeless often create a problem for the police, since the police are frequently called upon to remove homeless people from parks and streets. The homeless have a stifling effect on businesses, and often they attract crime because they create an appearance of community neglect, and the public generally looks to the police to take care of a problem that is often considered to be marginally criminal. On the other hand, the police are often obligated to provide services to this economically disenfranchised class of people.

Since 1981 when Acquired Immunodeficiency Syndrome (AIDS) was first recognized as a deadly disease, it has become one of our nations's most important health issues. The human body contracts the AIDS virus most frequently through sexual contact and by using needles or syringes that are contaminated with the virus when they are shared by intravenous drug users. It can also be contracted through blood transfusions with blood containing the virus, and possibly by virus-infected mothers passing the disease onto their new-born babies. Police officers who come into contact with AIDS victims must take precautions to avoid contracting the disease.

Since the 1970s police work has been recognized as stressful. Not only are police officers exposed to acts of aggression and violence, but the stressful circumstances of police-work include rotating shifts, poor pay, inadequate opportunities, and excessive paperwork. A by-product of stress can include marital difficulties, substance abuse, and suicide. Police officers suffering from stress need to develop strategies to deal with stress.

Key Terms

ADA
Commission on Accreditation
   for Law Enforcement
   Agencies
HIV
mandatory standards

National Advisory Commission
   of Criminal Justice
   Standards / Goals
non-mandatory standards
professionalism
stressors

Review Questions

1. Describe how discretion is important to police work.
2. Describe the value of police accreditation.
3. Describe multiculturalism.
4. Describe why the Americans with Disabilities Act is important to the police.

5. Describe how homelessness affects police work.
6. Describe how AIDS affects police work.
7. Describe how stress affects police work.

References

Bennett, Brad R. "Incorporating Diversity: Police Response to Multicultural Changes in Their Communities." *FBI Law Enforcement Bulletin* 64, No. 12 (December 1995).

Brown, Jennifer M. and Elizabeth A. Campbell. *Stress and Policing.* New York: John Wiley and Sons, 1994.

De Santo, Joseph A. and Lawrence J. Fennelly. "Stress and the Police." *Law and Order* (February 1979): 54.

Goldstein, Herman. "Police Discretion: The Ideal Versus the Real." *Public Administration Review* 123 (September 1963).

Goolkasian, Gail A., Ronald W. Geddes, and William De Jong. *Coping With Stress.* Washington: U.S. Government Printing Office, 1985.

Hammett, Theodore M. *AIDS and the Law Enforcement Officer: Concerns and Policy Responses.* Washington: National Institute of Justice, 1987.

Higginbotham, Jeffrey. "The Americans with Disability Act." *FBI Law Enforcement Bulletin* 60, No. 8 (1991).

Kennedy, Daniel B., Robert J. Homant, and George L. Emery. "AIDS Concerns Among Crime Scene Investigators." *Journal of Police Science and Administration* 17, No. 1 (1990).

Kinkade, Patrick T. and Matthew C. Leone. "To Protect and Serve? Public Perception of Policing Responsibility and the AIDS Patient." *American Journal of Police* XII, No. 4 (1994).

Manning, Peter K. "The Police: Mandate, Strategies, and Appearances." *The Police and Society: Touchstone Readings.* Ed. Victor K. Kappeler. Prospect Heights, IL: Waveland Press, 1995.

Melekian, Barney. "Police and the Homeless." *FBI Law Enforcement Bulletin* 59, No. 11 (1990).

Pound, Roscoe. "Discretion, Dispensation and Mitigation: The Problem of the Individual Special Case," 35 N.Y.U.L. Rev. 925, 926 (1960).

Rossi, Peter. *Down and Out In America.* Chicago: University of Chicago Press, 1989.

Rubin, Paula N. "The Americans with Disability Act and Criminal Justice: An Overview." *The Americans with Disability Act and Criminal Justice: An Overview* Washington: U.S. Department of Justice, September 1993.

Schneid, T. and L. Gaines. "The Americans with Disability Act: Implications for Police Administrators, *Police Liability Review.* (Winter 1994): 4.

Seyle, Hans. *The Stress of Life.* New York: McGraw-Hill, 1956.

Shusta, Robert M. et al. *Multicultural Law Enforcement: Strategies for Peacekeeping in a Diverse Society*. Englewood Cliffs, NJ: Prentice-Hall, 1995.

Standards For Law Enforcement Agencies. *The Standards Manual of the Law Enforcement Agency Accreditation Program*. Fairfax, VA: Commission on Accreditation for Law Enforcement Agencies, 1989.

Stratton, John G. "Police Stress: An Overview." *The Police Chief* XLV, No. 4 (1978).

Wilson, James Q. *Varieties of Police Behavior: The Management of Law and Order in Eight Communities*. Cambridge: Harvard University Press, 1968.

Whisenard, Paul M. *The Effective Police Manager*. Englewood Cliffs, NJ: Prentice-Hall, 1981.

Young, Alan and Ana Novas. "Accelerated Learning: A New Approach to Cross-Cultural Training." *FBI Law Enforcement Bulletin*. 64, No. 3 (1995).

CHAPTER 13

Police Misconduct

1. Police wrongdoing can be perceived by the general public as a serious impeachment of trust.
2. Police use of excessive force has been a national issue in the 1990s.
3. Police use of deadly force is an issue that is more important to minority groups than it is to the majority.
4. Police corruption remains a major issue in the 1990s.

Introduction

The police have a position of legal authority that requires them to maintain the trust of the public. Reports of misconduct by police officers cause citizens to lose their confidence in the police. Even the appearance of wrong-doing can justify a loss of respect for the police. It is extremely important, therefore, for the police to maintain the respect and trust of the people for whom they provide police service, because it is often the help of the community—the witnesses and the victims—that leads to the successful arrest and prosecution of offenders.

Police misconduct is wrongdoing committed by a police officer—whether the wrongdoing is a criminal violation or a violation of departmental rules. Misconduct can be unethical or amoral but yet not be criminal. Police history indicates that a wide variety of police misconduct has occurred since the initiation of policing in our country. Such incidents include violations of civil rights, corruption, the commission of crimes, and excessive use of force. Police misconduct can reflect either an individual police officer's behavior, a group of police officers' behavior, or it can involve an entire police organization. Regardless of the specific situation, police misconduct has taken place throughout the history of American policing and it still occurs in our police agencies today.

Academicians who are students of organizations advocate that most occupations provide their members with the opportunity for behavioral misconduct. Police departments are no exception. There are three elements of occupational misconduct: "(1) opportunity structure and its accompanying techniques of rule violations, (2) socialization through occupational experiences, and (3) reinforcement and encouragement from the occupational peer group, i.e., group support for certain rule violation."[1] Richard Lundman identifies five conditions that must be met before individual misconduct can be attributed to faults in the police department itself:

1. For an action to be organizationally deviant it must be contrary to norms or rules maintained by others external to the police department;
2. For police misconduct to be organizationally rather than individualistic in origin, the deviant action must be supported by internal norms which conflict with the police organization's formal goals and rules;
3. Compliance with the internal operating norms supportive of police misconduct must be ensured through recruitment and socialization;
4. There must be peer support of the misbehavior of colleagues;
5. For improper behavior to be organizationally deviant, it must be supported by the dominant administrative coalition of the police organization.[2]

Accordingly, if police officers are not to gain financially because of their positions (i.e., accepting discounts, etc.), Lundman suggests that informal rules often takes precedence over formal department rules. Although the police department may have a policy forbidding officers from accepting free meals, the informal peer support acceptance process may allow the officer to violate the departmental policy without thinking he or she did anything wrong. Even recruits are socialized into the informal misconduct process often without recognizing that their behavior violates departmental regulations and/or criminal laws. The "code of silence" which has been integrated into most police departments provides a passive acceptance of police misconduct by officers refusing to be a party to departmental rule violations. Misconduct often occurs in police departments because police administrators refuse to recognize the existence of misconduct by their officers and to take constructive action to stop in-

---

1. Thomas Barker, "Peer Group Support for Police Occupational Deviance," *Criminology* 15, No. 2, (November 1977), 356.

2. Richard J. Ludman, *Police and Policing: An Introduction,* (New York: Holt, Rinehart and Winston, 1980), 140–141.

appropriate police behavior.[3] Consequently, police misconduct can be defined as "*actions [that] violate external expectations for what the department should do. Simultaneously, the actions must be in conformity with internal operating norms, and supported by socialization, peers, and the administrative personnel of the department.*"[4]

Police Wrongdoing

Some types of police wrongdoing do not result in any monetary reward or material gain, yet police officers who commit these wrongful acts usually violate departmental policies and often criminal laws. According to Thomas Barker these forms of misconduct include perjury, sex on duty, sleeping on duty, drinking on duty, and police brutality.[5] Other types of misconduct may involve such activities as using drugs on duty.

Perjury

When a police officer intentionally lies or falsifies the truth under oath he or she commits the crime of perjury. This occurs most often when police officers are giving testimony in a courtroom. Perjury is sometimes committed by police officers in order to cover up their own illegal or inappropriate behavior—if an officer has planted evidence on a suspect or has questioned the suspect without informing him of his constitutional rights.

Sex on Duty

The police officer's position often allows him or her to come into contact with a variety of people. There are cases in which police officers have had sex on duty with a prostitute or with other individuals. For some police officers this may be an occasional act, while for others it can become a common occurrence. The author is aware of one police officer who roamed lover's lanes during the late

---

3. Ibid., 140–141.

4. Ibid., 141.

5. Thomas Barker, "An Empirical Study of Police Deviance Other Than Corruption," in Thomas Barker and David L. Carter, *Police Deviance,* (Cincinnati: Anderson, 1986).

evening or early morning hours searching for young couples. He would chase the male away and intimidate the female into having sex with him. This came to the attention of the police chief when the mother of one young lady informed him of the situation. The police chief used a female and a male police officer from another department, wired the female officer with an eavesdropping gadget, and instructed them to park in lover's lane. When the police officer approached the two undercover officers, chased the male officer away, and made sexual advances to the female, his conversation with her was recorded. The police officer was then given the opportunity to resign or to be prosecuted. The officer resigned.

Sleeping on Duty

Police departments usually have policies that forbid police officers from sleeping on duty. When police officers sleep on duty it generally takes place on the midnight to 8 a.m. tour. Usually the hours between 2:00 a.m. and 6:00 a.m. are quiet times when police are rarely assigned a call. It is during these hours that police officers will tend to take naps. Traditionally, many police officers have had second jobs to supplement their income. They work as painters, masons, car repairmen, and janitors. Often this means that the officer working the midnight tour has a difficult time keeping awake.

Drinking on Duty

Most police departments have a percentage of police officers who enjoy alcoholic beverages, whether it be beer or liquor. But some of these officers become addicted to drinking and will drink on duty. Since many communities have bars and liquors stores, these police officers have no difficulty obtaining alcoholic beverages while on duty. Most police officers sneak their drinking and make an attempt to hide their drinking from their fellow officers while others are fairly open about it.

Drugs on Duty

With the wide acceptance of drug use in our society it should be no surprise that there are police officers who are using drugs. Police officers have access to drugs by the contacts they make with drugs dealers and users. There are cases on record where police officers have confiscated drugs from drug dealers and users and have used those drugs themselves or sold them.

Police Brutality

The term "police brutality" is vague and tends to mean different things to different people. Some people consider verbal abuse to be a form of police brutality while others limit police brutality to physical abuse alone. Thomas Barker claims that when citizens charge police brutality they are referring to a number of police actions:

1. Profane and abusive language,
2. Commands to move or get home,
3. Field stops and searches,
4. Threats,
5. Prodding with a nightstick or approaching with a pistol, and
6. The actual use of Physical force[6]

Should profanity and abusive language by a police officer be considered brutality? Obviously it is inappropriate for an officer to use profane and abusive language with a citizen—this behavior does not endear the citizen to the police officer or the department he or she represents—but at a minimum, the officer who conducts himself or herself in an abusive manner toward citizens will be violating departmental policies.

Depending upon the circumstances and the situation it may be appropriate behavior for an officer to command that citizens move along or head for home. For example, if a city has a curfew for teenagers, and the youngster is violating the curfew, the officer has a responsibility to tell the juvenile to go home. Also, if a group of citizens, regardless of their age, are blocking a roadway or an entrance into a store, the officer has an obligation to keep open a passageway. However, there may be times when the officer's demands amount to nothing more than harassment.

The police have the legal right to make field stops to questions citizens about their reasons for being in a specific neighborhood. For instance, if a citizen is walking at 3:00 a.m. in a middle class neighborhood, an officer has the right to question the citizen about

6. Ibid., 71.

what he is doing in the neighborhood, even though the citizen may live in the neighborhood and have a legitimate reason for being there. So when an officer stops a citizen under these circumstances, he or she is simply doing his or her job. There may also be times when an officer may stop an individual simply because he looks out of place, because he is dressed shabbily, or because he looks un-kempt. Additionally, police officers do have the right to search individuals who they arrest or who they consider to be a danger to themselves or others. Of course, there may be officers who abuse this responsibility.

Police officers have no justifiable right to prod any citizen with a nightstick. This should be considered abusive behavior and not be condoned by the police agency. Officers who exhibit this behavior should be reprimanded. At times, for safety's sake, an officer may have to approach a citizen with his or her firearm drawn—if, for example, the citizen being stopped meets the description of a suspect who a few minutes ago robbed a convenience store. But when a police officer cannot provide a valid reason for having his weapon drawn on a citizen, the police department is responsible for taking disciplinary action.

There are times, however, when police officers are legally justified in using physical force upon a citizen. Police officers *do* have the right to use physical force to make an arrest. But when an officer uses unnecessary physical force it becomes known as excessive force.

Use of Excessive Force

The March 3, 1991, beating of Rodney King by Los Angeles police officers brought to the attention of the world the issue of excessive use of force by police officers. The beating of Rodney King was videotaped by a private citizen who first offered it to the Los Angeles Police Department. When the police department refused the tape, the citizen, George Holliday, brought it to a local television station which aired it. Eventually CNN obtained a copy of the videotaped beating of Rodney King and gave it national and international exposure. The incident itself began when the California Highway Patrol Officers chased and stopped Rodney King in the City of Los Angeles. Rodney King failed to cooperate with the officers, and in order to obtain his cooperation, the officers used an electronic TASER gun on him and repeatedly struck him with a metal truncheon (fifty-six blows) hitting his back, neck, head, feet, ankles, and kidneys.

Although the Rodney King case brought to the world the issue of excessive use of force by police officers, it had many historical precedents. The "use of excessive force" by agents of social control have been well documented in history, and throughout the brief history of policing, officers have been accused of physical abuse.

During this century the National Commission on Law Observance and Enforcement (the Wickersham Commission) in 1931 found evidence of considerable use of excessive force. In 1947, the President's Commission on Civil Rights arrived at similar findings. The Civil Rights Commission reported in 1961 that "use of excessive force" was a serious problem throughout the United States.[7]

Police officers are justified in using force only if it is "immediately necessary." The "necessity requirement" has two facets: "time" and the "amount" of force. Under New Jersey law a police officer may not use force until the suspect knows the purpose of the arrest or reasonably believes the suspect knows the reason for the arrest. The officer is only permitted to use force when and to the extent that such force may be necessary.[8]

Basically, a police officer should only use the amount of force necessary to make an arrest. Each arrest situation is unique and the amount of force, if needed, will vary from situation to situation. Nevertheless, the use of force by police officers will be necessary as long as there are members of society who refuse to obey our nation's laws and who resist the police, but the use of excessive force by police officers cannot be condoned.

There is a lack of statistical information describing the extent of the use of excessive force by police officers in the past. In fact, obtaining accurate data on excessive force used is rather difficult. In order to correct this deficiency the United States Congress enacted the *Violent Crime Control and Law Enforcement Act* in 1994 which compels the Attorney General to collect data on the use of exces-

---

7. The President's Commission on Law Enforcement and Administration of Justice, *Task Force Report: The Police*, (Washington, DC: U.S. Government Printing Office), 181.

8. Division of Criminal Justice, *New Jersey Law Enforcement Guidelines*, (Trenton, NJ: Division of Criminal Justice, Law Enforcement Section, 1993), 18–3.

sive force by the police and to publish an annual report of its findings. The federal law provides for the following:

1. The Attorney General shall, through appropriate means, acquire data about the use of excessive force by law enforcement officers.
2. Data acquired under this section shall be used only for research or statistical purposes and may not contain any information that may reveal the identity of the victim or any law enforcement officer.
3. The Attorney General shall publish an annual summary of the data acquired under this section.[9]

The President's Commission on Law Enforcement and Administration of Justice reported in their *Task Force Report: The Police* that physical abuse by police officers was not a serious problem, but it does exist. Commission observers accompanied patrol officers in a number of major cities observing their activities in high crime and slum areas for five to eight-week periods, and commission observers *did* observe instances when the use of excessive force was used when none was necessary. Most of those physically abused were poor, were drunks, were sexual deviates, or were youngsters who the police considered hoodlums. One key ingredient observers discovered was that those who were physically abused usually verbally challenged the police officers' authority.[10] Vance McLaughlin, Director of Training for the Savannah Police Department, in a study on the use of force by Savannah Police officers, drew the following conclusions:

1. Use of force is infrequent;
2. When force occurs, it is exercised in a reasonable way that reflects the training of a proactive police force to prevent excesses;
3. When force occurs, it is examined closely by superiors;
4. Citizens believing that their rights have been violated have recourse to certain courses of action, from departmental to the courts.[11]

---

9. Tom McEwen, *National Data Collection of Police Use of Force,* (Washington, DC: U.S. Department of Justice, 1996), 3.
10. *Task Force Report: The Police,* 181–182.
11. Vance McLaughlin, *Police and the Use of Force,* (Westport, CT: Praeger, 1992), 2.

Table 1
Reported Incidents of Police Use per 1,000 Sworn Officers
During 1991 in City Departments

Type of force	Rate per 1,000 sworn officers
Handcuff / leg restraint	490.4
Bodily force (arm, foot, or leg)	272.2
Come-alongs	226.8
Unholstering weapon	129.9
Swarm	167.7
Twist locks / wrist locks	80.9
Firm grip	57.7
Chemical agents (Mace or Cap-Stun)	36.2
Batons	36.0
Flashlights	21.7
Dog attacks or bites	6.5
Electrical devices (TASER)	5.4
Civilians shot at but not hit	3.0
Other impact devices	2.4
Neck restraint / unconsciousness-rendering holds	1.4
Vehicle rammings	1.0
Civilians shot and killed	0.9
Civilians shot and wounded but not killed	0.2

Source: National Data Collection on Police Use of Force, *1996, p. 34.*

There seems to be some agreement among those familiar with policing that the use of excessive force by police officers is more the exception than the rule. One reason offered by Elliott Spector, an attorney in private practice, for most cases of excessive use of force is the unwillingness on the part of the public to cooperate with police and active resistance. Spector claims, "The truth is that, for the most part the police are better trained and use more restraint than ever before; however, they face a dramatic increase in disrespect for the uniform and violence against the police."[12]

In a study on the "use of force" the Colorado Law Enforcement Training Academy found that officers who overreacted had high levels of stress and lacked control of the situation in which they

---

12. Elliott B. Spector, "Police Brutality Hysteria," *The Police Chief* 59, No. 10, (1992), 13.

used excessive force. The officers also lacked self-confidence.[13] The Colorado study concluded that pre-employment screening was extremely important and that those individuals who were predisposed to either overreact or underreact to a situation should be eliminated from consideration for police employment. Secondly, the study concluded that training that is repetitive in physical (tactical skills) and verbal (negotiating) skills needs to be conducted until the officer feels competent and comfortable in both the physical and verbal areas.[14]

The Use of Force Continuum

To control the use of force by police officers a *Use of Force Continuum* has been implemented for many police agencies. The "use of force continuum" provides officers with guidelines for the amount of force justified for the specific situations they will encounter:

1. Controlled Confrontation—represents the vast majority of police-citizen encounters. Other than the authority inherent in the position as perceived by the citizen, the presence of power, symbolic influence of police uniform, the squad car, etc., actual physical force remains non-existent.
2. Body Language—as much as 70 percent of communication occurs through non-verbal channels. A reluctant individual may be convinced into compliance by the actions of an officer; a body shift toward the offender, intensified eye contact with the individual,
3. Verbal Persuasion—a non-compliant individual can be verbally convinced by the officer into a pattern of control. The direction of the structured conversation may be toward the futility of resistance, the reassurance of the officer's authority, or utilizing time for more assistance to arrive, etc.
4. Contact Controls—a reluctant individual can be brought into compliance with the placement of "hands-on" and the assumption of an arrest posture. Generally the officer assumes control of the subjects's arm while positioning himself to the rear/side of the subject. This contact allows potential flexibil-

---

13. John Nicoletti, "Training for De-Escalation of Force," *The Police Chief* 57, No. 10, (1990), 37.
14. Ibid., 39.

ity if resistance is continued and in many cases adds a degree of
futility to further subject aggression.

5. Joint Restraint—a mildly resistant subject can be placed into a
controlled posture with a lavage domination technique. Usually the wrist or elbow joint are the focus of a variety of restraint tactics which can grow in tension or pain compliance
reciprocal to subsequent resistance.

6. Nerve Center Controls—aggressive resistant subjects may necessitate additional areas of pain compliance concentrated
upon isolated nerve centers throughout the body until an acceptable threshold of pain is experienced as a simultaneous
control tactic employed.

7. Weapon Assisted Pain Compliance Techniques—to facilitate
more rapid and/or effective pain compliance against a belliger-
ent subject, weapons; including yawara sticks, batons, etc., can
be utilized to conduct controlled strikes or pressure stimulation
into traditionally recognized nerve centers, muscle groups, or
joint locations in order to facilitate control.

8. Chemical Irritants—individual aero-canisters containing a tear
gas formulation can be used to subdue an aggressive non-compliant subject. They become more ideal for the subject who is
increasingly violent in his resistance while providing less opportunity for injury to either party.

9. Electrical Devices—a type of mechanism very effective on
physically agitated individuals are the electrical based weapons.
Via high voltage and safe, low amperage, these devices over-
ride the body's nervous system and cause muscle dysfunction
allowing for directed submission until control is assumed.

10. Intimate Impact Weapons—with a violent subject, striking or
punching techniques can normally be directed toward nerve
centers and are more efficient with the use of small weapons
under the generic heading of yawaras or yawara sticks. The
tactical use of these weapons necessitate close contact to be
functional but control and power tactics are significantly improved with a focused targeting of impact.

11. Extending Impact Weapons—an extremely violent subject en-
dangers close proximity techniques therefore strikes or thrusts
can be best made by extension designed weapons under the
generic heading of batons or nightsticks. With distancing, the
officer has the ability to control the subjects's violent actions
with a minimized risk potential.

12. Weaponless Techniques With Debilitating Potential—extremely violent subjects must be immediately subdued to minimize risks. These techniques attack life essential centers of the body and therefore, allow for total control. Perhaps the most widely used technique is the lateral vascular neck restraint. Once initiated it result in unconsciousness within several seconds, or possible death if tension is continued.

13. Weapon Technique With Debilitating Potential—again if distance is essential, a baton power strike to the knee joint can cause joint dislocation and prevent further movement.

14. Service Firearm—when necessity requires immediate curtailment of deadly, aggressive behavior the use of the service weapon in combination with the center-mass targeting of the perpetrator may be the most acceptable alternative.

15. Supplemental Firearms—a violent situation involving life threatening risk to the officer or others may necessitate the use of firearms with increasing power or flexibility. Normally these incidents relate to situations involving hostage encounters, barricaded subjects, etc.[15]

The "use of force continuum" provides for a progressive application of force—for each level of severity and danger that a situation might present the officer has a scale of reference for determining the amount of force that should be used. Since not all situations that an officer encounters are the same he or she will have to determine the severity of the situation and based upon the "use of force continuum" and then determine the amount of force that is appropriate.

The most extreme form of force is *deadly force*. When the use of excessive force can threaten to take an individual's life or when it actually takes a life, then it becomes deadly force.

Deadly Force

Deadly force can best be described as force capable of causing serious bodily injury or death. Generally, the police have the authority to use deadly force to save their lives or the lives of others. The

---

15. Greg Conner, "Use of Force Continuum," *Law and Order* 34, No.1–6, (1986), 19.

use of deadly force by those responsible for policing can be traced back to the common law of England, but the modern police officer's legal authority to use deadly force has been set forth in common law, statutory law, and case law. Under common law an officer may, when necessary, use deadly force to apprehend someone who he or she reasonably believes has committed a felony; deadly force is not permitted, however, to merely prevent the escape of a misdemeanant. The rationale behind this action was that up to 1800 virtually all felonies were punishable by death. If an officer killed an individual committing a felony, he was—in a sense—doing the state a favor, since the individual convicted of a felony would receive the death penalty anyway.

In contemporary society there are few crimes punishable by death. In order to receive the death penalty now an individual must be convicted of murder in the first degree, but even this is not uniform throughout the United States. There are some states that do not have capital punishment at all. Under those circumstances police officers who use deadly force to kill an individual may, in effect, have recourse to exercise more authority and more power than a judge or jury. The most severe punishment that an individual can receive is the loss of life. Because of this, the use of deadly force by police officers has been a controversial issue. James Fyfe, a noted scholar on police use of deadly force, claims that controversy over deadly force can be attributed to "presidential commissions, police practitioners, researchers contracted by police practitioners, radical criminologists, more traditional academics, social activists, law reviews and popular writers."[16] Additionally, Fyfe enumerates a number of recommendations that are still valid as we approach the twenty-first century:

1. Police departments should institute clear policy guidelines to limit the use of deadly force.
2. Policy guidelines should be related to the dangerousness of suspects, and should prohibit use of deadly force to apprehend nonviolent suspects.
3. Police departments should investigate thoroughly all incidents in which police weapons are discharged, whether or not anybody or anything is actually struck by bullets.

---

16. James J. Fyfe, "Observations on Police Deadly Force," *Crime and Delinquency* 27, No. 3, (1981), 376.

4. Reports of these investigations should minimize uncertainty about what has happened by making as complete use of witnesses and forensic techniques as possible.
5. All police shootings should be reviewed and adjudicated by police departments, with contributions from as many perspectives and levels of the police organization as possible. These adjudications should consider both the circumstances of the instant shooting and the record of the officer involved.
6. The findings of investigations and adjudicatory bodies should be made available to the public, and police departments should react to questioning and criticism openly and responsibly rather than defensively.
7. Police agencies should attempt to improve and use state-of-the-art psychological devices and techniques to screen and monitor personnel in order to identify those likely to use violence without proper justification.
8. Police supervisors and field commanders should be held accountable for monitoring and acting on the unjustifiable use of force or violence by personnel reporting to them.
9. Police training programs should be based upon social science principles to increase officers' skills in daily interaction and crisis intervention in the community, and to reduce the possibility that police actions will cause the escalation of violence.
10. Police firearms training programs should consider legal, administrative, and moral questions concerning use of the gun, and should encourage the use of less drastic alternatives where possible.
11. Police deployment policies and practices should be formulated in such a manner that the potential for police-citizen violence is reduced.
12. Police agencies should encourage citizens to make complaints about officers' use of abuse or unnecessary force, should thoroughly investigate all such allegations, and should advise complainants of finding and the action taken.[17]

There are a variety of ways in which the actions of a police officer could become deadly force. These can consist of neck holds which can cut off air circulation or blood flow enough to cause death. In Philadelphia in 1985, the police dropped an incendiary

---

17. Ibid., 388.

bomb from a helicopter onto a house which caught fire resulting in the death of eleven members of a militant group. But the most common way for the police to use deadly force is with a firearm.

Appellate court decisions, statutory law, and departmental policies all provide guidelines that police officers must follow in order for deadly force to be legally justifiable. In 1986 the U.S. Supreme Court struck down the *fleeing felon rule* which allowed police officers to use deadly force—that is, to shoot to kill a suspect escaping from the scene of a crime. In *Tennessee v. Garner* the court stated

> The use of deadly force to prevent the escape of all felony suspects, whatever the circumstances is unconstitutionally unreasonable. It is not better that all felony suspects die than they escape. Where the suspect poses no immediate threat and no threat to others, the harm resulting from failing to apprehend him does not justify the use of deadly force to do so.[18]

Although the U.S. Supreme Court banned the arbitrary shooting of an unarmed fleeing felon who posed no threat to the officer or any other citizens, the decision of the court was not absolute. The Supreme Court indicated in Tennessee v. Gardner that when a police officer has probable cause to believe that a suspect poses a threat of serious physical harm to either the officer or to another person that the officer could use deadly force to prevent escape.

Shootings by police officers occur in a variety of situations other than those in which there is a fleeing felon. They can occur during robbery attempts, burglaries, domestic disturbances, narcotics arrests, or traffic stops. Most progressive police departments have it as a policy that police officers are only justified in using deadly force when they reasonably believe that their lives or the life of another is in immediate danger.

Corruption

Corruption involves either a material or monetary reward or gain. In performing corrupt acts officers gain economically for providing services that they should already be performing or by failing

---

18. Tennessee v. Garner, 105 Supreme Court Reporter, 470 U.S. 901, 1701.

to perform services that are required by their position. Basically, acts of corruption are characterized in three ways: "(1) They are forbidden, by some norm, regulation or law, (2) They involve the misuse of the officer's position and (3) They involve a material gain no matter how significant."[19] Additionally, Tom Barker and Robert O. Wells claim there are ten types of corrupt behavior:

1. Corruption of Authority: Officers receive unauthorized free meals, services, or discounts and liquor;
2. Kickbacks: Officers receive money, goods, or services for referring business to towing companies, ambulances, garages, etc.;
3. Opportunistic Thefts: Opportunistic thefts from arrestees, victims, burglary scenes, and unprotected property;
4. Shakedowns: Officers take money or other valuables from traffic offenders or criminals caught in the commission of an offense;
5. Protection of Illegal Activities: Protection money accepted by police officers from vice operations or legitimate businesses operating illegally;
6. Traffic Fix: "Taking up" or disposal of traffic citations for money or other forms of material reward;
7. Misdemeanor Fix: Quashing of misdemeanor court proceedings for some material reward or gain;
8. Felon Fix: "Fixing" of felony cases for money or other forms of material gain;
9. Direct Criminal Activities: Officers engage in serious felonies such as burglary, robbery, and larcenies;
10. Internal Payoffs: The sale of days off, holidays, work assignments etc. from one officer to another.[20]

Similarly, Ellwyn Stoddard has identified ten forms of corruption:

1. Mooching: An act of receiving free coffee, cigarettes, meals, liquor, groceries, or other items either as a consequence of being in an underpaid, undercompensating profession or for the possible future acts of favoritism which might be received by the donor.

---

19. Tom Barker and Robert O. Wells, "Police Administrator's Attitudes Toward The Definition and Control of Police Deviance," Unpublished paper presented at the Academy of Criminal Justice Sciences, Philadelphia, Pennsylvania, (1981), 4.
20. Ibid., 4–5.

2. Chiseling: An activity involving police demands for free admission to entertainment whether connected to police duty or not, price discounts, etc.

3. Favoritism: The practice of using license tabs, window stickers, or courtesy cards to gain immunity from traffic arrest or citation (sometimes extended to wives, families, and friends of recipient).

4. Shopping: The practice of picking up small items such as candy bars, gum, or cigarettes at a store where the door has been accidentally unlocked after business hours.

5. Extortion: The demands made for advertisements in police magazines or purchase of tickets to police functions, or the "street courts" where minor traffic tickets can be avoided by the payment of cash bail to the arresting officer with no receipt required.

7. Bribery: The payment of cash or "gifts" for past or future assistance to avoid prosecution; such reciprocity might be made in terms of being unable to make a positive identification of a criminal, or being in the wrong place at a given time when a crime is to occur, both of which might be excused as carelessness but no proof as to deliberate miscarriage of justice. Differs from mooching in the higher value of a gift and in the mutual understanding regarding services to be performed upon the acceptance of the gift.

8. Shakedown: The practice of appropriating expensive items for personal use and attributing them to criminal activity when investigating a break-in, burglary, or an unlocked door.

9. Perjury: The sanction of the "code" which demands that fellow officers lie to provide an alibi for fellow officers, apprehended in unlawful activity covered by the "code."

10. Premeditated Theft: Planned burglary, involving the use of tools, keys, etc. to gain forced entry or a pre-arranged plan of unlawful acquisition of property which cannot be explained as a "spur of the moment" theft.[21]

---

21. Ellwyn R. Stoddard, "The Informal 'Code' of Police Deviancy: A Group Approach to 'Blue-coat Crime,'" *The Police and Society: Touchstone Readings,* Victor E. Kappeler, Ed., (Prospect Heights, Waveland Press, 1995), 190–191.

In a study of police corruption, Ellwyn Stoddard found that an informal *code* exists in police departments that supports and condones police misconduct. He believes that forms of police misconduct such as corruption are socially prescribed within the organization. When recruits are indoctrinated into the police subculture they soon recognize that the support of their fellow officers is important to ensure their personal safety and for their success as police officers. Furthermore, recruits are generally unfamiliar with police procedures and practices and are dependent upon the guidance of veteran officers who have been on the police force for several years. Like other members of our society, police officers want to be accepted by their fellow officers, so if a recruit observers a senior officer involved in misconduct he or she faces the option of looking the other way or reporting the senior officer—which may cause the recruit difficulties (loss of trust, for example) not only with fellow officers but also with superiors. Ultimately, new police officers soon learn that they all make mistakes—some of which may result in violations of departmental policy or criminal law, and most police recruits quickly comprehend that it is best to keep quiet if they observe misconduct by fellow officers.

Many states also have laws against police officers accepting gratuities. There are a number of police departments that have policies that don't permit officers to accept free meals, cigarettes, groceries, and other gratuities. However, since gratuities are an integral part of our society, there are members of our society who do not consider it corruption if police officers accept gratuities.

Although there are degrees of corruption. Some forms of corruption are much more serious than others. New York City police officers have used the term "grass-eaters" or "meat-eaters" in describing different forms of corruption. "Grass-eaters" are officers who accept gratuities from construction contractors, tow-truck operators, and gamblers but who are not actively seeking illicit payments. "Meat-eaters" are officers who aggressively seek out financial gain—including gains from gambling, narcotics, and other offenses—that can yield a substantial amount of money.[22] Generally, illegal activities such as gambling, narcotics, and prostitution cannot

---

22. *The Knapp Commission Report on Police Corruption,* (New York, NY: George Brazillier, 1973), 65.

exist for very long without police protection or without an arrangement in which the police agree to look the other way.

In large cities like New York many different types of gambling take place: there is the numbers game which is similar to the lottery; there is bookmaking which involves betting on horses, dogs, or sporting events; there are various card and dice games; and there is a wide variety of informal, friendly wagering between otherwise law-abiding citizens. Police officers have been known to shake down gambling operations on a regular and systematic basis usually because officers feel that society sees nothing wrong with gambling and even if gamblers are arrested and convicted they usually get nothing more than a slap on the wrist.

Narcotics also present the police with opportunities to engage in corrupt behavior. The following are the most common forms of narcotics-related corruption:

- Keeping money and/or narcotics confiscated at the time of an arrest or raid,
- Selling narcotics to addicts-informants in exchange for stolen goods,
- Passing on confiscated drugs to police informants for sale to addicts,
- "Flaking" or planting narcotics on an arrested person in order to upgrade an arrest,
- "Padding" or adding to the quantity of narcotics found on an arrested person in order to upgrade an arrest,
- Storing narcotics, needles and other drug paraphernalia in police lockers,
- Illegally tapping suspects' telephones to obtain incriminating evidence to be used either in making cases against the suspects or in blackmailing them,
- Purporting to guarantee freedom from police wiretaps for a monthly service charge,
- Accepting money or narcotics from suspected narcotics law violators as payment for the disclosure of official information, and
- Financing heroin transactions.[23]

Although police officers' involvement in drug corruption may not be a common occurrence, it does account for the largest per-

---

23. Ibid., 91–92.

centage of cases in which police corruption occurs. In some areas of the South Sheriffs have been known to run interference for drug dealers, and one sergeant on the Savannah, Georgia, police department operated his own drug gang. In another case, an officer provided information to a teenage drug dealer. If we search our newspapers and newsmagazines, we will find police officers in rural, in suburban, and in urban police departments who have succumbed to the temptation of easy drug money.

One New York City police officer, "Officer Otto," described police corruption to the *"Mollen Commission"* in the following manner: "Police officers view the community as a candy store, I know of police officers stealing money from drug dealers, police officers stealing drugs from drug dealers, police officers selling stolen drugs back to drug dealers. I also know of police officers stealing guns and selling them. I know cops committing perjury to conceal their crimes. I know of the use of excessive force."[24]

The Mollen Commission was created in 1992 by Mayor David Dinkin as a result of the discovery of a police drug ring in Brooklyn. One police officer was known to snort cocaine from the dashboard of his police cruiser. This same officer made $8,000 per week selling drugs and protection. Another group of rogue officers from Brooklyn known as the *Morgue Boys*—because they liked to do their drinking in an abandoned coffin factory—rampaged through black and Latino neighborhoods, snorting cocaine, stealing, dealing, and selling protection to drug dealers. They would knock down doors to gain entrance into apartments and then lie about their activities.[25] In a Harlem Precinct the New York City Police Commissioner reported that, of the 191 officers assigned to the precinct, 25 percent were rogue cops, and most of the officers assigned to the precinct were aware of the corruption. These corrupt officers were selling drugs, protecting drug dealers, and brutalizing citizens.[26] In one reported incident, an officer struck a drug dealer on the head and grabbed a bag of cocaine from him then shot him in the midsection, seriously wounding him. Another officer, over a three-year pe-

---

24. Eric Pooley, "The Extraordinary Story of How an Underfunded and Unloved Team of Mollen Commission Investigators Unearthed the Dirtiest Corruption of Them All: Untouchable," *New York* 27, (July 11, 1994), 17.

25. Ibid., 19.

26. Clifford Krauss, "Bratton Says Corruption Sweep Involves Dozens More Officers," *The New York Times*, (April 17, 1994), 1.

riod, made $60,000 stealing cash from drug dealers and selling drugs. Other officers accepted payoffs from neighborhood drug dealers who were trying to monopolize their area. Two officers divided $100,000 in cash that they took from an apartment that they illegally broke into.[27] During this same period of time sixteen police officers from a Bronx Precinct, including two sergeants, were charged with graft. The officers were charged with robbery, burglary, larceny, filing false police reports, and insurance fraud.[28] Another Brooklyn police officer was arrested on burglary charges and charges of grand larceny and insurance fraud. The nine-year police veteran took money from an open safe while responding to a burglary call, and he was also charged with mail fraud on an automobile insurance scheme.[29]

Police corruption can be found in other cities including Atlanta, Georgia. Six Atlanta police officers were arrested for extorting money from drug dealers and shaking down citizens for police protection. About the same time five Philadelphia police officers were charged with planting evidence on suspects, falsifying police records, and lying in court.[30]

Police officers have been charged with rapes, robberies, domestic violence, child abuse, and murder. For instance, police officers in Miami have been charged with murder, racketeering, robbery, cocaine trafficking, and aggravated battery.[31] In Detroit, four police officers were charged with the murder of a black motorist who was beaten to death. While robbing a Vietnamese restaurant, a New Orleans police officer put a bullet into the head of a security guard who happened to be her partner on the police force. She then killed all of the witnesses who could identify her. She was apprehended when a child of the owner who had been hiding during the robbery was able to identify her as the murderer.[32] Furthermore, in Sa-

---

27. Clifford Krauss, "12 Police Officers Charged In Drug Corruption Sweep; Bratton Sees More Arrests," *The New York Times,* (April 16, 1994), 24.

28. Clifford Krauss, "16 Police Officers Are Indicted In Bronx Precinct Graft Inquiry," *The New York Times,* (May 3, 1995), A1.

29. George James, "Police Officer Is Arrested on Burglary Charges in Sting Operation," *The New York Times* (September 7, 1995), B5.

30. Ronald Smothers, "Atlanta Holds Six Policemen In Crackdown," *The New York Times,* (September 7, 1995), A17.

31. "Slice of Vice," *Time* 127, (January 6, 1986), 72.

32. S.C. Gwynne, "Cops and Robbers," *Time* 145, (March 20, 1995), 45.

vannah, Georgia, a police officer placed his own child in scalding hot water. In Wichita, Kansas, a police officer was charged with child molestation. In Galesburg, Illinois, a police officer was charged with bank robbery, and in Chatham County, Georgia, a police officer was caught robbing convenience stores, including a convenience store on his own beat.

No one can say with certainty how serious or widespread police corruption is in our nation's police departments. In some instances, acts of police corruption are committed by single police officers, in others they are committed by groups of police officers, and in some situations entire police departments and city governments have been involved in corrupt behavior. Often, good officers refuse to come forward with evidence and supervisors refuse to take part in stopping corruption—in some situations they even condone it. In some communities corruption is a way of life and an acceptable way of doing business.

Summary

Police misconduct gives the public a negative attitude toward the police. The police have a position of legal authority that requires that they maintain the trust of the public. Reports of misconduct by police officers cause citizens to lose their confidence in the police. Even the appearance of wrongdoing provides a justification for many people to lose respect for the police.

Police misconduct is any wrongdoing committed by a police officer. Police history indicates that a wide variety of police misconduct has occurred since the initiation of policing in our country.

Misconduct covers police behavior that includes not only monetary or material gain but also inappropriate behavior that involves no monetary gain or reward. Police wrongdoing that involves no material gain or reward includes perjury, sex on duty, sleeping on duty, drinking on duty, using drugs on duty, and police brutality. Although police wrongdoing may not necessarily be criminal in nature, it should at least result in disciplinary action.

One form of misconduct that will result in the criminal prosecution of an officer is the use of excessive force. The Rodney King case provides an example of a case in which police officers were charged with a crime as a result of beating a motorist. Although the use of excessive force by police officers may not be extensive, it still occurs.

When the use of excessive force can threaten to take an individual's life or when it actually does take a life, it becomes deadly force. Deadly force can best be described as force capable of causing death or serious bodily injury. Generally, the police have the authority—set forth in common law, statutory law, and case law—to use deadly force to save their lives or the lives of others. There are a variety of ways in which police actions could be considered deadly force: neck holds which can cut off air circulation or blood flow and cause death or routine measures that have accidental consequences, but the most common way for the police to exercise deadly force is with a firearm.

Appellate court decisions, statutory law, and departmental polices all provide guidelines that police officers must follow for the use of deadly force to be legally justifiable.

Police misconduct that involves a material reward or gain is often referred to as corruption. No one can say with certainty how serious or widespread police corruption is in our nation's police departments. In some instances, acts of corruption are committed by a single police officer, other acts are committed by groups of police officers, and in some situations entire police departments and city governments may be involved in corrupt practices.

Corruption continues to exist because good officers often refuse to come forward and supervisors are often willing to look the other way. In some cities corruption may be a way of life.

Key Terms

code of silence	perjury
field stops	police brutality
Fleeing Felon Rule	Rodney King
Knapp Commission	Tennessee v. Gardner
Mollen Commission	use-of-force continuum
Morgue Boys	Wickersham Commission

Review Questions

1. Describe police misconduct.
2. Explain police wrongdoing.
3. Describe what is meant by the term excessive force.
4. Describe what is meant by the term deadly force.
5. Describe what is meant by police corruption.

References

Barker, Thomas. "Peer Group Support for Police Occupational Deviance." *Criminology* 15, No. 3, (1977).

Barker, Thomas and Robert O. Wells. "Police Administrators' Attitude Toward The Definition And Control Of Police Deviance." Unpublished paper presented at the Academy of Criminal Justice Sciences, Philadelphia, Pennsylvania, 1981.

Conner, Greg. "Use of Force Continuum." *Law and Order* 34, No. 1–6, (1986).

Division of Criminal Justice, *New Jersey Law Enforcement Guidelines*. Trenton, NJ: Division of Criminal Justice, Law Enforcement Standards Section, 1993.

Fyfe, James J. "Observations on Police Deadly Force." *Crime and Delinquency* 27, No. 3, (1981).

Gwynne, S.C. "Cops and Robbers." *Time* 145 (March 20, 1995).

James, George. "Police Officer Is Arrested on Burglary Charges in Sting Operation." *The New York Times* (September 7, 1995).

Knapp Commission Report on Police Corruption. New York: George Braziller, 1973.

Krauss, Clifford. "Bratton Says Corruption Sweep Involves Dozens More Officers." *The New York Times* (April 17, 1994).

Krauss, Clifford. "16 Police Officers Are Indicted In Bronx Precinct Graft Inquiry." *The New York Times* (May 3, 1995).

Krauss, Clifford. "12 Police Officers Charged In Drug Corruption Sweep: Bratton Sees More Arrests." *The New York Times* (April 16, 1994).

Lundman, Richard J. *Police and Policing*. New York: Holt, Rinehart and Winston, 1980.

McEwen, Tom. *National Data Collection on Police Use of Force*. Washington, DC: U.S. Justice Department, 1996.

McLaughlin, Vance. *Police and the Use of Force: The Savannah Study*. Westport, CT: Praeger, 1992.

Nicoletti, John. "Training for De-escalation of Force." *The Police Chief* 57,

No. 7, (1990).

Pooley, Eric. "The Extraordinary Story of How an Underfunded and Unloved Team of Mollen Commission Investigators Unearthed the Dirtiest Corruption Secret of Them All: Untouchables." *New York* 27 (July 11, 1994).

President's Commission on Law Enforcement and Administration of Justice, *The Task Force Report: The Police.* Washington, DC: U.S. Government Printing Office, 1967.

"Slice of Vice." *Time* 127 (January 6, 1986): 73.

Smothers, Ronald. "Atlanta Holds Six Policemen In Crackdown." *The New York Times* (September 7, 1995).

Spector, Elliott. "Police Brutality Hysteria." *The Police Chief* 59, No. 10 (1992).

Stoddard, Ellwyn R. "The Informal 'Code' of Police Deviancy: A Group Approach to 'Blue-coat Crime'" in Victor E. Kappeler's, *The Police and Society: Touchstone Reading.* Prospects Heights, IL: Waveland Press, 1995.

CHAPTER 14

Police Accountability

1. Why should the police be held accountable for their actions?
2. Are civilian review boards still needed for reviewing police misconduct?
3. Do the police need a Bill of Rights for police officers?
4. Can police/community relations be improved upon?

Introduction

The police must be accountable for their actions. Police administrators, supervisors, and police officers are responsible to a variety of public entities for their behavior, their policies, and their procedures, and the conduct of police officers has to be controlled so that individual rights are not violated. Essentially, the line police officer should be responsible to his or her supervisors, the supervisors to police administrators, administrators to the police chief, the chief to elected authorities, and elected authorities to the community itself, so that ultimately, the police are accountable to the citizens of their city.

The issue of police accountability continues to be on the political agenda of politicians and interest groups, and often the issue of police accountability becomes a matter of deciding who will have control over policing and who will make the decisions on which police actions are based. The debate itself involves complex issues and there are as many different perspectives on these issues as there are interested parties.

Accountability may be defined as "a concept applied to any organization [that] can refer to relations of direction and control, to internal discipline procedures, to arrangements for consultation and co-operation, and so on. When applied to the organization it can have a number of quite distinct meanings."[1]

Under this definition the police are "accountable" in three ways:

1. First, the police are "accountable to the law." Legal accountability refers to the extent to which the activities of the police

---

1. Steven P. Savage, "Political Control Or Community Liaison? Two Strategies in the Reform of Police Accountability ," The Political Quarterly 55, (Jan./March 1984), 49.

are subject to control through the courts: police apply the law but are not above it. Policing must or should take place within boundaries of both criminal and civil law.

2. Secondly, accountability can refer to the guidelines, regulations and sanctions which operate under police complaints procedures.
3. Third, political accountability.[2]

The police organization—through its police chief, administrators, supervisors, policies, procedures, and guidelines—control police behavior and hold them accountable for their behavior. Police officers who do not follow the policies and procedures of their agency can be disciplined with a written reprimand that is placed in their personnel file, with loss of vacation, or with a suspension of pay.

There are both internal police mechanisms and external mechanisms to maintain control over the police and to hold them accountable. First, the city government sets the hiring standards for the police department, it decides how many officers are needed to police the city, it decides how much training and what kind of training the officers should have, and it decides what kind of modern technology the police department can purchase. The city government also approves the police department's budget—which includes the salaries of police officers—and it plays an important role in determining the type of police service the community will receive.

Complaints against the police are usually reviewed in three ways: internally, internally with an external review of specific cases, and bilaterally[3]—

> *Exclusively internal mechanisms* are those in which citizens' complaints are entirely administered by the police with no external scrutiny,
>
> The second type of mechanism represents those systems that partially administer all complaints *internally but whose decisions are subject to formal external scrutiny in certain cases*, and

---

2. Ibid., 49.

3. Paul West, "Investigation of Complaints Against The Police: Summary Report of a National Survey," *American Journal of Police* 7, No. 2, (1988), 103–104.

Bilateral systems are those in which complaints are administered by both police departments and a formally constituted external agency.[4]

The techniques used to hold the police accountable can include any one or all of the following procedures: *internal affairs units, civilian review boards/civilian oversight of the police, the legal system, civil liability,* and *police unions.*

Internal Affairs Units

Most police departments provide for a complaint procedure that allows citizens to make legitimate complaints regarding police employees, and often police departments have policies that allow citizens to file complaints in person, by telephone, or by mail. But in all cases it is preferable that complainants identify themselves, since anonymous complaints do not have the same impact as identifiable complaints, and because citizens need to recognize that police officers and employees of a police department have the same rights that are guaranteed to all citizens and that they should have the opportunity to meet their accusers.

Ideally, every complaint, regardless of its nature, is impartially investigated, and generally, complaints are handled by the lowest appropriate level of the organization. For example, sergeants will handle complaints against officers, lieutenants will handle complaints against sergeants. Minor breaches of departmental policies and procedures are normally handled by the supervisor of the accused officer, while serious accusations are normally turned over to the Internal Affairs Unit. In any formal investigation all witnesses will be interviewed, all relevant physical evidence will be examined, and all information pertinent to the complaint will be obtained. Like other police departments, the Sacramento Police Department renders one of four possible findings as a result of its investigations of complaints:

Sustained: The investigation disclosed enough evidence to clearly prove the allegation,

---

4. Ibid., 104.

Not Sustained: The investigation failed to reveal enough evidence to clearly prove or disprove the allegation,

Exonerated: The act which provided the basis for the complaint did occur; however, investigation revealed the act was justified, lawful and proper,

Unfounded: The investigation has produced sufficient evidence to prove the act or acts alleged did not occur. This finding shall also apply when individual personnel named in the complaint were not involved in an act that did occur.[5]

The Sacramento Police Department notifies complainants of their findings in writing. When a finding of "Sustained" has been reached, the accused officer receives a hearing and the complainant is expected to testify. The type of disciplinary action that results depends upon the type and severity of the violation—whether it is a violation of department policy and procedure or a violation of a state or federal law. In some situations the Internal Affairs Unit is required to notify either the Distinct Attorney or the Attorney General.

In the latter part of the twentieth century it appears that it is almost compulsory for police departments to investigate all citizen complaints. The California Penal Code requires that "Each department or agency in this State which employs peace officers shall establish a procedure to investigate citizens' complaints against the personnel of each departments or agencies, and shall make a written description of the procedure available to the public."[6] The California Penal Code further states:

1. Citizens have the right to file a complaint against an officer for misconduct.
2. Police agencies are required to have a procedure to investigate citizen complaints.
3. Citizens have a right to the written description of the investigative procedure.
4. Citizens have the right to have a complaint investigated if they believe the officer behaved improperly.
5. The police agency must retain a citizen's complaint for five years.

---

5. www. quiknet.com/spd/complain.html, September 6, 1996.
6. California Penal Code Section 832.5 (a)

6. Citizens knowingly making false reports against police officers can be prosecuted on a misdemeanor charge.
7. The citizen filing a complaint must sign a statement that he read an information advisory that outlines the preceding six points.[7]

Citizen complaints of misconduct that get the attention of the Internal Affairs Unit often involve corruption or the use of excessive force by officers. In fact, Internal Affairs Units are generally assigned the responsibility of monitoring the use of force by police officers. For example, the Internal Affairs Unit of the Savannah Police Department has been charged with the duty of investigating citizen complaints that involve the use of force resulting in injury to citizens. Upon completion of a sworn complaint written in a citizen's own words and following a preliminary investigation, accused officers are notified in writing of an investigation. Officers being investigated are provided written information pertaining to their rights relative to the investigation—rights that are established by the department's rules and regulations. The Savannah Police Department gives police officers who are questioned immunity which means that any information supplied by the police officer cannot be used against him in a future criminal trial. The written notification of the complaint provides the officer with the date of occurrence of the action in question, its location, and a synopsis of the allegation. The officer is required to provide a written response to the allegations, to provide a narrative of the incident, and to respond to written questions requested by Internal Affairs.

Ultimately, the Savannah Police Department believed this process would be considered fair by both citizens and police officers.[8] The Internal Affairs procedures established by the Savannah Police Department served four purposes:

> The procedure permitted citizens to seek redress of their legitimate grievances against officers when the citizens felt they were subjected to improper treatment by an officer.
> The procedure provided the chief of police with an opportunity to monitor employee compliance with departmental

7. California Penal Code Section 148. 6(b).
8. Vance McLaughlin, *Police And The Use Of Force: The Savannah Study,* (Westport, CT: Praeger, 1992), 95–97.

procedures and rules. When violations were established, appropriate discipline, training and direction were applied as needed in order to correct the problem.

The procedure of investigating all citizen complaints, including anonymous complaints, helped perpetrate a positive image and ensure the integrity of the police department.

The procedure also helped protect the rights of departmental employees.[9]

Civilian Review Boards

The civilian review board concept dates back to the 1930s, and can be defined as "an independent tribunal of carefully selected outstanding citizens from the community at large."[10] The issue of establishing *civilian review boards* or *civilian oversight of the police* never seems to go away. Whenever the police are involved in turmoil with citizens, a civilian review board—if one is not already implemented—is usually recommended as one method of controlling police misconduct. Some of the same arguments for it made in the latter part of the twentieth century are similar to the arguments made in the 1960s and 1970s.

In the 1960s William Turner perceived the police as partial enforcers of the law and practitioners of injustices who require supervision by civilians. He had little faith in the ability or willingness of police administrators or internal grievance systems to control police malpractice. Turner considered civilian review boards necessary to control police abuses and as instruments to gain trust and respect for the police in ghetto communities.[11]

This decade has had its own advocates for civilian oversight of the Police. Richard Terrill claims that traditional procedures have not always worked in checking police powers—at least when it comes to police misconduct. Terrill views civilian oversight as a suitable strategy for checking the exercise of police power.

---

9. Ibid., 96.

10. William J. Bopp and Donald O Schultz, *A Short History of American Law Enforcement,* (Springfield, IL: Charles C. Thomas, 1972), 146.

11. William W. Turner, *The Police Establishment,* (New York: G.P. Putman's Sons, 1968), 209.

Those communities that have established civilian oversight bodies usually have two characteristics in common. First, civilian oversight has gained approval through a formal legal process—whether by the amendment of a city charter or by ordinance. Second, the civilian oversight board functions independently of the police department.[12]

There are, however, both pros and cons of the civilian review of the police behavior. The proponents of civilian review feel that

1. A lack of communication and trust exists between the law enforcement and minority group communities.
2. The lack of trust is accentuated by the belief that law enforcement agencies fail to discipline their own employees who are guilty of misconduct.
3. Civilian review would theoretically provide an independent evaluation of citizen complaints.
4. Civilian review would ensure that justice is done and actual misconduct is punished.
5. Civilian review would improve public trust in law enforcement.
6. Civilian review provides for better representation of the entire community.[13]

On the other hand, those opposed to civilian review feel that

1. Civilian review boards ignore other legal resources that citizens have for registering legal complaints, i.e., state attorney's office, federal EOC, civil suits, FBI civil rights investigation, and so forth.
2. It is difficult for citizens to understand operations of law enforcement agencies and have a thorough understanding of laws, ordinances and procedures which law enforcement officers must uphold and operate within.
3. Civilian review boards have a destructive effect upon internal morale.
4. Civilian review boards invite abdication of authority by line supervisors and lower-level management. These are the levels of supervision that should exercise maximum control.

---

12. Richard J. Terrill, "Alternative Perceptions of Independence in Civilian Oversight," *Journal of Police Science and Administration* 17, No. 2, (1990), 80.

13. Terry Hensley, "Civilian Review Boards: A Means to Police Accountability," *The Police Chief* 55, No. 9, (1988), 45.

5. Civilian review boards weaken the ability of upper- level management to achieve conformity through discipline.
6. The creation of a civilian review board is tantamount to admitting that the police cannot "police" themselves.[14]

In 1991, thirty of America's fifty largest cities had some type of Civilian Oversight Board. In addition, there are a number of smaller communities that have Civilian Oversight Boards.[15] The March 3, 1991, beating of Rodney King by Los Angeles police officers reignited the call for outside review of police misconduct, and as long as police are either actually involved in inappropriate behavior or as long as the public thinks that they are, there will be a call by citizens, interest groups, minorities, and politicians to establish civilian oversight boards or to give more power to those that already exist. Ultimately, the police can not run from the fact that there are citizens in our society who will not believe that the police are capable of cleaning their own house or that they are even willing to do so, and as long as there are members of the public who believe this, the call for a civilian oversight board will not go away.

The noted scholars Jerome Skolnick and James Fyfe believe that "No matter how effective civilian review, most of the time cops will be exonerated, and probably should be. Most complaints against police are not sustainable. The civilian review system in San Francisco nailed cops only 8 percent of the time in 1990, which means that accusers were upheld only one time in twelve."[16]

The Legal System

Although it is generally not discussed in most books on policing, the police are ultimately accountable to the legal system. The legal system holds the police accountable for enforcing the law according to guidelines established by the legislative branch and appellate court decisions. It also examines the manner in which the police

---

14. Ibid., 45.

15. Robert Snow, "Civilian Oversight: Plus or Minus," *Law and Order* 40, No. 12, (December 1992), 51.

16. Jerome H. Skolnick and James J. Fyfe, *Above The Law: Police and the Excessive Use of Force,* (New York: Freepress, 1993), 229.

enforce the law. The police are expected to impartially enforce state laws and federal laws and to protect the constitutional rights of all citizens, and when they do not, they are informed of such by the courts.

The first stage of the legal system, the prosecutor's office, a State's Attorney, or a District Attorney, is responsible for verifying that police arrests, the collection of evidence, the interviewing of witnesses, and the interrogation of those arrested follows criminal procedures and that any arrests made were for state laws currently on the books. Normally, the prosecutor cannot bring to trial a criminal case in which the police have failed to follow criminal procedures or in which they have violated a suspect's constitutional rights. If the police have acted improperly and have failed to follow criminal procedures, then it is the responsibility of the prosecutor to inform the police so that they can correct their errors. But if a suspect has been physically abused, the prosecutor may also conduct an investigation of the circumstances of the incident, and any time sufficient evidence exists to prove that a police officer used unnecessary or excessive physical force that causes injury to a citizen, the prosecutor can charge the officer with a crime.

The trial court can also hold the police officer accountable. This court reviews the criminal procedures carried out by the police officer—an extremely important matter in a criminal case. When a police officer does not follow criminal procedures, he or she is informed of such by the judge and his or her case is jeopardized. Essentially, all of the officer's reports pertaining to the case must be accurate and truthful and all testimony must be accurate and truthful. If the officer does not meet this criteria, his or her credibility as a competent police officer is usually damaged for future criminal cases. Furthermore, if it can be proven that the officer lied, then perjury charges can be leveled.

The third tier, the appellate courts of the various state and the federal governments, have played a major role in controlling police misconduct and in holding police officers accountable for their actions. Appellate courts often overturn lower-court decisions solely on the basis of police impropriety. For the last three decades The United States Supreme Court has had a great impact on criminal procedures (see Chapter Two for the Supreme Court cases that have impacted the police process). Its decision on civil liability has had a tremendous effect on police accountability.

Civil Liability

Since the 1970s the United States Supreme has applied *Title 42 US Code Section 1983* to check police misconduct. Essentially, the law forbids agents of the government to use any state law, ordinance, regulation, or custom as a method of denying citizens their constitutional rights. The United States Supreme Court described the purpose of *Section 1983* in the following terms:

> As a result of the new structure of law that emerged in the post-Civil War era—and especially of the Fourteenth Amendment, which was its centerpiece—the role of the Federal Government as a guarantor of basic federal rights against state power was clearly established. *Section 1983* opened the federal courts to private citizens, offering a uniquely federal remedy against incursions under the claimed authority of state law upon rights secured by the Constitution and the laws of the nation....
>
> The very purpose of Section 1983 was to impose the federal courts between the States and the people, as guardians of the people's federal rights—to protect the people from unconstitutional action under color of state law, 'whether that action be executive, legislative, or judicial.'[17]

Title 42 of the United States Code, *Section 1983* deals with procedural remedies rather than substantial remedies. The law provides an avenue of redress for violation of federal constitutional rights, as addressed in the Bill of Rights, and specific rights, as guaranteed by federal statutes. Although the law was passed in 1871 it was seldom used until 1961 because of the court's narrow interpretation of *Section 1983*.

In 1961 the restrictive interpretation of *Section 1983* began to be expanded. In the case of *Monroe v. Pape*[18] the Supreme Court broadened the interpretation and gave new meaning to *Section 1983*. A review of the scenario should help the reader comprehend the Supreme Court's interpretation.

James Monroe alleged that thirteen Chicago police officers forced their way into his home during the early morning, awoke him and

---

17. Sheldon H. Nahmond, *Civil Rights and Civil Liberties Litigation,* (New York: McGraw-Hill, 1986), 4.

18. 365 U.S. 167 5 L ed 2nd 492, 81 S Ct 473 1961

his family, and forced them to stand naked in the living room. The police officers then proceeded to ransack every room in the house, emptying drawers and ripping mattress covers. James Monroe was then taken to the police station and interrogated for ten hours about a two-day-old murder. Monroe was not charged with a crime, he was not taken to a magistrate even though one was available, and he was not allowed to call his family or attorney. Eventually he was released without having had any charges brought against him. Monroe claimed that the police officers did not have a search warrant nor any arrest warrant and that the officers acted wrongfully "under color of the statutes, ordinances, regulations, customs, or usages" of the state of Illinois and the City of Chicago.

The allegations by Monroe constituted a deprivation under color of state authority of a Fourth Amendment right guaranteed by the Fourteenth Amendment and satisfied a legal requirement of *Title 42* of the United States Code, *Section 1983*. This law confers upon the petitioner the right to take action against any person who—under color of state law, custom, or usage—subjects another person to the deprivation of any rights, privileges, or immunities guaranteed by the U.S. Constitution. In other words, the guarantees of the Fourth Amendment against unreasonable searches and seizures are equally applicable to the states via their judicial incorporation into the due process clause of the Fourteenth Amendment.

The U.S. Supreme Court has the authority to enforce the provisions of the Fourteenth Amendment against state representatives, which includes police officers, who in some way fail to act according to their authority or who abuse their authority. *Title 42 USC, Section 1983* provides a legal remedy to those who have been abused in some manner by police officers. *Section 1983* allows for a suit in equity, or other proper proceedings for redress, for individuals deprived of their Constitutional rights, privileges, and immunities by an official's abuse of position.

The U.S. Supreme Court in *Monroe v. Pape* concluded that *Title 42 USC* serves several purposes: 1) it overrides certain kinds of state laws; 2) it provides a remedy where state law is inadequate; 3) it provides a federal remedy if the state remedy, adequate in theory, is not available in practice.[19]

---

19. Monroe v. Pape, 365 US 167, 5 L Ed 2d 492, 81 S Ct 473, 1961.

Although *Section 1983* was enacted because of the conditions existing in the South following the Civil War, the law serves primarily as a limitation on states' authority. Although a state may have a law that, if enforced, guarantees an individual's rights, the federal remedy serves as a supplement to ensure that guarantee. Additionally, it provides that the individual need not seek the state's remedy prior to seeking the federal remedy.

The Supreme Court further found that the phrase "under color of any statute, ordinance, regulation, or custom" should be accorded the same meaning in both *Title 18 USC, Section 242* which provides for criminal punishment and *Title 42 USC, Section 1983* which gives an individual who has been deprived of Constitutional rights the right to take action. Specifically, action taken "under color" of state law describes a misuse of power not specifically prohibited by state law. Furthermore, for an officer to be liable for violating Constitutional rights, specific *intent* is not a necessary requirement.

In the Monroe case, the Supreme Court stated that "A municipal corporation is not within the ambit of *Rev. Stat. 1979 (42 USC 1983)* and is not a 'person' within the meaning of the statute.[20] The court however indicated that action could be taken against every "person" who deprived an individual of their U.S. Constitutional rights. In summary, the Court said the City of Chicago could not be sued or held liable under the law, but the Chicago police officers *could* be held liable for *their* actions. The case opened a pandora's box of civil rights law suits against police officers.

The U.S. Supreme Court was later to reverse its decision that governmental agencies could not be sued in the *Monell v. Department of Social Services of the City of New York et. al.*[21] The Supreme Court concluded that under *Section 1983* local government officials could be sued in their official capacity for damages and retrospective declaratory and injunctive relief even though the local governmental agency must ultimately pay. Essentially, a local government agency can be held liable for traditions and customs that are unwritten and carried out by an agency or its representative. But a

> Section 1983 plaintiff suing a local government (or, indeed, any defendant) has to show both duty and a cause in fact relationship between breach of duty and plaintiff's constitutional

20. Ibid., 494.
21. 436 US 658, 56 L Ed. 2d 611, 98 S Ct 2108, 1978.

deprivation. If only one of these is shown, plaintiff loses and defendant wins because a prime facie Section 1983 cause of action has been stated.[22]

In order to establish a *prima facie* case there must be sufficient evidence presented during the judiciary process either through the testimony of witnesses and/or the presentation of physical evidence.

The Los Angeles District Attorney and the U.S. Justice Department were both able to establish a *prima facie* case against the four Los Angeles police officers who gave Rodney King a beating on March 3, 1991. Initially the four Los Angeles police officers were charged under California criminal law, but they were acquitted by a California jury. Immediately after the verdict became known, a riot occurred in Los Angeles, and President Bush directed the Attorney General to examine the possibility of bringing federal charges against the four officers. The officers were then charged by the U.S. Government with violating the civil rights of Rodney King. They were eventually convicted in a federal court and sentenced to prison. Subsequently, the City of Los Angeles was required to pay Rodney King $3.8 million in compensatory damages for his beating.

Police officers are agents of the government and ultimately the governmental agency that employs them is responsible for their actions. County and city governments are sued since they generally have "deep pockets," and because they have a tax base to raise the money. Furthermore, suing a police officer does not usually result in a settlement involving large amounts of money. Police officers are usually not well off financially and the ability to collect funds from them can be difficult, if not impossible.

Unions

Although police unions are often associated with pay raises and benefits for police officers they also play a role in prohibiting activities that are inappropriate for those officers. Union agreements usually contain specific guidelines that all police officers in the organization must follow, and police unions can play a major role in

---

22. Jane Monell, et al. v. Department of Social Services of the City of New York, et al. *U.S. Supreme Court* 436 US 658, 56 L Ed 611, 98 S Ct, 1978, 351.

holding police officers accountable for their behavior or for any misconduct committed by them.

Prior to the adoption of civil service by county and city governments, police officers—who often owed their positions to political influence—found it impossible to belong to employee organizations. Police officers largely lacked job security and often lost their positions when they lost favor with their political mentors or when there was a change in political power.

Initially most of the police organizations were *benevolent associations* which were founded to protect police officers and to improve their working conditions. Generally, these associations were not offensive to the police administrators or local government officials. Often high ranking police officers had control of the benevolent associations. Some of the early benevolent associations had *slush funds* to influence politicians and governmental decision-making. For example, the New York Patrolmen's Benevolent Association (PBA) which was formed in 1894 did not have a conflict with city government until 1914 when the city administration wanted to eliminate the appeal process for patrolmen. The city's bid was defeated largely due to the efforts of the Patrolmen's Benevolent Association.[23]

At first, police organizations were formed to provide police officers with fringe benefits, such as death benefits, to lobby for pay raises, and to function as fraternal associations, and most big city departments between the years of 1890–1915 had formed police associations. Since politicians controlled the police departments and established their conditions and terms of employment, the collective bargaining process was not open to police associations. The only avenue open to the early police associations was political leverage which they used to achieve their goals.[24]

A major set-back for police organizations was the *Boston Police Strike* of 1919. The city administration of Boston offered an annual salary increase of $100, but the *Boston Social Club*, the police organization, wanted a $200 increase and decided to send a representative to the Mayor. During this period the Boston Social Club requested a union charter from the *American Federation of Labor* (AFL) and it

---

23. Allen Z. Gammage and Stanley L. Sachs, *Police Unions,* (Springfield, IL: Charles C. Thomas, 1972), 31–32.

24. Hervey A. Juris and Peter Feuille, *Police Employee Organizations,* (Evanston, IL: Northwestern University, 1973), 2.

was granted. The Police Commissioner, who was appointed by the governor, refused to recognize the union and banned it. The Commissioner then suspended nineteen men for joining the union in violation of his order. In order to show their support for the nineteen suspended men, the other officers voted to strike. The striking police officers lost their jobs and for the next twenty years the police union movement lay dormant.[25]

Police unionism became activated again in 1937 when the American Federation of State, County, and Municipal Employees (AFSCME) chartered its first police local in Portsmouth, Virginia. AFSCME had established thirty-one locals by 1945, and sixty-six locals by 1951.

But the American Federation of State, County, and Municipal Employees has never been able to recruit large numbers of police officers.[26] One reason for this might be that police officers have felt that their positions were unique and that their jobs could not be compared to those of other governmental workers.

The Fraternal Order of Police (FOP) founded in 1915 has not considered itself to be a labor union. It has operated as a loose confederation of local lodges and it has generally encouraged the local lodges to be autonomous.[27] Some of the FOP lodges are operated simply as meeting clubs for police officers while others function as bargaining units for police officers and/or provide legal assistance to police officers who have been brought up on charges by their police department or who have been sued under *Section 1983*. Currently, there are a variety of police union chapters, lodges, and associations and they fall into three major categories:

1. *Independent local police employees organizations* not affiliated with any larger group. Many state police agencies and large municipal departments are characterized by such large organizations. The Los Angeles Police Protective League and the New York City Patrolmen's Benevolent Association are examples of this type of organization.
2. *Local employee organizations* loosely affiliated with a parent organization that is statewide or national in scope. Unions in this category include those in the Fraternal Order of Police (FOP),

25. Gammage and Sachs, 34–44.
26. Harvey A. Juris and Peter Feuille, 44–49.
27. Ibid., 52.

which represents about 150,000 members in some 1,400 lodges, located in 44 states. All sworn members of a department, no matter what their rank, can be FOB members.

3. *Organizations affiliated with traditional labor unions* or with groups that have most of the characteristics of traditional labor unions. Examples of the former include the International Union of Police Associations (or IUPA, founded by the executive of the now-defunct International Conference of Police Associations and organized in 1978 as an affiliate of the AFL-CIO); chapter of the American Federation of State, County, and Municipal Employees (or AFSCME), also an affiliate of the AFL-CIO); and the International Brotherhood of Police Officers and the National Union of Police Officers.[28]

Police unions can bargain with governmental officials on grievance procedures, grievance resolutions, and disciplinary procedures. Union agreements can include the establishment of appeals processes for disciplinary actions taken against an officer. Unions can negotiate with departments over the operations of Internal Affairs Units in order to protect the rights of the police officer, and they can ensure that the police officer's *Bill of Rights* is recognized by municipal, county, or state officials.

Today, police officers are being held accountable for their actions by civilian review boards, internal affairs units, the courts, and civil liability laws; the police union, as the representative of the rank and file officer, should have as its goal the protection of officers from damage to their careers that comes from the inside and from the outside.

Police Officer's Bill of Rights

Since the 1960s police officers have been exposed to numerous challenges. These demands include an increasing crime rate, an increasing drug problem, a deterioration of our nation's infrastructures, and a downsizing of many police departments. One of the biggest threats to police officers for several decades has been the

---

28. James J. Fyfe, Jack R. Greene, William F. Walsh, et al., *Police Administration,* 5th ed., (New York: McGraw-Hill, 1997), 346–347.

dramatic increase in litigation involving police officers. In addition, police officers are often the targets of criminal actions such as shootings, they are subjected to false accusations of police misconduct, and they find themselves involved in law suits for simply following departmental polices. Because of these actions there are national and state movements to fight back.[29]

In 1974, Maryland became the first state to enact a police officer's *Bill of Rights*, and California, Florida, and Virginia all followed the lead. Currently, there is no national *Bill of Rights* for police officers but since 1970 there have been numerous attempts to establish one. More recently, one of the bills proposed would require all states to adopt a Bill of Rights for police officers. At the time of the printing of this book the United States Congress has not passed a bill of rights for police officers.

In order to protect the *rights of police officers* the *National Law Enforcement Officers Rights Center* was established on October 13, 1994. The Rights Center was founded by the *National Association of Police Associations* (NAPO) to protect police officers' legal and constitution rights that have been infringed upon by civil litigation. According to the Rights Center Director, Robert Scully, a twenty-six-year veteran of the Detroit Police Department, "police officers are increasingly becoming paralyzed by the prospect that they will be sued for doing their job." He continues, "Stopping violent crime requires empowering law enforcement officers, not immobilizing them. Police must have confidence that the legal system is their ally, not their enemy."[30] The need for the *National Law Enforcement Officers Rights Center* exists because obstacles have been placed in the police officer's path, including

- A litigation "explosion" resulting from "an entire cottage industry of trial lawyers who solicit the public to sue law enforcement officers, motivated by prospect of large damage awards and hefty fees."
- Lawsuits and disciplinary action against police officers "for doing nothing more than following existing police department policies to the letter."
- Employees forcing police officers to engage in political activity against their will. Scully cited a recent federal appeals court rul-

---

29. http://police.sas.ab.ca/pdhome/napo/overview.html September 18, 1996.
30. http://police.sas.ab.ca/pdhome/napo/release.html, September 18, 1996.

ing which upheld the dismissal of an Illinois deputy sheriff over his refusal to participate in the sheriff's reelection campaign.

- Officers who are denied their "constitutional right to live where they choose through restrictive residency requirements." A New Hampshire appeals court upheld such a rule last year, declaring that the right to live where one chooses is "fundamental" but not absolute.
- Unlawful firings, harassment and demotions resulting from officers' involvement in union organizing efforts. "A motivated work force requires that all officers enjoy the right to join a union and bargain collectively."[31]

The National Law Enforcement Officers Rights Center functions like public employers organizations, attorney organizations that have been effective in protecting the rights of their organization's members. In effect the Rights Center functions as a national lobbying entity for police officers. Since police unions, associations, and lodges are diversified, the Rights Center provides police officers with a competent ally to represent them on the national scene. The Rights Center was established to

- Be a clearinghouse on issues affecting the legal rights of law enforcement officer;
- Research labor and employment, contract, pensions, criminal and constitutional law as they affect police officers rights;
- Train law enforcement officers about proper techniques in search and seizure, use of deadly force and other key issues;
- Conduct legal education programs for attorneys representing police officers;
- Follow key legislation in Congress and state legislatures;
- Track important legal cases and file "friends of the court" briefs;
- Produce a law enforcement officer employment rights and responsibility manual; and
- Open new lines of communication between law enforcement officers and people they protect removing misunderstandings that keep police and the community at odds.[32]

---

31. Ibid.
32. Ibid.

Community Relations

Police/community relations is a concept that, when used effectively, can remove misunderstandings between citizens and the police. Constructive police/community relations offers an excellent opportunity for the police to open lines of communication with the community that will improve interaction and trust between the two groups. Three decades ago The President's Commission on Law Enforcement and Administration of Justice recognized the value of a positive police/community relationship. The Commission considered police indifference, police mistreatment of citizens, and citizen hostility toward the police to be disruptive influences in the community. Police officers who work in communities that are hostile toward them will have difficulty providing police protection to that community; conversely, citizens who are hostile toward the police will not report crimes to the police or provide them with the information necessary to solve crimes. When a community has negative feelings toward the police, tension rises and aggressive actions against the police begin to occur—which can, in turn, trigger irrational behavior on the part of police officers.[33] The President's Commission outlined several principles of community relations:

- A community relation program is not a *public relation* program to "sell the police image" to the people. It is not a set of expedients whose purpose is to tranquilize for a time an angry neighborhood by, for example, suddenly promoting a few Negro officers in the wake of a racial disturbance.
- Community relations are not the exclusive business of specialized units, but the business of an entire department from the chief down. Community relations are not exclusively a matter of special programs, but a matter that touches on all aspects of police work.
- The needs of good community relations and of effective law enforcement will not necessarily be identical at all times.
- Improving community relations involves not only instituting programs and changing procedures and practices, but re-exam-

---

33. The President's Commission On Law Enforcement and Administration of Justice, *The Challenge of Crime In A Free Society,* (Washington, DC: Government Printing Office, 1967), 100.

ining fundamental attitudes. The police will have to learn to listen patiently and understandingly to people who are openly critical of them or hostile to them, since those people are precisely the ones with whom relations need to be improved.

- The police must adapt themselves to the rapid changes in patterns of behavior that are taking place in America. This is a time when traditional ideas and institutions are being challenged with increasing insistence.[34]

The principles of community relations as outlined by the President's Commission still hold true as we approach the millennium as they did three decades ago. Many of the community relations principles have been incorporated into the new police strategy known as *community policing.*

Community policing, like community relations, emphasizes listening to people rather than telling them what to do. It stresses that the police need to take seriously the concerns and the input of citizens who live and work in the neighborhood or community. And the police are listening, because they now recognize that they need the cooperation of citizens to be successful in preventing and controlling crime. The police are also recognizing that

1. Citizens may legitimately have ideas about what they want and need from the police that may be different from what police believe they need;
2. Citizens have information about the problems and people in their areas that police need in order to operate effectively; and
3. Police and citizens each hold stereotypes about the other that, unless broken down by non threatening contacts, prevent either group from making effective use of the other.[35]

The police can also improve their relations with the community by establishing *citizen police academies* and *community advisory* councils. Citizen police academies that are operated by police departments offer courses to citizens on police subjects once a week for fifteen weeks. Citizens walk away with a better understanding of police problems. Graduates of citizen police academies are also a

---

34. Ibid., 100.

35. Mary Ann Wycoff, "The Benefits of Community Policing: Evidence and Conjecture," *Community Policing: Rhetoric or Reality,* Jack R. Greene and Stephen D. Mastrofski, Ed.s, (New York: Praeger, 1988), 105–106.

source of police volunteers who can perform a number of services that leave officers free to perform police tasks.

Community advisory councils meet with police operations personnel to work on decreasing the crime rate, eliminating disorder, and reducing the fear of crime. A partnership between a community advisory council and the police can be linked to improving the quality of life for community citizens. The community advisory council can identify and prioritize problems within the community that a majority of residents want rectified. Once the problems are identified, strategies can be developed to solve the problems.

Additionally, police departments need to understand that they need to be more open if they hope to gain the confidence and trust of the people they serve. The police must recognize that not all police information is confidential, but obviously, criminal investigations or any confidential information should not be discussed with citizens or even with officers who have no need to know. The police must also agree that they should be held accountable not only for any misconduct but also for any policies, procedures, or activities that are questionable. When a community-police partnership becomes a reality, we may then expect fewer complaints against the police and a greater success rate in solving crime.

Summary

The police must be accountable for their actions. Police administrators, supervisors, and police officers are responsible to a variety of public entities for their behavior, and the conduct of police officers has to be controlled so that individual rights are not violated. Ultimately, the police are accountable to the citizens of their city.

There are both internal mechanisms and external mechanisms to maintain control over the police and to hold them accountable. Techniques used to hold the police accountable can include any one or all of the following procedures: internal affairs units, civilian review boards, the courts, civil liability, and police unions.

Most police departments provide for a complaint procedure. A citizen complaint procedure allows citizens to make legitimate complaints regarding police employees. Often police departments have policies that allow citizens to file complaints in person, by telephone, or by mail. Serious accusations are handled by the Internal Affairs

Unit. The internal affairs unit works directly for the police chief and all findings pertaining to the complaint go directly to the police chief. Based on the findings of internal affairs investigations, disciplinary action, including criminal charges, can be brought against an officer.

One external mechanism used to control police misconduct is the civilian review boards. The support for civilian review lies in the belief that traditional procedures have not always worked in checking police powers—at least in cases of police misconduct—but there are both supporters and opponents of civilian review. The supporters feel the police cannot be trusted to police themselves. The opponents hold the view that there are sufficient mechanisms in place to review police complaints of misconduct and that another mechanism is not necessary.

Although it is not always considered by the public to be a mechanism to control police misconduct, the legal system is one of the most important methods of holding the police accountable. The police are expected to impartially enforce the law and both prosecutors and the courts oversee the police in this regard. The courts, especially the appellate courts, have established policies and procedures that the police are required to follow in criminal investigations.

An important legal avenue open to citizens who feel that their rights have been violated by police misconduct is *Title 42 US Code Section 1983*. This law forbids agents of the government to use any state law, ordinance, regulation, or custom as a method of denying citizens their constitutional rights. *Section 1983* provides an avenue of redress for violations of federal constitutional rights, as addressed in the Bill of Rights, and specific rights, as guaranteed by federal statutes. Both police officers and the governmental agencies can be sued for the wrongful acts a police officer.

Police unions can offer another mechanism for controlling police misconduct. Union agreements usually contain specific guidelines for conduct that must be followed by police officers. The police unions can play a major role in holding police officers accountable for their behavior or any misconduct committed by them. Police unions can also bargain with governmental officials on grievance procedures, grievance resolutions, and disciplinary procedures and they can negotiate with municipal, county, or state entities to ensure that a *Bill of Rights* for police officers is recognized.

Since the 1960s police officers have been exposed to numerous challenges. These include an increasing crime rate, an increasing drug problem, a deterioration of our nation's infrastructures, and a downsizing of many police departments. One of the biggest threats to police officers for several decades has been dramatic increase in litigation that has involved police officers. In addition, police officers are often targets of criminal action such as shootings, they are subjected to false accusations of police misconduct, and they are sued for simply following departmental policies. Consequently, national and state movements have begun to help them fight back. Supporters of the police are aggressively pursuing the adoption of a national Bill of Rights for police officers. As this book goes to print a national Bill of Rights has not been passed.

A concept that can go a long way in improving understanding between the police and the community is police/community relations. Constructive police community relations offer an excellent opportunity for the police to open lines of communication that can improve interaction and trust between the two groups. When the principles of community relations are applied, better relationships will take place.

Key Terms

accountability
AFL
AFSCME
Boston Social Club
civilian oversight
complaint
complainant
deep pockets
external review
immunity

internal review
James Monroe
Monell v. Dept. of Social Services
Monroe v. Pape
NABO
PBA
Rodney King
Section 1983
slush fund

Review Questions

1. Who are the police accountable to?
2. Explain the difference between external and internal review mechanisms.
3. Should complaints about the police be reviewed by an external body? Explain.
4. Discuss why police/community relations are important.

References

Fyfe, James J., Jack R. Greene, William F. Walsh, et al. *Police Administration.* New York: McGraw-Hill, 1997.

Gammage, Allen Z. and Stanley L. Sachs. *Police Unions* Springfield, IL: Charles C. Thomas, 1972.

Hensley, Terry, "Civilian Review Boards: A Means to Police Accountability." *The Police Chief* 55, No. 9, 1988.

Juris, Hervey A. and Peter Feuille. *Police Employee Organizations.* Evanston, IL: Northwestern University, 1972.

McLaughlin, Vance. *Police and the Use of Force: The Savannah Study.* Westport, CT: Praeger, 1992.

Nahmond, Sheldon. *Civil Rights and Civil Liberties Litigation.* New York: McGraw-Hill Book Company, 1986.

President's Commission on Law Enforcement and Administration of Justice. *The Challenge of Crime In A Free Society.* Washington, DC: U.S. Government Printing Office, 1967.

Savage, Stephen P. "Political Control Or Community Liaison? Two Strategies in the Reform of Police Accountability," *The Political Quarterly* 55 (Jan/Mar 1984).

Skolnick, James H. and James J. Fyfe. *Above the Law: Police and the Excessive Use of Force.* New York: Free Press, 1993.

Snow, Robert. "Civilian Oversight: Plus or Minus," *Law and Order* 40, No. 12, 1992.

Tertill, Richard J. "Alternative Perceptions of Independence in Civilian Oversight." *Journal of Police Science and Administration* 17, No. 2, 1990.

Turner, William W. *The Police Establishment.* New York: G.P. Putman's Sons, 1968.

West, Paul. "Investigation of Complaints Against The Police: Summary Report of A National Survey." *American Journal of Police* 7, No. 2, 1988.

Wycoff, Maryann. "The Benefits of Community Policing: Evidence and Conjecture." in Jack R. Greene and Steven D. Mastrofski's *Community Policing: Rhetoric or Reality.* New York: Praeger, 1988.

Index of Subjects

Index of Names